Man and Citizen
(De Homine and De Cive)

BERNARD GERT is Stone Professor of Intellectual and Moral Philosophy at Dartmouth College and Adjunct Professor of Psychiatry at Dartmouth Medical School. He is the author of *The Moral Rules: A New Rational Foundation for Morality* (1970, 1973, and 1975; German edition, 1983), coauthor, with Charles M. Culver, of *Philosophy in Medicine: Conceptual and Ethical Issues In Medicine and Psychiatry* (1982; Japanese edition, 1984), and the author of *Morality: A New Rational Justification of the Moral Rules* (1988).

CHARLES T. WOOD, Daniel Webster Professor of History at Dartmouth College, is the author of such works as *The Quest for Eternity: Manners and Morals in the Age of Chivalry* (1983) and *Joan of Arc and Richard III: Sex, Saints, and Government in the Middle Ages* (1988). Most recently he is coeditor, with David Lagomarsino, of *The Trial of Charles I: A Documentary History* (1989). Wood is also a Fellow of the Medieval Academy of America.

T. S. K. SCOTT-CRAIG, Emeritus Professor of Philosophy at Dartmouth College, is author of *Christian Attitudes to War and Peace* (1938) and *Sound and Sense* (1960).

Man and Citizen

(De Homine and De Cive)

Thomas Hobbes's *De Homine*,
translated by Charles T. Wood,
T. S. K. Scott-Craig, and Bernard Gert,
and the translation of *De Cive*
attributed to Thomas Hobbes,
also known as *Philosophical Rudiments
Concerning Government and Society.*

Edited with an Introduction by
Bernard Gert.

Hackett Publishing Company
Indianapolis / Cambridge

THOMAS HOBBES: 1588–1679

Reprinted from the 1972 Doubleday and Company
    Anchor Books edition: ISBN 0-8446-4756-X

For further information, please address

   Hackett Publishing Company
   Box 44937
   Indianapolis, Indiana 46244-0937

Cover design by Listenberger Design & Associates

Library of Congress Cataloging in Publication Data
Hobbes, Thomas, 1588–1679.
    [De homine. English]
    Man and citizen: Thomas Hobbes's De homine/translated by
Charles T. Wood, T.S.K. Scott-Craig, and Bernard Gert; and, De cive/
translated by Thomas Hobbes, also known as Philosophical rudiments
concerning government and society; edited with an introduction by
Bernard Gert.
        p.   cm.
    First work is a translation of: De homine. Second work is a
translation of: De cive.
    Reprint, with corrections. Originally published: Garden City, N.Y.:
Anchor Books, 1972.
    Includes index.
    ISBN 0-87220-112-0: ISBN 0-87220-111-2 (pbk.):
    1. Political science—Early works to 1800. 2. Natural law.
3. Authority. I. Wood, Charles T. II. Scott-Craig, T. S. K.
(Thomas S. K.) III. Gert. Bernard, 1934–   . IV. Hobbes, Thomas,
1588–1679. De cive. English. 1990. V. Title.
JC153.H5813   1990
320'.01'1—dc20   90-36836
                                                  CIP

The paper used in this publication meets the minimum requirements of American National Standard for Information Sciences—Permanence of Paper for Printed Library Materials, ANSI Z39.48-1984.

∞

CONTENTS

Introduction

3

On Man

33

The Citizen:
PHILOSOPHICAL RUDIMENTS CONCERNING
GOVERNMENT AND SOCIETY

87

Appendix

387

Introduction

INTRODUCTION

This volume contains the best version of Hobbes's moral and political philosophy available in English. It includes the only English translation of *De Homine* (Chapters 10–15), in which Hobbes expresses his most mature thoughts on human nature and morality. It also includes the complete English translation of *De Cive*, for which Hobbes himself is responsible.* Although as literature *De Cive* does not rival *Leviathan*, which is a masterpiece of English prose style, it is superior to it as philosophy. For example, in Chapter 14 of *Leviathan*, definitions of The Right of Nature and A Law of Nature are abruptly offered with no explanation of their aptness. However, in Chapter 1, Sections 7–10 of *De Cive*, Hobbes provides reasons for his definition of The Right of Nature and in Chapter 2, Section 1, he provides reasons for his definition of A Law of Nature. Thus, *De Cive* provides a much clearer account of these crucial concepts than *Leviathan*. What *De Cive* lacked was an account of human nature, for Hobbes had planned it to be the last book of a trilogy; and the second book of that series, *De Homine*, was to contain his account of human nature.

A few words about the translation of *De Homine*. Several years ago in looking for confirmation of my view that Hobbes did not maintain psychological egoism, I discovered *De Homine*. I tried translating it myself, but the result was unreadable. I then asked my colleague T. S. K. Scott-Craig for his help, and together we produced a translation. It was readable. We then decided to ask Charles Wood, a colleague in the history department, to join our effort. Professor Wood, in effect, made an en-

---

* Recent scholarship casts doubt on this assertion.

tirely new translation which, after considerable revision by the three of us working together, is the translation included in this volume. It was Professor Wood's idea to make the translation match that of Hobbes's own translation of *De Cive*, for from the very beginning we envisaged a volume containing both *De Homine* and *De Cive*.

Since our translation is the only English translation of *De Homine*, we have tried to keep it fairly literal, and have avoided, as much as possible, interpreting the text. We have used Hobbes's translation of *De Cive* entitled *Philosophical Rudiments Concerning Government and Society* (1651) as a guide whenever possible and also have taken advantage of the fact that Hobbes translated *Leviathan* from English into Latin. Indeed, *De Homine* is the only one of Hobbes's philosophical works that has not been previously available in English. Since he wrote it in 1658, it is later than both *De Cive* (1642, Notes and Preface added in 1647, translated in 1651) and *Leviathan* (1651) and has some claim to represent his final views of the matters discussed in all three.

Hobbes has been so consistently misinterpreted that it is now difficult to read him properly. In this introduction I shall attempt to counter the misleading interpretations by discussing several of the more important topics with which Hobbes deals. These include his account of human nature, reason, morality, rights, obligations, and laws. Throughout these discussions I shall refer to the passages in this volume that support, and sometimes to those that contradict, the view of Hobbes which I put forward. Although Hobbes was not completely consistent, his moral and political philosophy is remarkably coherent and still deserves the serious attention of anyone concerned with moral and political philosophy. I shall, in general, refrain from putting forward my own moral and political views, which are expressed in my book, *The Moral Rules* (Harper & Row, 1970).

The most serious misinterpretation of Hobbes concerns his view of human nature. Hobbes has served for both philosophers and political scientists as the paradigm of someone who held an egoistic view of human nature. This made it impossible to provide a coherent account of his moral and political philosophy, so that most commentators were led to reinterpret his philosophy in order to reconcile it with his egoism. Once we recognize that Hobbes did not maintain psychological egoism, then we are relieved of the task of reconciling Hobbes's moral and political views with egoism, and so we can accept what he says without reinterpretation.

Before I can show that Hobbes's psychology is not egoistic, I must provide some account of psychological egoism. This is not as easy as it seems, for psychological egoism, though often explicitly attacked, seems to be one of those views that no philosopher explicitly defends. The philosophical interest of psychological egoism rests upon its claim that men *never* act in order to benefit others, or because they believe a certain course of action to be morally right. To say only that *most* actions of *most* men are motivated by self-interest presents no philosophical problems, though it states a pessimistic view of human nature which may not be justified by the facts. It is the claim that *all* actions of *all* men are motivated entirely by self-interest that is philosophically interesting; only when the claim is presented in this manner is it correct to talk of psychological egoism or of an egoistic view of human nature. I do not deny that Hobbes held a pessimistic view of human nature; I do deny that he held an egoistic view.

If we take psychological egoism to entail that an honest answer to the question, "Why did you do that (voluntary) act?" always would be, "I thought it was in my best interest," then psychological egoism is obviously false. We often act in ways that we know to be contrary to our best interest. Giving in to temptation is a common phenomenon, e.g., going to a movie when we know we ought to be studying, taking a second helping when we know we ought to watch our weight. Hobbes is constantly lamenting that men's passions often lead them to act contrary to their best interests (*De Cive*, III, 12, 25, 32)* so that he certainly cannot be held to be a psychological egoist if this means that he holds that all men always act from motives of self-interest.

If psychological egoism is to be at all plausible, it must permit acting on individual passions, ambition, lust, etc., as well as acting out of self-interest. As striking as this enlargement seems, it does not materially affect the main point of psychological egoism. Though psychological egoism is phrased positively, i.e., holding that all men always act out of motives of self-interest, its point is most clearly expressed negatively, i.e., as denying the existence of certain kinds of motives, viz., genuine benevolence, or the belief that an action is morally right. Recognizing the point of psychological egoism leads to the formulation that probably comes closest to saying what the psychological egoist wants to say: *Man always acts in order to satisfy his desires.* This formulation has the added advantage, to the psychological egoist, that it is importantly ambiguous. The ambiguity I am concerned with here lies primarily in the phrase "his desires." "His desires" can be opposed to "the desires of someone else," thus denying all benevolent actions. They can be opposed to "his moral sense," thus denying all action done because one believes it is the morally right thing to do. The psychological egoist must interpret "his desires" as opposing both "the desires of someone else" and "his moral sense," thus denying that any actions are done from either of these motives. The important ambiguity arises when "his desires"

* References are by chapter and paragraph.

are not opposed to anything. On this interpretation we no longer have psychological egoism, but a view which I shall call "tautological egoism," i.e., a view which sounds like psychological egoism but which has no empirical consequences. I do not deny that Hobbes was a tautological egoist; I do deny that he was a psychological egoist.

Tautological egoism is a direct consequence of Hobbes's definition of "will." "The last appetite (either of doing or omitting), the one that leads immediately to action or omission, is properly called the *will*" (*De Homine*, XI, 2). Thus, it necessarily follows that we always act on our desires. Since Hobbes further holds that "The common name for all things that are desired, in so far as they are desired, is good" (*D.H.*, XI, 4), it follows necessarily that every man seeks what is good to him. But though these definitions suggest an important kind of psychological egoism, they do not, in fact, impose any limits on the desires of men or on what they consider to be good, and hence entail only tautological egoism. It is perfectly compatible with these definitions for a man to desire to help another, that is, to act from charity or benevolence. It is also possible for a man to desire to act justly, i.e., to act out of a moral sense. And Hobbes explicitly allows for both of these kinds of persons or actions.

There is no denying that Hobbes sometimes makes statements that seem to commit him to psychological egoism. But generally these are most plausibly interpreted as a kind of rhetorical exaggeration (see, e.g., *D.C.*, XIII, 13 where he says "all things obey money"). Hobbes was writing to persuade, and was not always as precise as he should have been. For example, in explaining certain common ways of behaving, he makes general statements that, if taken literally, contradict each other. Thus he says, "To grieve because of another's evil, that is to feel another's pain and to suffer with him, that is to imagine

that another's evil could happen to oneself, is called compassion" (*D.H.*, XII, 10). But he also says, "To see evil
done to another is pleasing; but it pleaseth not because it
is evil but because it is another's" (*D.H.*, XI, 12). Yet this
general remark, which not only seems to deny the fact of
compassion, but to make everyone a kind of sadist, is understood only when we read the next sentence, "Whence
it is that men are accustomed to hasten to the spectacle
of the death and danger of others." Hobbes is simply trying to explain why this happens, for it is incomprehensible to him that one should simply enjoy the suffering of
another. There is a similar conflict when he claims, "It is
displeasing to see another's good; not because it is good,
but because it is another's" (*D.H.*, XI, 12) and later mentions the kind of love "when we wish well to others"
(*D.H.*, XII, 8). But if we simply take the first remark as
explaining envy, the second, benevolence, the conflict disappears, just as the former conflict disappears when we
take the earlier remarks as explaining compassion and
sadism. That Hobbes tries to explain one's feelings toward others by bringing in thoughts about oneself should
not be used to show that he held that we had no such feelings. To explain something is not to explain it away.

Hobbes's political theory is often thought to require
an egoistic psychology, whereas what it actually requires
is only that all men be concerned with their own self-
interest. That is, though Hobbes's political theory requires that all men be concerned with their own self-
interest, especially their own preservation, it does not
require that they cannot be concerned with anything else.
Nothing in Hobbes's political theory requires that men
not have friends for whom they are willing to make some
sacrifice. When talking of the right of punishing in which
". . . every man contracts not to assist him who is to be
punished," Hobbes observes, "But these kind of contracts men observe well enough, for the most part, till

either themselves or their near friends are to suffer" (*D.C.*, VI, 5). This is not psychological egoism. What Hobbes does deny is an undifferentiated natural benevolence. He says, "For if by nature one man should love another (that is) as man, there could no reason be returned why every man should not equally love every man, as being equally man" (*D.C.*, I, 2). Hobbes's argument is that since it is obvious that all men do not love all other men equally, we do not love other men simply because they are men (see *D.C.*, IX, 18). His point is simply that love of others is limited and cannot be used as a foundation upon which to build a state.

Since Hobbes's main practical concern is to provide a theory that will persuade men to obey the law, it is not surprising that he does not make use of limited benevolence for it provides little support for obeying the law. But because Hobbes does not concern himself with benevolence, this is no reason for holding that he denies its existence. We have already quoted from the definition of love in *De Homine*. In *De Cive* Hobbes says, "They who love their neighbors cannot but desire to obey the moral law, which consists . . . in the prohibition of pride, ingratitude, contumely, inhumanity, cruelty, injury, and the like offenses, whereby our neighbors are prejudiced" (*D.C.*, XVIII, 3; see also *D.C.*, XVII, 8). But Hobbes does not think that such love is widespread enough to play any role in his political theory. Since Hobbes's political theory does not require the denial of limited benevolence, and since the quotations given above strongly indicate that he did not deny the existence of such benevolence, we may safely conclude that in so far as egoism denies the existence of any benevolent actions Hobbes is not an egoist.

Psychological egoism not only denies benevolent action, it also denies action done from a moral sense, i.e., action done because one believes it is the morally right

thing to do. I shall label the view that denies only this
latter kind of motive, *psychological inclinationism*. Inclinationism does not deny benevolent action, only action done because of a moral sense. That Hobbes is not
an inclinationist is clear from his discussion of justice.
"But when the words are applied to persons, to be just
signifies as much as to be delighted in just dealing, to
study how to do righteousness, or to endeavor in all
things to do that which is just; and to be unjust is to neglect righteous dealing, or to think it is to be measured
not according to my contract, but some present benefit"
(*D.C.*, III, 5). Hobbes's pessimism about the number of
just men is primarily due to his awareness of the strength
of man's passions and his conviction that most people
have not been properly educated and disciplined.

When Hobbes offers as "a principle, by experience
known to all men, and denied by none, to wit, that the
dispositions of men are naturally such, that except they
be restrained through fear of some coercive power, every
man will distrust and dread each other" (*D.C.*, Preface, p.
99), he certainly seems to be holding an egoistic psychology. But when we look at how he supports this principle,
we see that he is not maintaining that all men are naturally evil, but rather that in any large group you will find
some evil men, and "though the wicked were fewer than
the righteous, yet because we cannot distinguish them,
there is a necessity of suspecting, heeding, anticipating,
subjugating, self-defending, ever incident to the most honest and fairest conditioned" (*D.C.*, Preface, p. 100).
Hobbes's political theory does not require that no one will
obey the law unless there is fear of punishment, but
rather the much less controversial position that when
dealing with the *large groups* of people necessary for a secure state, there will always be some who will not obey the
law unless they are threatened by punishment (*D.C.*, V,
3). Though we may be aware of small communities in

which mutual trust and respect make law enforcement unnecessary, this is never the case when we are dealing with a great multitude of men. Hobbes's point is that if a great multitude of men are to live together, there must be a common power set up to enforce the rules of the society. That there is not now, nor has there ever been, any great multitude of men living together without such a common power is sufficient to establish Hobbes's point.

One of Hobbes's most important distinctions is that between natural man and civilized man. The importance of this distinction can be seen from his remark, "To speak impartially, both sayings are very true; that *man to man is a kind of God;* and that *man to man is an arrant wolf.* The first is true, if we compare citizens among themselves; and the second, if we compare cities" (*D.C.,* Dedicatory, p. 89). That natural men can be substituted for cities is clear from several passages (*D.C.,* Preface, p. 99, I, 13, XIV, 4). Natural man is man considered as if he were simply an animal (*D.H.,* X, 3, 5), not modified in any way by education or discipline. Though obviously an abstraction, natural man is fairly well exemplified by children. "Unless you give children all they ask for, they are peevish, and cry, aye and strike their parents sometimes; and all this they have from nature . . ." (*D.C.,* Preface, p. 100). It is natural men that behave like arrant wolves; whether citizens, i.e., civilized men, will behave in this way depends on how they are brought up.

This point is made most explicitly when Hobbes explains why he denies the common opinion "that man is a creature born fit for society" (*D.C.,* I, 2). This explanation, which is contained in a footnote to his denial, is very important. He does not deny that men actually live in society, nor does he say that society is a collection of misfits and that that is why we have all the trouble that we do—a position which would be congenial to the psychological egoist or inclinationist. He does not deny

". . . that men (even nature compelling) desire to come together," but he points out that men are not born apt for society because they are born infants, and infants are incapable of entering the compacts necessary for society. However, the main point of the passage is that "Many also (perhaps most men) either through defect of mind, or want of education, remain unfit during the whole course of their lives; yet have they, infants as well as those of riper years, a human nature; wherefore man is made fit for society not by nature, but by education." Natural man may be unfit for society, but this does not mean that man is; man may become civilized, he may by education change from one that acts only according to inclination to one that acts according to contracts and laws. Thus, Hobbes's equanimity about the character of natural man is explained.

If Hobbes is not an egoist, what is he? The answer has already been strongly indicated. Hobbes believed that human nature was malleable, that one could train, educate, and discipline people into good citizens. Granted this conditioning must take into account the strong passions of natural man, still through such training man could become quite different from what he was originally (see *D.C.*, Preface, p. 100 f.). In *De Homine* he gives a detailed analysis of how character is formed. "Dispositions, that is, men's inclinations toward certain things, arise from a sixfold source: namely from the constitution of the body, from experience, from habit, from the goods of fortune, from the opinion one hath of oneself and from authorities. When these things change, dispositions change also" (*D.H.*, XIII, 1). From this list of character-forming forces, Hobbes gives special importance to the influences of man in society. This importance is shown in the passage where Hobbes is considering authorities (*D.H.*, XIII, 7). Here Hobbes shows a clear understanding of the way in which character is formed, noting the importance of good precepts, but aware of the greater importance of a good example. I grant that Hobbes was sometimes misled by his tautological egoism and that his pessimism *may* be greater than is justified. But it seems to me incredible that anyone with the understanding of human nature that Hobbes displays in this and numerous other passages, could be found guilty of the traditional charge of holding as crude a theory as psychological egoism. An unbiased look at the evidence—textual, philosophical, and historical—shows beyond any reasonable doubt that the traditional charge has not only not been proven, but that the evidence *against* his holding psychological egoism overwhelmingly outweighs the evidence for his holding it.

Hobbes's concept of reason has more in common with the classical philosophical tradition stemming from Plato and Aristotle than with the modern tradition stemming from Hume. For Hobbes, reason provides a genuine guide to conduct, one applicable to all rational men (*D.C.*, I, 7 and II, 1); it is not merely a method whereby each man attempts to harmonize or maximize his particular passions. That is, for Hobbes reason is not, or at least should not be, the slave of the passions, rather the passions are to be controlled by reason (see *D.C.*, VII, 18). This is not to deny that "every man by reasoning, seeks out the means to the end which he propounds to himself" (*D.C.*, XIV, 16); but reason does more than this, it has an end of its own, avoidance of violent death.

Reason is very complex; it has a goal, lasting preservation, it discovers the means to this goal. It also discovers the means to ends set by the passions, but it governs the passions, or tries to (*D.C.*, III, 32), so that its own goal is not threatened. Since its goal is the same in all men, it is the source of rules applying to all men. All of this is surprisingly close to the generally accepted account of rationality. We generally agree that someone who follows

his passions when they threaten his life is acting irration-
ally, and we think that though men have different desires, the goal of reason is the same in all. We also believe
that everyone always ought to act rationally, though we
know that they do not do so. Perhaps it was just the
closeness of Hobbes's account of reason to the ordinary
view of the matter that has led to it being so completely
overlooked.

The failure to recognize that the avoidance of violent
death is the end of reason has distorted almost all accounts of Hobbes's moral and political philosophy, yet it
is a point on which Hobbes is completely clear and consistent. In the Epistle Dedicatory to *De Cive*, he says that
reason "teaches every man to fly a contra-natural dissolution [*mortem violentam*] as the greatest mischief that
can arrive to nature" (*D.C.*, p. 93). At the end of Chapter
I he says that it is a dictate of right reason to seek peace
when possible and if not to prepare for war, because men
cannot "expect any lasting preservation continuing thus
in the state of nature, that is, of war" (*D.C.*, I, 15; see
also *D.C.*, III, 29). And he calls temperance and fortitude
precepts of reason because they are means tending to
one's preservation (*D.C.*, III, 32).

One of the reasons why it has not generally been rec-
ognized that Hobbes regarded it as an end of reason to
avoid violent death is that he often talks of the avoidance
of death in a way that makes it seem merely an object of
a passion. Thus, he says that man shuns death "by a certain impulsion of nature, no less than that whereby a
stone moves downward" (*D.C.*, I, 7). And it is assumed
that this "impulsion of nature" cannot be rational, but
must be merely a passion. But in the sentence immediately following, Hobbes concludes that "It is therefore
neither absurd, nor reprehensible, neither against the dictates of true reason, for a man to use all his endeavors
to preserve and defend his body and the members thereof

from death and sorrows." What is overlooked is that Hobbes regards reason as "no less a part of human nature, than any other faculty, or affection of the mind" (*D.C.,* II, 1). For Hobbes, reason dictates that one take all those measures that are necessary for his preservation; peace if possible, if not, defense. Reason's dictates are categorical; it would be a travesty of Hobbes's view to regard the dictates of reason as hypothetical judgments addressed to those men whose desire for their own preservation happens to be greater than any conflicting desire. He explicitly talks about irrational appetites (*D.C.,* III, 32) and expressly declares that the seventh law of nature, which is a dictate of reason, prohibits scorning others because "most men would rather lose their lives (that I say not, their peace) than suffer slander" (*D.C.,* III, 12). He does not say if you would rather avoid slander than death, it is rational to do so.

Since reason has a goal of its own, it would seem as if it must possess some power of its own to move us to act. However, Hobbes seems to consistently hold "that the actions of men proceed from the will, and the will from hope and fear" (*D.C.,* V, 1). Further, he explicitly contrasts "fear, hope, love, or some other perturbation of the mind" with "true reason" (*D.C.,* II, 1). Since it is only the passions or appetites that move us and since reason is not a passion or appetite, how can it have any effect on our actions? My suggestion is that reason somehow uses the passions in order to achieve its goal. It can do this because some strong natural passions have the same end as reason. For Hobbes, emotions and appetites are primarily reactions to present stimuli and only reason can determine what should be done in the long run (*D.H.,* XII, 1). Reason does this by finding out the facts, that is, the consequences of various courses of actions. The passions, though primarily determined by present stimuli, can be influenced by beliefs about the future; and it is by providing these beliefs that reason influences the passions. On this view, the rational man, or the one who follows reason, will be one whose passions and appetites, and hence, will and action, is based on the beliefs about the future provided by reason (*D.H.*, XII, 4).

On many views, reason simply finds out the facts and then is indifferent to what is done with these facts by the passions. For example, Hume's view seems to be that as long as we are aware of the consequences of our actions, any course of action is as rational as any other. This is not Hobbes's view. On Hobbes's view, reason not only discovers the facts and their relationship to our lasting preservation, it also determines how we should act. And how we should act is determined solely by the situation reason discovers, not at all by the way one happens to feel about the situation. Where preservation is concerned, reason tells all men in the same situation to act in the same way; this is an important feature of the concept of reason. This universality of reason makes it possible for Hobbes to formulate general rules of reason that apply to all men. It also allows Hobbes to hold an objective view of morality, even though he holds "that good and evil are names given to things to signify the inclination or aversion of them by whom they were given" (*D.C.*, III, 31).

Hobbes, following Aristotle, regards morality as concerned with character traits or habits. Since morality is objective for Hobbes, it is only those habits that are called good by reason that are moral virtues. "Reason declaring peace to be good, it follows by the same reason, that all the necessary means to peace be good also; and therefore that modesty, equity, trust, humanity, mercy (which we have demonstrated to be necessary to peace), are good manners or habits, that is, virtues" (*D.C.*, III, 31). Moral virtues are those habits of acting that the reason of all men must praise. It is interesting to note that it is only in *De Homine* that Hobbes explicitly acknowledges that on this account, prudence, temperance, and courage are not moral virtues. In *De Cive* he distinguishes temperance and fortitude from the other virtues and does not call them moral (*D.C.*, III, 32), but he does not explicitly deny that they are moral virtues. But in *De Homine*, he explicitly points out that one should not "demand that the courage and prudence of the private man, if useful only to himself, be praised or held as a virtue by states or by any other men whatsoever to whom these same are not useful" (*D.H.*, XIII, 9).

That morality is determined by reason and that reason has as its goal self-preservation seems to lead to the conclusion that morality also has as its goal self-preservation. But this conclusion is false. It is not the self-preservation of individual men that is the goal of morality, but of men as citizens of a state. That is, moral virtues are those habits of a man that make it rational for all other men to praise him. These habits are not those that merely lead to an individual's own preservation, but to the preservation of all; that is, to peace and a stable society. Thus, Hobbes says "Good dispositions are those that are suitable for entering into civil society; and good manners (that is, moral virtues) are those whereby what was entered upon can be best preserved" (*D.H.*, XIII, 9). And in *De Cive*, when talking of morality, he says, "The goodness of actions consist[s] in this, that it [is] in order to peace, and the evil in this, that it [is] related to discord" (*D.C.*, III, 32).

The nature of morality is a complex and vexing question. If we consider morality as applying primarily to manners or habits as Hobbes does, then his view that the moral virtues are those habits which reason declares to be good, that is, that all rational men, in so far as they are rational, must call good, seems to me to be very satisfactory. It yields, as Hobbes notes, all of the moral virtues that are ordinarily considered to be such, and further, it allows one to distinguish courage, prudence, and temperance from the moral virtues. Perhaps most important, it provides, in almost self-evident fashion, the justification of morality. For what is it to justify morality but to show that reason favors it. Reason, seeking self-preservation, must favor morality which seeks peace and a stable society. For reason knows that peace and a stable society are essential for lasting preservation. This simple and elegant justification of morality does not reduce morality to prudence; rather it is an attempt, in a great philosophical tradition stemming from Plato, to reconcile reason or rational self-interest and morality. It is, in my view, one of the most successful of all such attempts.

Hobbes's attempt to reconcile reason or rational self-interest and morality is as successful as it is because of the limited view he takes of the goal of reason or of rational self-interest. As I have emphasized, it is primarily self-preservation, not self-interest in some wider sense, that he puts forward as the goal of reason or as the content of rational self-interest. Only when self-interest is interpreted in this narrow sense does Hobbes's claim that reason supports being moral, i.e., obeying the natural and civil laws, become at all plausible. It is extremely implausible to maintain that it is never in one's self-interest, widely conceived, to violate the law. But it is not quite so implausible to maintain this, when self-interest is limited to self-preservation. Further, if one's life is clearly threatened by obedience to the law, then Hobbes holds that one is justified in violating the law. Thus, with the exception provided, Hobbes has a strong case for saying that reason always supports acting morally.

The importance of reason in Hobbes's thought will become even more apparent in what follows. For I shall now attempt to clarify several of the key terms in Hobbes's philosophy. The two most important are "right" and "obligation." There are both natural rights and acquired rights, and there is both natural or rational obligation and contractual obligation. In interpreting Hobbes, one of the most important matters is determining the nature and relationship of these rights and obligations. Then one must decide whether a given right, e.g., the right to punish, is a natural or acquired right and whether a given obligation, e.g., the obligation to obey the civil law, is a rational or contractual obligation. Closely related to these matters is the interpretation of the nature of law and duty, and the different methods of giving up a right. My hope is that by pointing out the difficulties in Hobbes's terms, I can make his philosophy easier to understand.

Hobbes defines "a right" as "That liberty which every man hath to make use of his natural faculties according to right reason" (*D.C.*, I, 7). The kind of right that Hobbes is talking about here is natural right, that right which all men had "in the bare state of nature or before such time as men had engaged themselves by any covenants or bonds" (*D.C.*, I, 10). When Hobbes says that in the state of nature all men have the right to everything, this must be understood as following directly from his definitions of "right" and "state of nature." That is, the liberty that occurs in the definition of right must be that liberty which is the opposite of contractual obligation. For it follows from his account of the state of nature as the time before there were any contracts that all men were free of any contractual obligation; that is, they had complete contractual liberty. They had the contractual liberty to do whatever was in accord with right reason. Thus, natural right is best defined as freedom from contractual obligation.

However, in a footnote to his account of natural right, Hobbes makes clear that to be free from contractual obligation is not necessarily to be free from rational obligation (*D.C.*, I, 10, note). The right of nature is not the right to do anything one feels like doing; it is the right to

do anything compatible with the dictates of reason. These
dictates of reason, which are the laws of nature, oblige
us to act in ways that best lead to our lasting preservation. The right of nature allows us to do anything we
think will best help us to attain the goal of reason, lasting preservation. Thus, reason provides us with both obligation and liberty, the obligation to seek lasting preservation, and the liberty of doing whatever we think will help
us to attain this goal.

We have already seen that it is necessary to distinguish
two senses of obligation, rational and contractual. (There
is also a third kind of obligation, physical obligation, i.e.,
actually being physically controlled [see *D.C.*, XV, 7],
but it plays almost no part in Hobbes's views and I shall
not mention it again.) Hobbes usually does not regard
rational obligation as limiting natural right, only contractual obligation limits natural right. That it does so,
is again a matter of definition, for one becomes contractually obliged by giving up some of one's natural right.
When one gives up his natural right in any of the ways
that Hobbes discusses in Chapter II of *De Cive* then he
is most properly said to be obliged, for contractual obligation is by far the most important sense of obligation in
Hobbes's view. Also something else happens: The person
who received the right you gave up, and to whom you are
contractually obliged, is now said to have an acquired
right. And an acquired right is as different from a natural right as a contractual obligation is from natural or
rational obligation.

In the state of nature each man is and ought to be
governed only by his own reason. Reason dictates that
he seek peace, but it also allows him to use any means he
sees fit to best preserve himself (*D.C.*, I, 10). "Yet cannot
men expect any lasting preservation continuing thus in
the state of nature, that is, of war, by reason of that equality of power, and other human faculties they are endued

withal" (*D.C.*, I, 15). In order to gain lasting preservation, men must engage in those contracts that lead to a stable society; that is, they must give up some of their natural rights. (In what follows I am concerned only with those contracts that lead to the establishment of a state.) In practical terms, to have a natural right is to be able to decide for oneself what is most favorable to one's own preservation, i.e., to follow one's own reason. To give up a natural right is to oblige oneself to follow what someone else says. That person then has the acquired right to tell one what to do. There is a great possibility of confusion here, for prior to any contract, any person had the natural right to tell anybody what to do. This right, however, was completely vain, for no person was obliged to follow what anyone else told him to do. The acquired right is not vain, for then the person to whom one gives orders is obliged to obey. Someone who has an acquired right, also has a related natural right; that is, an acquired right seems to be simply a natural right plus someone else being contractually obliged to you.

In talking about the right of ruling or of punishing or, indeed, of any of the rights of sovereignty, Hobbes sometimes talks of them simply as natural rights; sometimes as acquired rights. Thus, he says, "For all right over others is either from *nature*, or from *contract*. How the right of governing springs from *contract*, we have already showed in chap. vi. And the same right is derived from *nature*, in this very thing, that it is not by nature taken away" (*D.C.*, XV, 5). Here it seems that Hobbes thinks it unimportant to distinguish between natural and acquired rights, as if they are simply different ways of obtaining power. This passage, in which Hobbes is discussing the sovereignty of God, is one of many in which, by trying to place God into his system, Hobbes's view is not only confusing, but seems much harsher than it really is. For in dealing with men, Hobbes has no doubt that sover-

eignty derives from contract solely (see *D.C.*, XIV, 19).
His attempt to allow God to punish atheists also results
in the confusion of two senses of punishment: the normal
one in which punishment is appropriate only when someone has broken a contractual obligation, and that which
we might call natural punishment, where the right to
punish is simply the natural right to inflict harm, as in
war (see *D.C.*, VI, 12 and *D.C.*, XIV, 19).

This tension between natural and acquired rights,
sometimes only the former being necessary for having the
right to rule, govern, punish, etc., and sometimes the latter, also has a parallel in Hobbes's account of law. He
says, "Law is the command of that person (whether man
or court) whose precept contains in it the reason of
obedience; as the precepts of God in regard of men, of
magistrates in respect of their subjects, and universally
of all the powerful in respect of them who cannot resist
may be termed their laws. . . . Law belongs to him who
hath power over them whom he adviseth" (*D.C.*, XIV,
1). It certainly sounds as if all that is required to make
laws is the natural right to rule plus the power to do so.
When these remarks are followed by the statement "To
follow what is prescribed by law, is duty," we can certainly see why Hobbes is sometimes accused of holding
the view that might makes right. And, indeed, he does
hold it, but only with regard to God (*D.C.*, XV, 5). And
even here it may be best to say that might gives right,
rather than might makes right, for what Hobbes holds is
that God has the natural right to do anything he wishes.
And though it is true that man ought to do what God
commands, this is a rational rather than a contractual
obligation (*D.C.*, XV, 7).

But when dealing with men, Hobbes almost always
treats the right of ruling or sovereignty as if it were not
merely a natural right, but also an acquired right. He
says that "both right and might" are necessary to coercive

power (*D.C.*, XVI, 15). He also holds that the obligation to obey the law involves a contractual obligation on the part of the ruled or subjects to obey. Thus, he says, "Contracts oblige us; laws tie us fast being obliged. A contract obligeth of itself; the law holds the party obliged by virtue of the universal contract of yielding obedience" (*D.C.*, XIV, 2). And in Article 1 of Chapter VIII he insists that of the three logically possible ways that a state can be formed, all involve contract. He goes on in Article 3 to maintain that "all obligation derives from contract." He is not always so clear, however, for he says, "The obligation to perform this [obedience] grows not immediately from that contract, by which we conveyed all our right on the city, but immediately from hence, that, without obedience, the city's right would be frustrate, and by consequence there would be no city constituted" (*D.C.*, VI, 13). Here he seems to be saying that we have a rational rather than a contractual obligation to obey the laws.

Thus, just as it sometimes is unclear whether the right of ruling is a natural or an acquired right, so it is sometimes unclear whether the obligation of obeying is a rational or contractual obligation. One reason for this seeming confusion is that an acquired right always includes a natural right, and a contractual obligation always includes a rational obligation. That there can be no acquired right without a natural right, nor a contractual obligation without a rational obligation again shows the importance of reason in Hobbes's view. One cannot have the right to do anything unless it includes the right to act as one thinks rational. Nor can one be obliged to do anything unless it is dictated by reason that one do that thing. Reason sets the limits to both liberty and obligation. An acquired right is the right to decide for others, as well as for oneself, what is the rational way to act, and reason always dictates that we perform our contractual

obligation because otherwise we are back in the state of
nature. Of course, if a contract requires us to do something that threatens our life, it is no longer valid and
hence imposes no obligation (*D.C.*, II, 18). The fact that,
for Hobbes, acquired rights are so closely tied to natural
rights and contractual obligations to rational obligations
makes him less careful in distinguishing between them
than seems desirable.

Hobbes always contrasts the obligation of the sovereign and subject, the latter having an obligation beyond
that of the sovereign. Both have a rational obligation,
but the subject also has a contractual obligation. It is by
virtue of his contract that the subject can commit injustice. For to commit an unjust act is to violate a contract. Hobbes is so clear on this point that he denies that
disobedience to God's laws by atheists, etc., is injustice
(*D.C.*, XIV, 19, note). Since Hobbes considers it to be
unjust to violate the civil law, it follows that violating a
law must be considered by him to necessarily involve the
violating of a contract; and hence it must be that laws
can be made only by those whom we have contracted to
obey. Thus, the right to rule, to make laws, etc., must be
an acquired right, and the laws must be not merely commands of the powerful, but of those whom we have contracted to obey, and hence the obligation to obey the
laws must be not merely a rational obligation, but also
a contractual one.

I have already pointed out that the subject seems to
have a contractual obligation while the sovereign does
not, yet if the obligation of the subject comes from contract, why doesn't the sovereign have a contractual obligation also? The answer to this lies in another ambiguity in Hobbes. In discussing the various ways in which
one can give up a right and become contractually obliged,
Hobbes mentions simple renunciation (*D.C.*, II, 4),
free gift (*D.C.*, II, 8), contract (*D.C.*, II, 9), and cove-

nant (*D.C.*, II, 9). In renunciation, the man simply gives up his right, not caring who gets it. In free gift he gives it to another because of some benefit or because of hope or fear, and the party to whom he gives it does not give up any of his natural right. Only in contract and covenant is there a mutual conveying of rights, and perhaps, strictly speaking, it is only in a covenant of mutual trust that there is any important mutual conveying of rights. However, even though he makes these distinctions with care, he ignores them in his actual discussion (as I have in the previous discussion), and generally uses the word "contract" to cover any transfer of right, whether mutual or not. However, though he talks of contract when discussing the formation of a state, it is clear that the most important transferring of right is not strictly speaking a contract, but a free gift. That is, there is never a contract between subject and sovereign, no matter which of the logically possible ways a state is formed, but the subject always makes a free gift of his rights to the sovereign either from fear of present death or in hope of gaining lasting preservation. This is why the sovereign can never be unjust, for he has never made a contract and hence cannot violate it. The subject has, however, transferred his right to the sovereign, and hence not to obey the sovereign is unjust (except, of course, where one's life is threatened).

The subject thus has a contractual obligation to obey the sovereign, which is a result of free gift, while the sovereign has not conveyed any right on the subjects. However, the sovereign, in accepting the free gift of the subject, comes under the third law of nature prohibiting ingratitude. Thus, he is required to act so "that the giver shall have no just occasion to repent him of his gift" (*D.C.*, III, 8). And in talking of the duties of the sovereign, Hobbes says, "Now all the duties of the rulers are contained in this one sentence, the safety of the people is the supreme law" (*D.C.*, XIII, 2). For it was for safety's sake that people made a free gift of their natural right to the sovereign. Thus, though sovereigns have no contractual obligations, "yet it is their duty in all things, as much as possibly they can, to yield obedience unto right reason, which is the natural, moral, and divine law" (*ibid.*).

This brings up another of the ambiguities in Hobbes; that of "duty," where duty is sometimes limited to contractual obligation, but in the passage quoted above also seems to be used with regard to rational obligation. As can be seen, this ambiguity, like several of the others, e.g., "right" and "obligation," is one in which the term has both a narrow or strict sense and a looser or wider sense.

Hobbes recognizes this dual sense of many of his terms. He says, "Sin, in its largest signification, comprehends every deed, word, and thought against right reason" (*D.C.*, XIV, 16). Yet in the next article, "But when we speak of the laws, the word sin is taken in a more strict sense, and signifies not every thing done against right reason, but only that which is blameable, and therefore is called *malum culpae,* the evil of fault." Thus, "right," "obligation," "law," and "duty," in their largest signification, are related generally to right reason, but in a more strict signification, they are related to contracts, or the giving up of rights.

There is one other ambiguity in Hobbes that must be mentioned before we leave this topic. This is with regard to some terms that Hobbes explicitly says are ambiguous, viz., "just," and "unjust." But the ambiguity that Hobbes is concerned with is that these terms "signify one thing when they are attributed to persons, another when to actions" (*D.C.*, III, 5). I am concerned with two other ambiguities. The first is similar to the ambiguities we have already discussed, i.e., "just" sometimes means doing what one is rationally obliged to do, sometimes what one is contractually obliged to do. But it is only rarely that Hobbes uses "just" in the looser sense (*D.C.*, III, 30), so that this ambiguity need not concern us. The more important ambiguity with regard to justice is that it sometimes applies to one who fulfills his contractual obligations, and sometimes to one who does not violate any contractual obligations. It may seem as if there is no ambiguity here, since whoever meets the first condition will necessarily meet the second one also. However, the ambiguity arises because someone who meets the second condition may not meet the first. This is the case with regard to all those who have no contractual obligations. Thus it is that Hobbes can say that both God and the sovereign are just, not because they keep their contractual obligations but because they have no contractual obligations to break.

The fact that neither sovereigns nor God can commit injustice is important for Hobbes because it is only injustice that can properly be punished. Hobbes does not deny that sovereigns can be immoral, but he does deny that the immorality of sovereigns can properly be punished. This is important, for otherwise any immoral act by the sovereign would serve as a pretext for punishing the sovereign, that is, for civil war. It is to avoid this possibility that Hobbes denies that the sovereign can be unjust or that there can be unjust laws. He never claims that the sovereign can't be immoral or that there can't be immoral or bad laws. What is just and unjust may be determined by the laws of the state, what is moral and immoral is not. Morality is a wider concept than that of justice and is determined by the reason of all men. However, to let justice be determined by the reason of all men rather than by the reason of the sovereign would be to invite discord and civil war, which is contrary to the goal of morality which is a stable society and peace. One can create an air of paradox by saying that for Hobbes it is immoral to attempt to punish certain immoral acts, viz., those of the sovereign. Hobbes is willing to accept this seeming paradox for he never loses sight of the goal of morality.

For Hobbes, moral and political philosophy were not merely academic exercises; he believed that they could be of tremendous practical importance. In his Preface to the Reader in *De Cive*, he maintains that "questions concerning the rights of dominion, and the obedience due from subjects [were] the true forerunners of an approaching war" (103). And he explains his writing of *De Cive* prior to the works that should have preceded it as an attempt to forestall that war. He genuinely believes that errors in moral philosophy are one of the main causes of civil war with its resulting evils (96–98). Thus, Hobbes's moral and political philosophy is informed by a purpose, the attainment of peace and the avoidance of war, especially civil war. When he errs, it is generally in his attempt to state the cause of peace in the strongest possible form. In this day of nuclear weapons, when whole nations can be destroyed almost as easily as a single man in Hobbes's day, we would do well to pay increased attention to the one philosopher to whom the attaining of peace was the primary goal of moral and political philosophy.

I shall now present a very brief summary of Hobbes's system. Men, in so far as they are rational, want to live out their natural lives in peace and security. In order to do this, they must come together into cities or states of sufficient size that they cannot be attacked by any group without some doubt about who will win. But when men come together in such a large group there will always be some that cannot be trusted, and thus it is necessary to set up a government with the power to make and enforce laws. This government, which gets both its right to govern and its power to do so from the consent of the governed, has as its primary duty the safety of the people. As long as the government provides this safety the citizens are obliged to obey the laws of the state in all things. Thus, the rationality of seeking lasting preservation requires the seeking of peace; this in turn requires the setting up of a state with sufficient power to keep the peace. Anything that threatens the stability of the state is to be avoided. The most important criticism of Hobbes's moral and political philosophy does not deny anything in the above system; rather, it is that by overemphasizing the fragility of the state, Hobbes imposed unnecessary restrictions on the liberty of subjects. But even though I have some sympathy with this criticism, it should be clear that philosophically speaking it requires no major change in Hobbes's system in order to meet it.

I have so far said very little about the place of God and religion in Hobbes's philosophy. As a practical matter, Hobbes took religion very seriously, for he thought it provided some of the strongest motives for action. Thus, it is not surprising that he spends so much time trying to show that his moral and political views are supported by Scripture. Nor is it surprising that he tries so hard to discredit those religious views that may lead to civil strife. There has been some debate concerning Hobbes's own thoughts concerning religion, but I find no reason to doubt his sincerity. There is good reason to believe that he honestly thought that reason and the Scriptures must agree (*D.C.*, IV, 1), for both came from the same source, God. But, accepting the sincerity of Hobbes's religious views does not require one to hold that God plays an essential role in Hobbes's philosophy. He explicitly denies that atheists and deists are subject to the commands of God (*D.C.*, XV, 2), but he never denies that they are subject to the laws of nature or of the civil state. Once one recognizes the role of reason in Hobbes, that by itself it provides a guide to conduct to be followed by all men, there is absolutely no need to bring in God. For in his moral and political theory there is nothing that God can do that is not already done by reason. Indeed, as I pointed out previously, Hobbes's attempts to fit God into his system usually result in some confusion and misleading remarks.

One of Hobbes's outstanding characteristics seems to me to be his intellectual honesty. Though he may have been a timid man (he himself claims that he was, which he explains by saying that his mother gave birth to him [April 5, 1588] because of fright over the coming of the Spanish Armada), his writing shows no trace of it. And he seems willing to hold views that he must have known would cause him some considerable trouble. He engaged in many academic controversies, which required considerably more courage in Hobbes's day than at the present time. Both the Roman Catholic Church and Oxford University banned the reading of his books and there was talk not only of burning his books but of burning Hobbes himself. He lived to ninety-one, dying on December 4, 1679, and seems to have been involved in controversy for more than half his life.

There is a charming account of Hobbes's life by John Aubrey in Aubrey's *Brief Lives*, and there are also excellent accounts of his life in two books both called *Hobbes*, one by George Croom Robertson and the other by John Laird. There is also a third book with the same title by R. Peters. There are a number of books on Hobbes's moral and political views, and though almost all regard him as a psychological egoist, they provide many valuable insights into Hobbes's views. Howard Warrender's book, *The Political Philosophy of Hobbes; His Theory of Obligation*, gives the fullest exposition of the view that God is essential in Hobbes's political theory. This view was first put forward by A. E. Taylor in his article "The Ethical Doctrine of Hobbes" (*Philosophy*, Vol. XIII, pp. 406–24). This article is reprinted in both *Hobbes Studies*, edited by K. C. Brown, and *Hobbes's*

Leviathan: Interpretation and Criticism, edited by Bernard H. Baumrin. This latter collection also includes my article, "Hobbes and Psychological Egoism" (*Journal of the History of Ideas,* XXVIII, 4), from which part of this introduction is taken. There are two other books on Hobbes which deserve to be noted: *Political Philosophy of Thomas Hobbes: Its Basis and Genesis,* by Leo Strauss, where Hobbes's debt to Aristotle is well brought out; and *Hobbes's System of Ideas,* by J. W. N. Watkins, which almost clarifies the nature of Hobbes's egoism. The most interesting edition of *Leviathan* is that edited by Michael Oakeshott, for he has a long and significant introduction. The complete works of Hobbes were brought out by Sir William Molesworth between 1839 and 1845. *The English Works,* with an index, fill eleven volumes. Volume Two contains Hobbes's translation of *De Cive* and with very minor revisions is the text that is reprinted in this volume. The revisions were made by comparing the Molesworth text with that of the original English text printed in 1651. I am very grateful to the Folger Shakespeare Library in Washington, D.C., for providing me with a microfilm copy of this edition. The *Opera Latina* has five volumes. Volume Two contains both *De Homine* and *De Cive,* and it was this text of *De Homine* that we used in making the translation that appears in this volume. There is no previous English translation of *De Homine.* Volume Four of the *English Works* contains a work called *Human Nature,* but this is the first half of an early work of Hobbes, the second half being *De Corpore Politico,* and the two together known as *The Elements of Law.* Even though it was never officially published by Hobbes, it is the account of human nature in *Human Nature* that has been most often used to support the claim that Hobbes was an egoist.

I wish to thank Sterling Lamprecht for his help and encouragement and for the pictures of Hobbes that he gave me. My colleagues Tim Duggan and Páll Árdāl have helped me to improve my introduction. And, of course, without T. S. K. Scott-Craig and Charles Wood there would have been no translation of *De Homine*. My wife, Esther, not only helped me to check the different editions of *De Cive*, but has also helped me check all the proofs.

This reprint of *Man and Citizen* is a tribute to the increasing vitality of the study of the philosophy of Thomas Hobbes. A new journal, *Hobbes Studies*, published its first volume on the four hundredth anniversary of his birth. Included in that volume is my article "The Law of Nature as the Moral Law," which provides an expanded discussion of Hobbes's account of the moral virtues contained in pages 16–18 of this introduction. In 1989, the papers presented at a conference in Nantes in 1987 were published in a volume entitled *Thomas Hobbes, De la Métaphysique a la Politique*, edited by Martin Bertman and Michel Malherbe. In that volume, I have an article, "Hobbes's Account of Reason and the Passions," (pp. 83–92) which corrects some misleading remarks about the relationship between reason and the passions that I make on page 15 of this introduction. A conference on Hobbes was convened by François Tricaud in Lyon in 1989. The volume containing those papers should be out shortly. In that volume I have a paper, "The Right of Nature," which clarifies Hobbes's account of the right of nature and of the obligation to obey the sovereign, which I discuss on pages 19–24 of this introduction.

I hope that this volume, which was originally published in 1972, will continue to play some role in the resurgence of Hobbes studies which has resulted in so many excellent books on Hobbes having been published in the last twenty years.

On Man

THE INDEX.

X. On speech and sciences   37
XI. On appetite and aversion, pleasure and displeasure and
    their causes   45
XII. On the emotions, or perturbations of the mind   55
XIII. On dispositions and manners   63
XIV. On religion   71
XV. On artificial man   83

TO THE MOST EXCELLENT WILLIAM,
EARL OF DEVONSHIRE,
MY MOST WORSHIPFUL LORD.

Having completed this section, *On Man,* I have finally fulfilled my promise. For you now possess the prime *Elements* of my philosophy in all its divisions and subdivisions. Moreover, it happens that the two parts whereof this section consists are very dissimilar. One is very difficult, the other very easy; one consists of demonstrations, the other of experience; one can be understood by few, the other by all. They are therefore somewhat abruptly conjoined; but this was necessary, granted the method of my work as a whole.*

For man is not just a *natural body,* but also a part of the state, or (as I put it) of the *body politic;* for that reason he had to be considered as both man and citizen, that is, the first principles of physics had to be conjoined with those of politics, the most difficult with the easiest. The first part of this section was long since ready for the press. "Why, then," you may ask, "since the remainder was easy, have we had to await publication so long? What have you been doing in the meantime?" I reply, "I have been fighting the beasts (ἐθηριομάχησα)." For I too have my Demetriuses and Alexanders, whose trifling works (ἐργασίαις) I am thought, though falsely, to wish to oppose. Yet since I had to answer their clamorings and insults, the long, drawn-out controversy hath caused excessive delay in publication. I had decided that, when these

* Chapter 1 of *De Homine* contains out-of-date biology. Chapters 2 to 9 are concerned with optics. Since they are irrelevant to Hobbes's moral and political philosophy, they have been omitted [Eds.' note].

Elements were finished, I would cast my pen aside. But when I see the current manners of those that teach science, I cast this hope aside and retain my pen; for peradventure these things may also have to be defended. Flies have always been a nuisance at sacrificial offerings. Therefore, like the Emperor Domitian, I shall transfix flies with my pen. So say I, unless perchance you yourself were to improve my efforts.

Thus I remain,
Your Excellency's Most Humble Servant
THOMAS HOBBES
24th June, 1658

X

On Speech and Sciences

1. Definition of speech: peculiar to man. 2. The origin
of speech. 3. The advantages and disadvantages of
speech. 4. Science and demonstration arise from the
knowledge of causes. 5. Theorems are demonstrable for
things only insofar as their causes are in our power;
in other cases it can be demonstrated only that such and
such is possible.

1. Speech or language is the connexion of names constituted by the will of men to stand for the series of conceptions of the things about which we think. Therefore,
as a name is to an idea or conception of a thing, so is
speech to the discourse of the mind. And it seems to be
peculiar to man. For even if some brute animals, taught
by practice, grasp what we wish and command in words,
they do so not through words as words, but as signs; for
animals do not know that words are constituted by the
will of men for the purpose of signification.

Moreover the signification that does occur when animals of the same kind call to one another, is not on that
account speech, since not by their will, but out of the
necessity of nature, these calls by which hope, fear, joy,
and the like are signified, are forced out by the strength
of these passions. And since among animals there is a
limited variety of calls, by changing from one call to another, it comes about that they are warned of danger so
that they may flee, are summoned to feeding, aroused to
song, solicited to love; yet these calls are not speech since

they are not constituted by the will of these animals, but burst forth by the strength of nature from the peculiar fears, joys, desires, and other passions of each of them; and this is not to speak, which is manifest in this, that the calls of animals of the same species are in all lands whatsoever the same, while those of men are diverse.

Therefore other animals also lack understanding. For understanding is a kind of imagination, but one that ariseth from the signification constituted by words.

2. Because, however, I would say that names have arisen from human invention, someone might possibly ask how a human invention could avail so much as to confer on mankind the benefit speech appears to us to have. For it is incredible that men once came together to take counsel to constitute by decree what all words and all connexions of words would signify. It is more credible, however, that at first there were few names and only of those things that were the most familiar. Thus the first man by his own will imposed names on just a few animals, namely, the ones that God led before him to look at; then on other things, as one or another species of things offered itself to his senses; these names, having been accepted, were handed down from fathers to their sons, who also devised others. But when, in the second chapter of Genesis, God is said to have prohibited the eating of the fruit of the tree of knowledge of good and evil before Adam had given names to anything, in what manner could Adam have understood that command of God, when he did not as yet know what was meant by *eating, fruit, tree, knowledge,* and lastly, *good* or *evil?* It must be, therefore, that Adam understood that divine prohibition not from the meaning of the words, but in some supernatural manner, as is made manifest a little later from this: that God asked him who had told him that he was naked. Similarly, how could Adam, the first mortal, have understood the serpent speaking of death,

whereof he could have had no idea? Hence these things could not have been understood in any natural way; and as a consequence, speech could not have had a natural origin except by the will of man himself. This is made even clearer by the confusion of languages at Babel. For from that time the origins of language are diverse and have been brought by single men to single peoples. What others say, however—that names have been imposed on single things according to the nature of those things—is childish. For who could have it so when the nature of things is everywhere the same while languages are diverse? And what relationship hath a *call* (that is, a sound) with an *animal* (that is, a body)?

3. Of the advantages related to language the following are pre-eminent. *First*, that the power of numeral words enables man not only to count things, but also to measure them, whatsoever they may be; so with bodies (insofar as they have any dimensions), whether they be long, or long and wide, or long, wide, and thick; and similarly he can add, subtract, multiply, divide, and compare them with one another; similarly he can also subject times, motion, weight, and degrees of increase and decrease to calculation. From these things the enormous advantages of human life have far surpassed the condition of other animals. For there is no one that doth not know how much these arts are used in measuring bodies, calculating times, computing celestial motions, describing the face of the earth, navigating, erecting buildings, making engines, and in other necessary things. All of these proceed from numbering, but numbering proceeds from speech. *Secondly*, one may teach another, that is, communicate his knowledge to another, he can warn, he can advise, all these he hath from speech also; so that a good, great in itself, through communication becomes even greater. *Thirdly*, that we can command and understand commands is a benefit of speech, and truly the greatest. For

without this there would be no society among men, no
peace, and consequently no disciplines; but first savagery,
then solitude, and for dwellings, caves. For though among
certain animals there are seeming polities, these are not
of sufficiently great moment for living well; hence they
merit not our consideration; and they are largely found
among defenseless animals, not in need of many things;
in which number man is not included; for just as swords
and guns, the weapons of men, surpass the weapons of
brute animals (horns, teeth, and stings), so man surpass-
eth in rapacity and cruelty the wolves, bears, and snakes
that are not rapacious unless hungry and not cruel unless
provoked, whereas man is famished even by future hunger.
From this it is easily understood how much we owe to
language, by which we, having been drawn together and
agreeing to covenants, live securely, happily, and elegantly; we can so live, I insist, if we so will. But language
also hath its disadvantages; namely because man, alone
among the animals, on account of the universal signification of names, can create general rules for himself in the
art of living just as in the other arts; and so he alone
can devise errors and pass them on for the use of others.
Therefore man errs more widely and dangerously than
can other animals. Also, man if it please him (and it will
please him as often as it seems to advance his plans), can
teach what he knows to be false from works that he hath
inherited; that is, he can lie and render the minds of men
hostile to the conditions of society and peace; something
that cannot happen in the societies of other animals, since
they judge what things are good and bad for them by
their senses, not on the basis of the complaints of others,
the causes whereof, unless they be seen, they cannot understand. Moreover, it sometimes happens to those that
listen to philosophers and Schoolmen that listening becomes a habit, and the words that they hear they accept
rashly, even though no sense can be had from them (for

such are the kind of words invented by teachers to hide their own ignorance), and they use them, believing that they are saying something when they say nothing. Finally, on account of the ease of speech, the man who truly doth not think, speaks; and what he says, he believes to be true, and he can deceive himself; a beast cannot deceive itself. Therefore by speech man is not made better, but only given greater possibilities.

4. *Science* is understood as being concerned with theorems, that is, with the truth of general propositions, that is, with the truth of consequences. Indeed, when one is dealing with the truth of fact, it is not properly called *science*, but simply *knowledge*. Therefore it is science when we know a certain proposed theorem to be true, either by knowledge derived from the causes, or from the generation of the subject by right reasoning. On the other hand, when we know (insofar as possible) that such and such a theorem may be true, it is knowledge derived by legitimate reasoning from the experience of effects. Both of these methods of proof are usually called demonstrations; the former kind is, however, preferable to the latter; and rightly so; for it is better to know how we can best use present causes than to know the irrevocable past, whatsoever its nature. Therefore science is allowed to men through the former kind of *a priori* demonstration only of those things whose generation depends on the will of men themselves.

5. Therefore many theorems are demonstrable about quantity, the science whereof is called geometry. Since the causes of the properties that individual figures have belong to them because we ourselves draw the lines; and since the generation of the figures depends on our will; nothing more is required to know the phenomenon peculiar to any figure whatsoever, than that we consider everything that follows from the construction that we ourselves make in the figure to be described. Therefore,

because of this fact (that is, that we ourselves create the figures), it happens that geometry hath been and is demonstrable. On the other hand, since the causes of natural things are not in our power, but in the divine will, and since the greatest part of them, namely the ether, is invisible; we, that do not see them, cannot deduce their qualities from their causes. Of course, we can, by deducing as far as possible the consequences of those qualities that we do see, demonstrate that such and such *could* have been their causes. This kind of demonstration is called *a posteriori*, and its science, physics. And since one cannot proceed in reasoning about natural things that are brought about by motion from the effects to the causes without a knowledge of those things that follow from that kind of motion; and since one cannot proceed to the consequences of motions without a knowledge of quantity, which is geometry; nothing can be demonstrated by physics without something also being demonstrated *a priori*. Therefore physics (I mean true physics), that depends on geometry, is usually numbered among the mixed mathematics. For those sciences are usually called mathematical that are learned not from use and experience, but from teachers and rules. Therefore those mathematics are pure which (like geometry and arithmetic) revolve around quantities in the abstract so that work in the subject requires no knowledge of fact; those mathematics are mixed, in truth, which in their reasoning also consider any quality of the subject, as is the case with astronomy, music, physics, and the parts of physics that can vary on account of the variety of species and the parts of the universe.

Finally, politics and ethics (that is, the sciences of *just* and *unjust*, of *equity* and *inequity*) can be demonstrated *a priori*; because we ourselves make the principles—that is, the causes of justice (namely laws and covenants)—whereby it is known what *justice* and *equity*, and their opposites *injustice* and *inequity*, are. For before covenants and laws were drawn up, neither justice nor injustice, neither public good nor public evil, was natural among men any more than it was among beasts.

XI

On Appetite and Aversion, Pleasure and Displeasure and Their Causes

1. What appetite and aversion are, and their causes. 2. They are not dependent on our will. 3. Appetite is born of experience. 4. Till now, good and evil have been diversely named. 5. The various names for good: *pulchrum*, pleasant, useful. 6. The greatest good to each is his own preservation; the greatest evil, with respect to nature, is his own destruction. 7. Riches. 8. Wisdom. 9. The arts. 10. Letters. 11. Work. 12. What pleasures are. 13. What *pulchra* are. 14. Goods compared. 15. The greatest good.

1. Appetite and aversion do not differ from delight and annoyance otherwise than desire from satisfaction of desire, that is, than the future differs from the present. For appetite is delight, and aversion, annoyance; but the former differs from pleasure, the latter from displeasure, as being not yet present, but foreseen or expected. Moreover, delight and annoyance, although they are not called senses, nevertheless differ only in this: that the sense of an object, as external, comes from the reaction or resistance that is made by an organ; and hence it consists in the endeavour of an organ to push outward; delight, however, consists in the passion made by the action of an object, and is an endeavour inwards.

2. Therefore the causes, as of sense, so of appetite and aversion, delight and annoyance, are these same objects of the senses. From this it can be understood that neither our appetite nor our aversion causeth us to desire or shun this or that; that is, we do not desire because we will. For will itself is an appetite; and we do not shun

something because we will not to do it, but because now
appetite, then aversion, is generated by those things desired or shunned, and a preconception of future pleasure
and displeasure necessarily follows from those same objects. What then: Do we desire food and the other necessities of nature because we will? Are hunger, thirst,
and desires voluntary? When desiring, one can, in truth,
be free *to act*; one cannot, however, be free to *desire*; a
fact that is made so obvious to anyone by his own experience that I cannot but be amazed that there are so many
people who do not understand how this can be. Whenever we say that someone hath free-will to do this or that,
or not to do it, it must always be understood with this
necessary condition: *if he wills.* For to talk of having free-
will to do this or that whether one wills or not is absurd.

Whenever it is asked of someone whether he ought to
do a certain proposed thing or to let it pass, he is said to
deliberate, that is, he hath the liberty of putting aside
either choice. In this deliberation, accordingly as advantages and disadvantages show themselves this way and
that, so appetite and aversion will alternate, until the
thing demands that a decision be made. The last appetite
(either of doing or omitting), the one that leads immediately to action or omission, is properly called the *will.*

3. According to the method of nature, sense is prior to
appetite. For it cannot be known whether or not what
we see as a pleasure would have been so, except by experience, that is, by feeling it. Therefore it is commonly said
that there is no desire for the unknown. In truth, however, there can be a desire to experience the unknown.
Whence it is that infants desire few things while youths
try many new things, and with increasing age, mature
men (especially educated ones) experiment with innumerable things, even with those that are unnecessary; experienced people know what every pleasure is, and, by
drawing on memory, they afterwards desire more often.

Even if first experiences of something be sometimes displeasing, especially when new or rare, by habit they are rendered not displeasing, and afterwards pleasing; that much can habit change the nature of single men.

4. The common name for all things that are desired, insofar as they are desired, is *good;* and for all things we shun, *evil.* Therefore Aristotle hath well defined *good* as that which all men desire. But, since different men desire and shun different things, there must needs be many things that are *good* to some and *evil* to others; so that which is *good* to us is *evil* to our enemies. Therefore *good* and *evil* are correlated with desiring and shunning. There can be a common *good*, and it can rightly be said of something, *it is commonly a good*, that is, useful to many, or good for the state. At times one can also talk of a good for everyone, like health: but this way of speaking is relative; therefore one cannot speak of something as being *simply good;* since whatsoever is good, is good for someone or other. In the beginning everything that God created was good. Why? Because all His works pleased Him. It is also said that God is good to all who invoke His name, but not to those who blaspheme His name. Therefore good is said to be relative to person, place, and time. What pleaseth one man now, will displease another later; and the same holds true for everyone else. For the nature of good and evil follows from the nature of circumstances (συντυχίαν).

5. The names of *good* and *evil* also vary in a number of different ways. For the same thing that, as desired, is said to be good, is said to be *pleasing* as acquired; the thing that, as desired, is said to be good, is said to be *pulchrum* when contemplated. For *pulchritudo* is that quality in an object that makes one expect good from it. For whatsoever things are seen as similar to those that have pleased, seem as though they would please. Therefore *pulchritudo* is an indication of future good. This, when

it is viewed in action, is called honesty; when it dwells in a form, it is called *beauty*; and it pleaseth by imagination, even before the good of which it is a sign is acquired. For the same reason *evil* and *turpe* are spoken about in the same way. Furthermore, the thing that, when desired, is called good, is, if desired for its own sake, called pleasing; and if for some other thing, it is called useful. For the good that we desire for its own sake we do not *use*, since *usefulness* is applied to means and instruments, while *enjoyment* applies to something proposed as an end. Moreover, good (like evil) is divided into *real* and *apparent*. Not because any apparent good may not truly be good in itself, without considering the other things that follow from it; but in many things, whereof part is good and part evil, there is sometimes such a necessary connexion between the parts that they cannot be separated. Therefore, though in each one of them there be so much good, or so much evil; nevertheless the chain as a whole is partly good and partly evil. And whenever the major part be good, the series is said to be good, and is desired; on the contrary, if the major part be evil, and, moreover, if it be known to be so, the whole is rejected. Whence it happens that inexperienced men that do not look closely enough at the long-term consequences of things, accept what appears to be good, not seeing the evil annexed to it; afterwards they experience damage. And this is what is meant by those who distinguish good and evil as *real* and *apparent*.

6. Moreover, the greatest of goods for each is his own preservation. For nature is so arranged that all desire good for themselves. Insofar as it is within their capacities, it is necessary to desire life, health, and further, insofar as it can be done, security of future time. On the other hand, though death is the greatest of all evils (especially when accompanied by torture), the pains of life can be

so great that, unless their quick end is foreseen, they may lead men to number death among the goods.

Power, if it be extraordinary, is good, because it is useful for protection; and protection provides security. If it be not extraordinary, it is useless; for what all have equally is nothing.

Friendships are good, certainly useful. For friendships, among many other things, confer protection. Therefore enemies are evil, as they bring dangers and remove security.

7. Riches, if immense—certainly as Lucullus defined the wealthy man as one that can support an army on his own —are useful. For they are almost certain protection. Moderate wealth, to those willing to use it for protection, is also useful; for it acquires friendships; friendships, moreover, are protection. Those unwilling to use riches for protection, however, provoke envy. Therefore to that extent they are an *apparent good*.

Riches that are not inherited, but acquired by one's own industry, are good; for they are pleasing. For they seem to everyone an argument for his own prudence. Destitution or even poverty, lacking necessities, is evil, since to need necessities is evil. Poverty without need is good; it delivers its owner from envy, calumny, and plots.

8. Wisdom is useful. For some protection is to be had from it. It is also desirable for its own sake, that is, pleasing. It is also *pulchrum* because it is difficult to acquire. Ignorance is bad; as in it there is no protection, or foresight of approaching evil.

The love of riches is greater than wisdom. For commonly the latter is not sought except for the sake of the former. And if men have the former, they wish to seem to have the latter also. For it is not as the Stoics say, that he who is wise is rich; but, rather, it must be said that he who is rich is wise.

The glory of wisdom is greater than riches. For the lat-

ter are usually had as a sign of the former. Want is less
a disgrace than stupidity; for the former can be attributed
to the inequity of fortune; the latter is attributable to
nature alone. Stupidity is, however, more bearable than
want; for the former, as they say, is not characteristically
a burden.

9. The sciences and arts are good. For they are pleasing. For nature hath made man an admirer of all new
things, that is, avid to know the causes of everything. So
it is that science is the food for so many minds, and is
related to the mind as food is to the body; and as food is
to the famished, so are curious phenomena to the mind.
They differ in this, however, that the body can become
satiated with food while the mind cannot be filled up by
knowledge.

Again, every art is useful insofar as it is possible to apply it to matter. They are also of the greatest public util-
ity, since it is to them that we owe nearly all the useful
tools and trappings of mankind. It ought to be understood, however, that not all men have the science where-
unto they profess; for those that discuss the causes of
things on the basis of others' writings, and those that
make discoveries by copying others' sentences, are utterly
worthless. For to do what hath been done, hath nothing
good about it in itself; but on the contrary, this is sometimes evil, since by confirming ancient errors they obstruct
the path of truth.

10. Letters are also good, especially languages and histories; for they are pleasing. They are useful, too, especially histories; for these supply in abundance the
evidence on which rests the science of causes; in truth,
natural history for physics and also civil histories for civil
and moral science; and this is so whether they be true or
false, provided that they are not impossible. For in the
sciences causes are sought not only of those things that
were, but also of those things that can be. The languages

that are in use among neighbouring peoples are also useful, for commerce and negotiations. Also Latin and Greek, assuredly the languages of the sciences, for science.

11. Work is good; it is truly a motive for life. Therefore unless you walk for the sake of walking, you do so for your work. *Where shall I turn, what shall I do?* are the voices of people grieving. Idleness is torture. In all times and places, nature abhors a vacuum.

12. To progress is pleasing; for it is an approach to an end, that is, to what is more pleasing. To see evil done to another is pleasing; but it pleaseth not because it is evil, but because it is another's. Whence it is that men are accustomed to hasten to the spectacle of the death and danger of others. In the same way, it is displeasing to see another's good; not because it is good, but because it is another's. Imitation is pleasing; for it recalls the past. It is pleasing to represent the past, if it was good, because it was good; and if it was evil, because it is past. Therefore music, poetry, and painting are pleasing.

Novelties are pleasing; for they are desired as food for the mind. To think well of one's own power, whether rightly or wrongly, is pleasing. For if one judgeth oneself truly, one seems to have provided for one's own protection; and if falsely, it is still pleasing; for those things that please when true will also please when false.

Therefore victory is pleasing; for it makes one think well of himself; and all games and contests are pleasing; since those that compete always imagine victory. Especially pleasing, however, are contests of talents; as in them everyone thinks that first place will be assigned to him. Therefore, to be vanquished in a contest of talents is displeasing.

To be praised is pleasing; for it makes us think well of ourselves.

13. Signs or indications of good are *pulchrum*. There-

fore a sign of extraordinary power is *pulchrum*. Also,
therefore, to do what is both good and difficult
is *pulchrum*; for it is an indication of uncommon power.
Extraordinary form is *pulchrum*; for it is a sign in all
things of the extraordinary execution of the work where-
unto one was born. That is finely formed, moreover, that
hath the form of that thing which we have proved to be
the best of its kind.

To be praised, loved, and magnified is *pulchrum*; for
they are testimonies to virtue and power. To be summoned to public office is *pulchrum*; for it is a public
testimony to virtue.

In the arts, new inventions, if useful, are *pulchrum*:
for they are a sign of extraordinary power. Trifles, on the
other hand, though more difficult, are less *pulchrum*: they
are indeed signs of power, but useless, and at the same
time indicate a mind of no great will and purpose.

To have learned the arts from others, that is, to have
been taught, is certainly useful, but not *pulchrum*; as
there is nothing extraordinary about it. For few are those
who cannot be taught.

To be bold in danger when the situation demands it is
pulchrum: for it is not common. If the situation doth not
demand it, it is stupidity, that is, *turpe*. To act everywhere
according to one's disposition and profession is *pulchrum*
in conspicuous men; as it is an indication of a free disposition. To do the contrary in conspicuous persons is
turpe and is the sign of a servile mind and of having something to hide: for no one hides a thing that is
pulchrum. To find fault with things that are right, a sign
of ignorance, is *turpe*: for knowledge is power. Moreover, to taunt is more *turpe*, a sign of lack of education.
To err is not *turpe*, since it is common to all. For a
teacher, to err too often is *turpe*, since it is contrary to his
profession.

Self-confidence is *pulchrum*: being a certain sign of

one conscious of his own virtue. Ostentation is *turpe:* for it ariseth from a need for praise.

Contempt for all but the greatest riches is *pulchrum:* for it is an indication of a person who has no need of small amounts. The love of money is *turpe:* it is the sign of one that can be led anywhere by a bribe. Furthermore, it is a sign of need, even in wealthy men.

To ignore a favour-seeker, is *pulchrum;* for it is an indication of self-confidence. To placate enemies with gifts is *turpe.* For it is a ransoming of oneself, or a purchasing of peace, a sign of need; for men are not accustomed to purchase, except those things that they need.

14. If good and evil be compared, other things being equal, the greater is that which lasts longer, as the whole is to the part.

And, other things being equal, that which is stronger, for the same reason. For larger and smaller differ as greater and less.

And, other things being equal, what is good for more is greater than what is good for fewer. For the more general and the more particular differ as greater and less.

To regain a good is better than not to have lost it. For it is more rightly esteemed because of the memory of evil. Therefore it is better to recover one's health than not to have been sick.

15. Concerning the pleasurable things whereof there be satiation, such as the pleasures of the flesh, I shall say nothing, because they are excessively well known, their pleasure is balanced by loathing, and because some of them are offensive. The greatest good, or as it is called, felicity and the final end, cannot be attained in the present life. For if the end be final, there would be nothing to long for, nothing to desire; whence it follows not only that nothing would itself be a good from that time on, but also that man would not even feel. For all sense

is conjoined with some appetite or aversion; and not to feel is not to live.

For of goods, the greatest is always progressing towards ever further ends with the least hindrance. Even the enjoyment of a desire, when we are enjoying it, is an appetite, namely the motion of the mind to enjoy by parts, the thing that it is enjoying. For life is perpetual motion that, when it cannot progress in a straight line, is converted into circular motion.

XII

On the Emotions, or Perturbations of the Mind

1. Perturbation of the mind and what it is. 2. Joy and hate. 3. Hope and fear. 4. Anger. 5. Fear of the invisible. 6. Pride and shame. 7. Laughter and weeping. 8. Love of external things. 9. Self-esteem. 10. Compassion. 11. Emulation and envy. 12. Admiration.

1. Emotions or *perturbations* of the mind are species of appetite and aversion, their differences having been taken from the diversity and circumstances of the objects that we desire or shun. They are called *perturbations* because they frequently obstruct right reasoning. They obstruct right reasoning in this, that they militate against the real good and in favor of the apparent and most immediate good, which turns out frequently to be evil when everything associated with it hath been considered. For though judgment originates from appetite out of a union of mind and body, it must proceed from reason. Therefore, although the real good must be sought in the long term, which is the job of reason, appetite seizeth upon a present good without foreseeing the greater evils that necessarily attach to it. Therefore appetite perturbs and impedes the operation of reason; whence it is rightly called a *perturbation*.

Moreover, emotions consist in various motions of the blood and animal spirits as they variously expand and contract; the causes of these motions are phantasms concerning good and evil excited in the mind by objects.

2. When it is conceived that a good is coming to oneself from outside, without any compensatory evil con-

sequences when the good is to be enjoyed, the emotion is called *joy*. On the other hand, to the extent that a person conceives that evil is impending upon him without any idea of a good to compensate for that evil, his emotion is called *hate*; and all evil, to the extent that it is impending, is called *hateful*. Therefore evil that we can neither overcome nor avoid, we hate.

3. Whenever, in truth, we simultaneously conceive of an evil and of some means whereby that evil may be avoided, the motion that ariseth we call *hope*. Similarly, if, with good impending, we conceive of some means whereby it may be lost, or if we imagine that some connected evil may be drawn to it, the emotion is called *fear*. And so it is manifest that *hope* and *fear* so alternate with each other that almost no time is so short that it cannot encompass their interchange. And so *hope* and *fear* must then be called perturbations, when both are encompassed in the briefest time; and these perturbations are named after the prevailing emotion, simply *hope* or *fear*.

4. If, when one is pressed or assaulted by evil, a sudden hope is conceived that the evil may be overcome by opposition and resistance, the passion ariseth that is called *anger*. And, in truth, it ariseth most often from the belief that one is contemned. Thus an angry man wishes to do as much as he can or hopes that he can, so that he will not seem to be suitable for, and subject to, the mockery of others, namely by doing evil to the contemner to the degree that seems to him sufficient for making the contemner repent of the evil he had done him. But anger is not always so conjoined with contempt. For, if anything whatsoever obstructs the progress of those proceeding to any proposed goal whatsoever (even if the obstacles be inanimate and therefore incapable of contemning), as soon as hope appears that such obstacles can be removed from the path, those proceeding summon strength, that

is, they show the anger whereby these things can be removed.

Related to anger is the emotion that is called μῆνις by
the Greeks, namely the desire for vengeance, that is, the
constant and long-term will of doing evil to someone so
that he will repent of the supposed injury done by him,
or it will frighten others away from doing injury. Such
was the anger of Achilles against the Greeks because of
the injury done him by Agamemnon. This differs, however, from the former anger in that the former is sudden,
while this is, on the contrary, most constant, as long as
the conversion to our will can be expected of the mind
of him with whom we are angry. And so, to kill him who
did the injury doth not satisfy vengeance; for the dead
never repent of anything. Therefore the object of anger
is displeasing to one, but only until he is overcome by
force. For him that you provoke with insults when you
are exposed, you will make angry; but you will make him
tremble when you are armed. As hope brings out *anger*,
so fear controls it; that is, just as through imagination
the animal spirits are poured into the nerves to make
them strong against attacking evil, so through imagination of greater evil they are withdrawn to the heart for its
defense, or for flight. The object of hope is an apparent
good; the object of fear, an apparent evil. Whence the
hoped-for good that is expected to come to us we never
perceive with security; for if we so perceived it, it would
then be certain, and our expectation would more properly
be called not hope, but joy. Even the most insubstantial
arguments are sufficient for hope. Yea, even what the
mind cannot truly conceive can be hoped for, if it can be
expressed. Similarly, anything can be feared even though
it be not conceived of, provided that it is commonly said
to be terrible, or if we should see many simultaneously
fleeing; for, even though the cause be unknown, we ourselves also flee, as in those terrors that are called panic-

terrors. For we believe that those that first fly have seen some danger as a cause for flight. Therefore in this instance the emotions need to be governed by reason. For reason is that which, by measuring and comparing both our powers and those of the objects regulates the amount now of hope and then of fear, so that we may neither be mocked by hopes nor lose by fear without just cause those goods that we have. For it is only our ignorance that makes us so frequently to experience false hope and treacherous fear.

5. All men are of the opinion that there is an invisible something or invisible things, from which (accordingly as they be favourable or unfavourable) all goods are to be hoped and all evils are to be feared. For men, whose power is small, when they saw those enormous works, heaven and earth, the visible universe, the motion and intellect of animals of most subtle devising, and the most ingenious fashioning of the organs, could not contemn their genius (since they can imitate none of them), and hence it is neither incomprehensible nor to be wondered at that all good is expected from Him by whom the greatest things are made when He is gracious, and all evil when He is angered. And this is the emotion that is called natural piety, and is the first foundation of all religions.

6. Sometimes the animal spirits are in concert transported by a certain joy that ariseth from their thinking themselves to be honoured (εὐδοκιμεῖν); this elation of the mind is called glory, and hath this as its cause, that the spirits, because they feel that the things they say and do are approved, rise from the heart to the face as a witness of the good opinion conceived of themselves.

The contrary emotion is shame, wherein the spirits, being suddenly transported by a consciousness or suspicion of something unseemly having been let slip, are disordered, and they force blood into the muscles of the

face, which is to blush. Therefore shame is displeasing
that happens to those who love praise when they are discovered saying or doing something that is unseemly in
word or deed. Therefore blushing is the sign of one that
desires to speak and act decently in all things; hence is it
praiseworthy in youths, but not so in others. For not only
is it demanded of mature men that they study how to be
seemly, but also that they know how.

7. Moreover, when the animal spirits are suddenly
transported by the joy arising from any word, deed, or
thought of one's own that is seemly, or of a stranger that
is unseemly, this passion is laughter. For if someone hath
said or done something extraordinary, as it seems to him,
he is inclined to laugh. In the same way, if someone else
hath said or done something unseemly, in comparison
with which he is made more commendable to himself
than hitherto, he can scarcely keep himself from laughter. And universally the passion of laughter is sudden
self-commendation resulting from a stranger's unseemliness. Therefore almost nothing is laughed at again and
again by the same people. One doth not laugh, however,
at the unseemliness of friends and kindred, since they
are not strangers. Therefore there are three things conjoined that move one to laughter: unseemliness, strangers,
and suddenness.

Weeping is the contrary passion, and it ariseth whenever someone believes that he hath suddenly been deprived of some vehement hope. And so the animal spirits,
dilated by hope, contract when hope suddenly fails, and,
making an attack on the tear-producing organs, they force
the humour that is in them to overflow in the eyes. Those
that weep the greatest amount and more frequently are
those, such as women and children, who have the least
hope in themselves and the most in friends. Those who
laugh the most are those who collect the fewest arguments for their virtue from their own praiseworthy deeds

and the most from the *turpe* deeds of others. Friends also weep at some time or other when returning to favour after anger. For in returning to favour there is a sudden banishing of revenge from the mind. Therefore they weep, like boys who have gone unavenged.

8. Love, if it be conspicuous, may be divided into almost as many passions as there are objects of love. Such as love of money, love of power, love of knowledge, etc. The love of money, if it exceeds moderation, is called covetousness; the love of political power, if immoderate, ambition; for these perturb and pervert the mind.

Moreover, the love, whereby man loves man, is understood in two ways; and good will appertains to both. But it is called one kind of love when we wish ourselves well, and another when we wish well to others. Therefore a male neighbor is usually loved one way, a female another; for in loving the former, we seek his good, in loving the latter, our own.

Again, love of fame or renown, if it be excessive, needs be placed among the perturbations; but moderation, both in the desire for fame and in the desire for other external things, is useful; certainly insofar as it can offer protection. But even though we think of fame after death as being neither unpleasing nor useless for others, we are nevertheless mistaken in looking at the future like the present, because we shall not experience it, nor can we mere mortals estimate its worth. For we would be making the same mistake as we would were we to be grieved because we had not been famous before we were born.

9. Excessive self-esteem impedes reason; and on that account it is a perturbation of the mind, wherein a certain swelling of the mind is experienced because the animal spirits are transported. The contrary emotion is excessive diffidence or a shrinking of the mind. Therefore solitude usually pleaseth the latter, and crowds of men, the former. Proper self-esteem, however, is not a

perturbation, but a state of mind that ought to be. Those, moreover, who estimate their own worth correctly, do so on the basis of their past deeds, and so, what they have done, they dare to try again. Those who estimate their worth too highly, or who pretend to be what they are not, or who believe flatterers, become disheartened when dangers actually confront them.

10. To grieve because of another's evil, that is, to feel another's pain and to suffer with him, that is, to imagine that another's evil could happen to oneself, is called compassion. And so those who have become accustomed to similar evils are more compassionate; and conversely. For evil that hath been less experienced one fears less. In the same way, we are less compassionate toward those who receive judicial punishments, either because we hate malefactors, or because we believe that no similar fault lies in us. Therefore, that almost no one is compassionate toward those who are said to suffer eternally in hell, and this by the most intense tortures, can be explained either because we believe that the same thing could not happen to us, or because those tortures are not sufficiently strongly comprehended by our imagination, or because those who teach that these things are so do not live as though they themselves believed in it for themselves under any circumstances.

11. Grief because another hath been preferred to oneself, when conjoined with suitable endeavours, is emulation; but when conjoined with the wish to have that preference withdrawn, it is envy.

12. Admiration is the passion of joy in novelty; for it is natural for men to love novelty. Moreover, we call things novel that happen rarely; further, in each kind of thing the best are also rare. Moreover, this passion is almost peculiar to men. For even if other animals, whenever they behold something new or unusual, admire it as far as they are able to judge whether it be harmful or

harmless to them; men, when they see something new, seek to know whence it came and to what use they can put it. And so they rejoice in novelty as an occasion for learning about causes and effects. Whence it follows that he who admires more things than others may be either more ignorant or more talented than others; to wit, more ignorant, if more new things happen to him; and more talented, if those same new things give him more to admire.

There would be an almost infinite number of passions, if we gave different names to all of them, however insignificant the differences between them. But since none there be that are not related to some one of those that we have described, we shall be content with what we have said concerning them.

XIII

On Dispositions and Manners

1. Definition of disposition. 2. The diversity of dispositions ariseth: from the constitution of the body: 3.
From habit: 4. From experience: 5. From the goods of
fortune: 6. From the opinion one hath of oneself: 7.
From authorities. 8. Virtues differ for different people.
9. Law is the standard of manners.

1. Dispositions, that is, men's inclinations toward certain things, arise from a six-fold source: namely from the
constitution of the body, from experience, from habit,
from the goods of fortune, from the opinion one hath of
oneself, and from authorities. When these things change,
dispositions change also.

2. From the constitution of the body: those of warmer
constitution are, other things being equal, for the most
part more daring; those of colder constitution are more
timid. Dispositions differ in two ways due to the mobility
of the animal spirits (that is, from the swiftness of imag-
ining things): first, because some dispositions are more
acute; whence some people are of a lively disposition, and
others of a slow one; secondly, of those that are of a
quick disposition, because some let their thoughts wander
over vast spaces, and some let them revolve around only
one thing; whence fancy is praiseworthy in some, while
judgment is commendable in others. And so the disposition of the latter people is suitable for resolving controversies, and for philosophy of all kinds (that is, for reasoning); of the former, for poetry and invention; both
alike are suitable for oratory. And, indeed, judgment

subtly distinguisheth among similar objects while fancy pleasingly confounds dissimilar objects. The former is characteristic, for the most part, of age, and the latter of youth. Often, however, both are found in both. Fancy, if it exceeds moderation, ends in stupidity, like those who cannot finish a speech, once begun, because their thoughts lead them from one proposition to others. Slowness, on the other hand, if it exceeds moderation, gives itself over to another kind of stupidity, dullness.

What is commonly said, that old men by disposition are excessively attentive to riches, is not true. For just because a great part of old men are wont to amass riches that they, least of all, are about to use, they do so not out of the disposition of old age, but from perpetual application; for before old age they applied themselves in the same way, namely so that, by trying to see how far they could proceed in the acquiring of riches through their prudence and talent, they could under all circumstances approve of themselves and enjoy their riches, not as riches, but as a sign of the prudence whereby they had collected them. Nor ought this to seem surprising; for those who apply themselves to letters, to the extent that they advance to greater age, usually in the same proportion grow greater in knowledge, as they see in knowledge, as in a glass, the virtue of their minds. And so all men, insofar as they have the strength, are accustomed to extol and cultivate whatsoever mode of life they have chosen as most pleasing for old age; and in old age they accomplish the most, not because they are older, but because they have more fully perfected their techniques in doing those things that, by their nature, the longer you work at them, the faster they are always accomplished.

3. From habit: because of this, that those things that offend when new (that is, those things that man's nature initially resists) more often than not whet that same nature when repeated; and those things that at first are

merely endured soon compel love. Something that is most fully perceived in the regulating of the body, but also in the operations of the mind. And so those accustomed to wine from youth by no means easily break the habit; and those imbued with no matter what opinions from boyhood retain them even in old age, especially men who are not particularly solicitous about the truth or falsity of things unless they pertain to something familiar. Therefore among all peoples' religion and doctrine, which everyone hath been taught from their early years, so shackle them forever that they hate and revile dissenters: as is made manifest principally from the books of theologians (for whom, of all people, it is least fitting), which are full of the most atrocious abuse. The disposition of these men is not suited to peace and society.

In the same way, habit makes those who have often lived in danger for a long time have a less fearful disposition; and those who have lived with honours for the longest time are less insolent in disposition, as by now they have ceased to admire themselves.

4. From experience of external things: whereby it happens that the disposition is rendered cautious. Those, on the contrary, who have but little experience are frequently foolhardy in disposition. For the human mind proceeds in its reasoning from the known to the unknown; and it cannot perceive the long-term consequences of things without knowledge from the senses, that is, without experience of many consequences. Whence it happens that men's dispositions are corrected by adverse events, namely a daring disposition by frequent misfortune, an ambitious one by repeated setbacks, and an impudent one by repeated coldness; finally, it is by the rod that boys' dispositions toward all things are shaped as parents and teachers wish.

5. From the goods of fortune, that is, from riches, nobility of birth, and civil power it happens that disposi-

tions are in some measure made various; for dispositions
are frequently made more proud by riches and civil power;
for those who can do more demand that they be allowed
more, that is, they are more inclined to cause injuries,
and they are more unsuited for entering into a society of
equitable laws with those who can do less. Ancient nobility makes the disposition affable, because in bestowing
honour on someone, they can be bountiful and kind to
all, since under all circumstances they are secure enough
about the honour due to themselves. The disposition of
new nobility is more suspicious, like those who, not yet
certain enough of how much honour ought to be bestowed
on themselves, often become excessively harsh toward inferiors and excessively diffident toward equals.

6. From the opinion that one hath of oneself. Whence
it also happens that those who to themselves seem wise,
and are not, have a disposition unsuited for correcting
their own faults. For they do not believe that anything in
them needs correcting. On the contrary, they are inclined
either to correct others' deeds, or to be vituperative or
scornful about them, like those who believe that whatsoever they see being done contrary to their own opinion is
being done improperly. And so they judge a state to be
badly governed which is not governed as they themselves
wish; and as a result they are more suited than other men
to new things. Those who to themselves seem learned
have the same disposition; for to themselves they seem
wise; for no man desires to be learned unless learning
leads to wisdom. Whence it happens that pedagogues
are most frequently censorious and antisocial in disposition, like those who, because they see that they have been
selected to regulate the manners of youths, scarcely abstain from censuring the manners of their own fathers,
even though dead. Also those, who are called to regulate
public morals by their teaching (especially doctors of the
Church and they not knowing by whom they are called to

so great a ministry), demand that kings themselves, the supreme governors of the Church, be ruled by them; yea, with the greatest danger to the state, they wish it to seem that this office hath been granted to them, not by kings, and by those whom God hath commissioned for the care and safety of the people, but directly by God. Similarly, those who are elected by the state to interpret the laws cannot but seem to themselves wiser than other men, so great is the testimony that they have received from the state. And so they demand to use their office not so much for declaring what is right, that is, for explaining the laws (that is, the state's mandates), but often even for laying down what is right, that is, for commanding the highest, that is, for compelling order in the state: something that frequently is wont to be the start of civil wars, especially when the rulers of the state are accused of injustice by those who are considered to be most expert in law, but who are in fact a most inexpert mob. They, by leading those to whom new things and civil war are useful, either because of pleasing ambition or for some other familiar and shameless cause, are taking arms against the rulers of the state, that is, against the state itself.

7. From authorities. Moreover, I call authorities anyone in any subject whose precept or example is followed, because one hath been led thereto by a belief in their wisdom. From them, if good, the dispositions of youths are well formed, and deformed, if deformed; they are either teachers, or fathers, or anyone whomsoever that youths hear commonly praised for wisdom; for they revere those who are praised and they imitate those whom they think worthy. Whence it must be understood, first, not only how much fathers, teachers, and tutors of youths must imbue the minds of youths with precepts which are good and true, but also how much they must bear themselves justly and in a righteous manner in their presence, for the dispositions of youths are not less, but much more

disposed to bad habits by example than they are to good ones by precept. Secondly, the books that they are to read must be sound, pure, and useful. There are, however, books which were written by citizens of Rome, when democracy was flourishing or recently extinct (and also by Greeks, when the republic of Athens was flourishing), that are filled with both examples and precepts that make the people's disposition hostile to kings; and this from no other cause than this, that in those books they see praised the shameful acts perpetrated by perfidious men, and especially regicides (provided that they called the kings tyrants before they killed them). In truth, the people's disposition hath up to now been greatly corrupted by the reading of books and the listening to siren songs of those who want supreme power in the kingdom to belong to an ecclesiastic in civil form. For it is on this account that, for Cassiuses and Brutuses, there arise Ravaillacs and Cléments, who announced they were serving God when, in killing their kings, they were really serving another's ambition.

8. Dispositions, when they are so strengthened by habit that they beget their actions with ease and with reason unresisting, are called *manners*. Moreover, manners, if they be good, are called *virtues*, if evil, *vices*. Since, however, good and evil are not the same to all, it happens that the same manners are praised by some and condemned by others, that is, are called good by some, evil by others, virtues by some, vices by others. So, just as the proverb hath it, "So many men, so many opinions," one can also say, "Many men, many different rules for vice and virtue." Nevertheless, what is to be understood about men insofar as they are men, is not applicable insofar as they are citizens; for those who are outside of a state are not obliged to follow another's opinion, while those in a state are obliged by covenants. Whence it is to be understood that they, who consider men by themselves

and as though they existed outside of civil society, can have no moral science because they lack any certain standard against which virtue and vice can be judged and defined. For all sciences begin with definitions, or otherwise they must not be called sciences, but mere verbiage.

9. Therefore a common standard for virtues and vices doth not appear except in civil life; this standard cannot, for this reason, be other than the laws of each and every state; for natural law, when the state is constituted, becomes part of the civil law. Nor is there any impediment to such a thesis in the fact that laws are innumerable and that once there were states with different laws. For, whatsoever the laws are, not to violate them is always and everywhere held to be a virtue in citizens, and to neglect them is held to be a vice. Although it is true that certain actions may be just in one state, and unjust in another, nevertheless, justice (that is, not to violate the laws) is and shall be everywhere the same. Moreover, that moral virtue, that we can truly measure by civil laws, which is different in different states, is justice and equity; that moral virtue which we measure purely by the natural laws is only charity. Furthermore, all moral virtue is contained in these two. However, the other three virtues (except for justice) that are called cardinal—*courage, prudence,* and *temperance*—are not virtues of citizens as citizens, but as men, for these virtues are useful not so much to the state as they are to those individual men who have them. For just as the state is not preserved save by the courage, prudence, and temperance of good citizens, so is it not destroyed save by the courage, prudence, and temperance of its enemies. For courage, like prudence, is more a strength of the mind than a goodness of manners; and temperance is more a privation of those vices that arise from the greedy dispositions of those that harm not the state, but themselves, than it is a moral virtue. For just as every citizen hath his own private good, so hath

the state its own public good. Nor, in truth, should one demand that the courage and prudence of the private man, if useful only to himself, be praised or held as a virtue by states or by any other men whatsoever to whom these same are not useful. So, condensing this whole teaching on manners and dispositions into the fewest words, I say that good dispositions are those which are suitable for entering into civil society; and good manners (that is, moral virtues) are those whereby what was entered upon can be best preserved. For all the virtues are contained in justice and charity. Whence it can also be understood that dispositions contrary to these are wicked; and that contrary manners and vices are all contained in injustice and in a mind insensible to another's evils, that is, in a lack of charity.

XIV

On Religion

1. Definition of religion. 2. What it is to love and fear God. 3. What faith is. 4. Faith depends on laws. 5. Justice is inscribed in the heart by God. 6. God can remit sins without injustice, with no punishment exacted. 7. No one's just works are sins. 8. Definition and subdivisions of worship. 9. What public worship is. 10. The parts of worship: prayers, thanksgiving, public fasts, offerings. 11. Various superstitious cults. 12. The end of worship is to allay anxieties about the future. 13. What things there are that change religions.

1. Religion is the external worship (*cultus*) of men who sincerely honour God. Moreover, they sincerely honour God who believe not only that He exists, but also that He is the omnipotent and omniscient creator and ruler of all things, and, further, that He is by His own will the distributor of prosperity and adversity. Therefore religion as such (that is, natural) consists of two parts; whereof one is *faith* (or the belief that God exists and that He governs all things), the other is *worship*. Moreover, the first part, which concerns faith in God, is usually called *piety* toward God. For he who believes the above cannot not endeavour to obey Him in all things; neither can he not endeavour to give thanks in prosperity nor to utter supplications in adversity; for these things are the most characteristic works of piety; in them are contained the love and fear wherewith we are commanded to love and fear God.

2. But God is not to be loved by man, as man is by man. For we always understand by the love of man to-

ward man either the desire for embraces or benevolence,
both whereof would be unsuitable for understanding love
toward God. To love God is to keep His commandments
gladly. To fear God is to watch lest we fall into sin, in
the same way as we are accustomed to fear the laws.

3. Moreover, faith, save for our belief that God hath
made and rules all things, because it concerns things that
are placed beyond the grasp of human nature, is opinion
which ariseth from the authority of the speakers. So unless there hath been an antecedent opinion that he who
speaks, learned what he saith by some supernatural
means, there can be no reason why we ought to believe
him. Therefore we believe no one about supernatural
things, unless we believe that he hath previously done
some supernatural deed. Moreover, how can someone be
believed who saith that the things he saith or teacheth
are confirmed by miracles unless he himself hath worked
miracles? For if a private person is to be believed without
a miracle, why should the various teachings of one man
be any better than those of another? Therefore the greatest part of our religion and most gratifying faith in God
must not depend on private persons, unless they work
miracles.

4. If religion, beyond what consists in natural piety,
doth not depend on private persons, miracles now having ceased, it must depend on the laws of the state. And
so religion be not philosophy, but rather in all states law;
and on that account it is not to be disputed but observed. For it can neither be doubted that God must be
thought of with honour, nor that He ought to be loved,
feared, and worshipped. For these things are common to
religions among all peoples. Only those things are to be
disputed wherein one man disagrees with another; which,
because of this, do not concern faith in God. In these disputations, moreover, while we are seeking scientific knowledge of those things that do not belong to science, we

are destroying faith in God, as much as we have any in us. For such knowledge bears the same relationship to faith as success doth to hope; for, as the apostle teacheth of the three virtues, *faith, hope,* and *charity,* when the kingdom of God is at hand, *faith* and *hope* will no longer exist, and *charity* alone will abide. Therefore questions about the nature of God, the creator of nature, are excessively inquisitive and do not increase the works of piety; those moreover which dispute about God, wish to win people over not so much to faith in God (in whom all believe already) as to faith in themselves.

5. Since, however, to love God is the same as to keep His commandments, and to fear God is the same as to fear lest we do something against His commandments, it can further be asked how one can know what things God hath commanded. To this question it can be replied, God himself, because He hath made men rational, hath enjoined the following law on them, and hath inscribed it in all hearts: that no one should do unto another that which he would consider inequitable for the other to do unto him. In this precept are contained both universal justice and civil obedience. For who would not judge it inequitable, if he were constituted by the people with the highest sovereignty in the state, in order to rule and to issue laws, for his laws to be spurned, or his authority overlooked, not to mention disputed, by any subject whatsoever? Therefore, if, when you were a king, you judged this to be inequitable, would you not have, in law, a most certain rule for your actions? Moreover, that law is also divine, which orders obedience to supreme powers, that is, to the laws of those in supreme command.

6. But since men now violate the commandments of God and sin daily, how can it be consistent with divine justice, someone may ask, that God doth not require punishment of them for their sins? But do we consider a man to be unjust or more holy if he never punisheth the harms

done him, and if he be so forgiving that he demands no revenge of any kind nor, indeed, any repentance? Therefore, unless we say that God be less compassionate than men, there is no reason why God cannot forgive sinners, at least the repentant, without any punishment having been received by them or by others in their place. Though God formerly demanded sacrifices for the people's sins, those sacrifices did not have punishment as their purpose, but were constituted as *signs* that those sinning were by themselves turning back to God and were returning to their former obedience. And so the death of our Saviour was not a punishment for sins, but a sacrifice for sins. And although He is said to bear our sins, this is not to be understood as a punishment any more than were the sacrifices of old, which did not consist in the punishments of animals for the sins that the Jews committed, but in the offerings of thankful men. Every year God required two he-goats of the Israelites; of these, one, which was for an offering, was burned, and the other, which was burdened with the sins of the people, was driven into the wilderness as though it were about to bear away the people's sins. Similarly Christ, insofar as He was offered on the cross, was killed; but insofar as He was burdened with our sins, He rose again. For, as the apostle saith, unless Christ be risen again, our sins remain.

7. Therefore, since piety consists of faith, justice, and charity, and since justice and charity are, moreover, moral virtues, I cannot agree with those who call them splendid sins. For if, indeed, they were sins, insofar as a man be holier than others, by that much less ought he to be believed as less just. What is it, therefore, that displeaseth God in those who do justice? For the most part, that which is displeasing to faith, (that is, to piety) is the simulation of justice by those lacking in it. For those who do just works and give alms only for glory or for the acquiring of riches or for the avoidance of punishment are

unjust, even though their works are very frequently just. Therefore, God is said to have hated the sacrifices of His people, which, however, because they had been commanded by God, could not have been sins. But, as just works without faith are an abomination to God, so also are sacrifices and all worship without justice and charity.

8. We are properly said to cultivate (*colere*) that thing, whatsoever it is, that we strive by services and labour to make as beneficial for us as we can. Thus we cultivate (*colimus*) the land so that it may be more fruitful for us; we cultivate or worship (*colimus*) powerful men for the sake of the power or protection that may accrue to us; so also we worship (*colimus*) God, that we may have His favour for ourselves. Therefore cultivation (*cultus*) of the divine, or divine worship, is to perform those actions that are signs of piety toward God. For these are pleasing to God, and by them alone can His favour be returned to us. Moreover, these actions are for the most part of the same kind as those we perform whenever we cultivate (*colimus*) men, but also in each way the best; for by our nature we are unable to show any other signs of piety. One kind of worship (*cultus*), however, is *private*, another *public*. It is private when men exhibit it according to their own individual will. It is public when the same is exhibited by the command of the state. Private worship is exhibited either by one person in secret or by many collectively; it is a sign of their sincere piety; for of what use is simulation that is seen by no one save Him who also sees the simulation? Such simulation can only be vain. In secret worship there are no ceremonies. I call ceremonies those signs of the act of piety that arise not from the nature of the act, but from the will of the state; for nature hath given everyone, to whom it hath given the belief that God exists, to fall prostrate and to genuflect when praying or adoring, as a sign of humility and subjection in the presence of God. In the private wor-

ship of many together, there can be ceremonies, since
men can jointly decide among themselves about the fit-
tingness of common performance; only provided that they
do nothing contrary to the laws of the state. But such a
situation is an invitation to simulation, which is, however, sometimes without fault. For men, if many be
gathered together in one place at the same time, are so
possessed by the nature of a crowd that individuals con-
ceal their timidity and demand that no one speak scurri-
lously, inconsiderately, boorishly, or in a disorganized
manner to them or in their presence; but rather most
elegantly as far as they understand that; and they demand a fitting seriousness of gesture, such as no one useth
in his own home. Wherefore, he who speaks to a crowd
or in their presence when all others are silent, must adopt
a role graver and holier than he otherwise might; this is,
indeed, a kind of play-acting, but without fault, since
when a crowd demands something, the many are more
powerful than the one.

9. There can be no public worship without ceremonies;
for public worship is what the state hath commanded to
be exhibited by all citizens at constituted places and
times, as a sign of the honour had by God. Therefore the
right to judge what is fitting and what is not, in the public
worship of God is within the power of the state. Ceremonies are signs of the acts of piety, not so much those
that are commanded by the nature of the act (which is
rational worship), but rather those that are commanded
by the will of the state. And on that account, when considering many peoples it necessarily follows that there
may be many things in the worship of God among one
people that do not exist among another; and that the
worship of some people will often be laughed at by others.
No worship hath at any time been directly ordained by
God save among the Jews, when He Himself was reigning. The ceremonies of other peoples were rational (some,

indeed, more than others); but among all it was rational to use ceremonies established by civil law.

10. The parts of worship are either rational or superstitious, if not fantastic. The rational parts are, first, *prayers*; for by them we signify that we believe that all future goods that are to be hoped for come from God, and from Him alone. Secondly, *thanksgiving*; for by this we signify that we believe that all past goods were given to us by God, and through His grace alone. Moreover, pious men are sometimes said to prevail on God, or even to overcome Him, with prayers; not that they at any time compelled God to change His mind or His eternal decrees; rather, God, the ruler of all things, wishes His gifts at some times to precede men's prayers, and at others, to follow them. Hence it is not improper that both prayers and thanksgiving are called by one name, *supplications*. Thirdly, *public fasts*, and other acts of those lamenting sins. For they are a sign of repentance, that is, of one's shame about one's sins; thereafter, being conscious of past failings, we rely less on our own strength, and wish to be cautious in the future so that we shall not again fall into sin. Moreover, we are accustomed to signify our humility and grief by ashes, sackcloth, and prostration; not that shame and humility are not genuine without them; but because nature herself teaches us to worship God (who sees into our hearts), in the same ways that we see cultivated or worshipped, men who cannot judge whether repentance is genuine save by such signs. In truth, those who savour their sins as soon as they know for a certainty that they are forgiven, know that they will savour them again, and are unable to grieve further about them, unless the grief be of a kind that also includes shame: for if they grieve, it is manifestly a sign that they grieve because they see themselves reduced to such misery that either they themselves or the sins they love must be abandoned; just as the merchant grieves at sea, when-

ever he sees that either himself or his merchandise is about to be lost. And so in divine worship sadness after sins is fitting and natural, but that sadness must not be of a contrary mind, but of one that is ashamed and humble. Fourthly, *offerings*, that is, sacrifices and oblations, are a rational part of public worship of the divine. For it is not rational that those from whom we have accepted everything should get nothing in return, that is, that we should consecrate nothing to God, that is, that we should set aside no portion from public worship of the divine for the support of ministers, for the honour of that ministry. For so it was in the Church that the ministers of Christ were supported by the Gospels, that is, by those things that were freely given by men because of the Good News; and so it was among the Jews and many other peoples that priests were supported by oblations and sacrifices; hence it is rational that in all states ministers of divine worship are supported by things consecrated to God, which on that account ought to be the most perfect of each kind.

11. On account of the different opinions held by those men who believed that there were many gods (especially those who thought that there once was a heavenly people, more or less a state of aerial men), superstitious worship hath greater variety than can be told. They also believed that those deities had a tongue of their own in heaven, and what was named one thing by men was named another by the deities; so that the man who was called Romulus on earth was in heaven named Quirinus; a similar thing is seen with other names, both among the Greek poets and the Fathers of the heathen church; in almost the same way, what we call the *state*, the clergy call the *church*, what in the state is called a *law* is in the church called a *canon*, and what in a kingdom is called *majesty* is in the church called *holiness*. And not content with a single state for the gods, they established another

for the sea gods under the rule of Neptune, and a third in hell under Pluto. As a result, there was almost no creature that they did not invoke as a god or goddess; there was almost no virtue without altar or temple, save labour and industry, divine powers that are in and of themselves propitious. Finally, whatsoever was nameable was by the same token deifiable. There is no man who doth not understand that all of this is inconsistent with natural reason. Nevertheless, local law was able to have this superstition called religion, and all other worship, superstition.

12. The end that all states allege for divine worship is this, that by it their god or deities may be made favourable, sometimes to the state itself, sometimes to individual citizens. For many, however, divine favour by itself is not enough. For, they think, *God is about to give me certain gifts, but perhaps other than I myself wish; He turns away evil, but only through my own prudence. Would that I might know, therefore, which of the things He prepares to give me—and that are about to come to me—are good, and which of them evil, as it may be necessary to ward them off.* Therefore they so worship that they always seem to be doubting either divine wisdom or divine kindness. And this is why almost all mortals, anxious about the future, turn to more kinds of prophecies than can be easily enumerated. There is, however, only one kind of prophecy that is certain, namely the voice of a prophet, but only if that prophet shall have performed a miracle; other prophecies are false. Astrology which dares by contemplating the stars, to predict about chance future events or to pronounce either way is not a science; it is, rather, the stratagem of a man to steal money from stupid people in order to escape poverty. Those who pretend that they are prophets, when they have performed no miracles, have the same purpose. That dreamers who have produced no miracle hold their own

dreams to be prophecies of the future is stupidity; that
they demand to be believed is insane; that they rashly
predict evil for the state is a crime. It is not true, as many
believe, that malicious people harm those to whom they
wish evil; rather, when the evils that they call down
actually happen as they wish, then they themselves assert
—confessing as though they had at some time done these
things themselves—that those evils were done as a result
of their own prayers by a demon they have seen while
dreaming and employed by a covenant for their work.
Therefore these people do not know the future; rather,
what they select, they hope the future will be. Nevertheless, both because of their wish to harm and because of
their impious worship, not undeservedly are they punished. Further, forebodings of the mind, that is, hope and
fear, and even each and every dream, are held as prophecies. In the same way, the chance flight of birds was an
augury. Men gaped at the entrails of cattle as predictions
of the future. Unintentional words in speaking were believed an omen of the future. Everything unusual was
said to be a portent and prodigy because through them
the deities seemed to be showing what was about to happen. They even used various kinds of lots, that is, they
put their luck to the test in all chance things. For the rest,
I pass by the innumerable other kinds of divination lest
I linger overlong on men's stupidity.

13. There are two things, usually, that change religions,
both to be found in priests: absurd dogmas, and manners
contrary to the religion that they teach. For the prudent
men of the Roman Church erred when they decided that
they could take advantage of the people's ignorance to
such an extent that they might hope not only then, but
always to be able to make the people believe contradictory
language. Little by little the people became educated, and
at last sometimes came to understand the meaning of the
words that they used. Whence it happened, that when

they saw not only that the doctors of religion themselves said contradictory things, but also that they religiously ordered others so to speak, the latter were first inclined sometimes to contemn themselves as ignorant and then to suspect their religion to be false, and either to correct it or to expel it from the state. Therefore doctors of religion must especially take care lest they mix anything from the teachings of physics into the rules for worshipping God. For, since they have no scientific knowledge of natural things, at times they can hardly avoid falling into absurd propositions; afterwards such men make everything that they teach to be contemned, especially when detected by the untaught; just as the ignorance of Roman doctors, detected by Luther, not only abolished a great part of the Roman religion both in our nation and among other peoples, but also separated those same peoples from their Roman dependency. If, however, they had kept silent about transubstantiation (that is, about the nature of body and place), about free-will (that is, about the nature of will and understanding), and about other things that I pass over for the sake of brevity, they could have retained what they had acquired. As for what concerns the other cause for change in religions, namely manners, it is manifest that no one from the people is so stupid as not to think one an imposter (who doth not believe what he orders to be believed) when he sees that one ordering him to believe things otherwise difficult to believe, living as though he himself did not believe; especially if his believing is useful to the one ordering him to believe. If, therefore, they teach, as they do everywhere, that it needs be believed that one should be less covetous than others, less ambitious, less proud, less indulgent of the senses, less mixed up in worldly business (that is, in secular affairs), less insulting, less envious, more simple in heart (that is, more open), more compassionate, more truthful—and yet do not themselves behave in such a manner—they should not complain if after them people do not join the faith. Truly, I believe that the Christian religion grew remarkably at the time of the Holy Apostles in large part because the lives of the heathen priests were not holy. That is to say, over and beyond the vices that they shared with the people, they embroiled themselves in the controversies that states had with each other; and they watched over the gods, just as nurses are wont to watch over children, especially so that no one save whom they wished might approach the gods, or so that the gods might love no one save those that they themselves had commended. Moreover, these covetous men commended only those from whom they received favours.

XV

On Artificial Man

1. Definition of person. 2. What author and authority are. 3. What a guarantor or surety is. 4. Other things besides man can be understood to have a person.

1. What the Greeks called πρόσωπον the Latins sometimes call man's *facies* (face) or *os* (countenance), and sometimes his *persona* (mask): *facies* if they wished to indicate the true man, *persona* if an artificial one, such as comedy and tragedy were accustomed to have in the theatre. For in the theatre it was understood that the actor himself did not speak, but someone else, for example, Agamemnon, namely the actor playing the part of Agamemnon in a false face who was, for that time, Agamemnon; nevertheless, afterwards he was also understood without his false face, namely being acknowledged as the actor himself rather than the person that he had been playing. And, on account of commercial dealings and contracts between men not actually present, such artifices are no less necessary in the state than in the theatre. Moreover, because the concept of person is of use in civil affairs, it can be defined as follows: *a person is he to whom the words and actions of men are attributed, either his own or another's: if his own, the person is natural; if another's, it is artificial.* Therefore, just as the same actor can play different persons at different times, so any one man can represent many. *I*, said Cicero, *bear three persons, my own, my adversary's, and the judge's.* As if he had said one Cicero can be considered to be me, my adversary, and the judge.

2. Of those who bear persons in the state, some do so at the command of him whose person they bear, and others do so not by command. Therefore whatsoever someone doth in the person of one who doth not wish to be represented by him is to be imputed to himself, that is, to the actor alone. But what he doth at the command of another is always the act of the one commanding, though sometimes of the representative also, that is, of both author and actor. For *he is called the author, that hath declared himself responsible for the action done by another according to his will:* and he that is called the *author* with regard to actions is called the *owner* with regard to possessions. Hence they are said to have authority that act by right of another. For unless he that is the author hath the right of acting himself, the actor hath no authority to act. Therefore if someone covenants or shall have made any contract whatsoever with an actor, not knowing whether that actor hath authority or not, he doth so at his own peril. If someone sins at another's command, both sin, since neither did right; unless, by chance, the state commanded it to be done, so that the actor ought not to refuse.

3. Again, with regard to guaranties, the guarantor assumes the person of him for whom he stands guaranty. For he is the author of the faith that one has who believes the promisor and, at his own peril, he commands belief in himself as guarantor. Whence he is called a surety (*fidejussor*).

Not only can a single man bear the person of a single man, but one man can also bear many, and many, one. For if many men agree that, whatsoever be done by some one man or group out of the many, they themselves will hold it as an action of each and every one of them, each and every one will be the author of the actions that the man or group may take; and therefore he cannot complain of any of their actions without complaining of himself. In the same way, all kings and supreme governors of any kind of states whatsoever bear the person of God, if they acknowledge God as ruler. In particular, first it was Moses and then Christ that bore the person of God reigning, and now, after the Holy Ghost descended visibly on the Apostles on the day of Pentecost, it is the Church, that is, the supreme governor of the Church in every state. Therefore, according to the custom of men, God among all peoples hath as His possessions the lands, rights, and other goods especially consecrated to Him. But He doth not have these things unless it be so constituted by the state. For, since the will of God is not known save through the state, and since, moreover, it is required that the will of Him that is represented be the author of the actions performed by those who represent Him, it needs be that God's person be created by the will of the state.

4. Even an inanimate thing can be a person, that is, it can have possessions and other goods, and can act in law, as in the case of a temple, a bridge, or of anything whatsoever that needs money for its upkeep. And caretakers constituted by the state bear its person, so that it hath no will except that of the state.

We shall speak, however, of such artifices as are used in the state (which is, moreover, the greatest of them) in the third section, which is entitled *De Cive.*

Albeit that natural laws consider man as man, we have made no mention of them in this section, save as they are contained in good manners. But since they cannot be observed save through pre-existing civil laws and the power of coercion, we shall treat of them as laws with sufficient amplitude in that same third section.

The Citizen:

PHILOSOPHICAL RUDIMENTS CONCERNING GOVERNMENT AND SOCIETY

TO THE RIGHT HONOURABLE
WILLIAM EARL OF DEVONSHIRE,
MY MOST HONOURED LORD.

May it please your Lordship,
It was the speech of the Roman people, to whom the
name of *king* had been rendered odious, as well by the
tyranny of the Tarquins as by the genius and decretals of
that city; it was the speech, I say, of the public, however
pronounced from a private mouth (if yet Cato the censor
were no more than such): *that all kings are to be
reckoned amongst ravenous beasts.* But what a beast of
prey was the Roman people; whilst with its conquering
eagles it erected its proud trophies so far and wide over
the world, bringing the Africans, the Asiatics, the
Macedonians, and the Achæans, with many other despoiled nations, into a specious bondage, with the pretence of preferring them to be denizens of Rome! So that
if Cato's saying were a wise one, it was every whit as wise,
that of Pontius Telesinus; who flying about with open
mouth through all the companies of his army in that
famous encounter which he had with Sylla, cried out: *that
Rome herself, as well as Sylla, was to be razed; for that
there would always be wolves and depredators of their
liberty, unless the forest that lodged them were grubbed
up by the roots.* To speak impartially, both sayings are
very true: that *man to man is a kind of God;* and that
man to man is an arrant wolf. The first is true, if we compare citizens amongst themselves; and the second, if we
compare cities. In the one, there is some analogy of similitude with the Deity; to wit, justice and charity, the twin
sisters of peace. But in the other, good men must defend

themselves by taking to them for a sanctuary the two
daughters of war, deceit and violence: that is, in plain
terms, a mere brutal rapacity. Which although men object to one another as a reproach, by an inbred custom
which they have of beholding their own actions in the
persons of other men, wherein, as in a mirror, all things
on the left side appear to be on the right, and all things
on the right side to be as plainly on the left; yet the
natural right of preservation, which we all receive from
the uncontrollable dictates of necessity, will not admit it
to be a vice, though it confess it to be an unhappiness.
Now that with Cato himself, a person of so great a renown for wisdom, animosity should so prevail instead of
judgment, and partiality instead of reason, that the very
same thing which he thought equal in his popular state,
he should censure as unjust in a monarchical; other men
perhaps may have leisure to admire. But I have been long
since of this opinion; that there was never yet any more
than vulgar prudence, that had the luck of being acceptable to the giddy people; but either it hath not been understood, or else having been so hath been levelled and
cried down. The more eminent actions and apothegms,
both of the Greeks and Romans, have been indebted for
their eulogies not so much to the *reason*, as to the *greatness* of them; and very many times to that prosperous
usurpation, (with which our histories do so mutually up-
braid each other), which as a conquering torrent carries
all before it, as well public agents as public actions, in the
stream of time. Wisdom, properly so called, is nothing
else but this: *the perfect knowledge of the truth in all
matters whatsoever.* Which being derived from the
registers and records of *things*; and that as it were through
the conduit of certain definite appellations; cannot possibly be the work of a sudden acuteness, but of a well-
balanced reason; which by the compendium of a word,
we call *philosophy.* For by this it is that a way is opened

to us, in which we travel from the contemplation of particular things to the inference or result of universal actions. Now look, how many sorts of things there are, which properly fall within the cognizance of human reason; into so many branches does the tree of philosophy divide itself. And from the diversity of the matter about which they are conversant, there hath been given to those branches a diversity of names too. For treating of figures, it is called *geometry*; of motion, *physic*; of natural right, *morals*; put altogether, and they make up *philosophy*. Just as the British, the Atlantic, and the Indian seas, being diversely christened from the diversity of their shores, do notwithstanding all together make up *the ocean*. And truly the geometricians have very admirably performed their part. For whatsoever assistance doth accrue to the life of man, whether from the observation of the heavens or from the description of the earth, from the notation of times, or from the remotest experiments of navigation; finally, whatsoever things they are in which this present age doth differ from the rude simpleness of antiquity, we must acknowledge to be a debt which we owe merely to geometry. If the moral philosophers had as happily discharged their duty, I know not what could have been added by human industry to the completion of that happiness, which is consistent with human life. For were the nature of human actions as distinctly known as the nature of *quantity* in geometrical figures, the strength of *avarice* and *ambition*, which is sustained by the erroneous opinions of the vulgar as touching the nature of *right* and *wrong*, would presently faint and languish; and mankind should enjoy such an immortal peace, that unless it were for habitation, on supposition that the earth should grow too narrow for her inhabitants, there would hardly be left any pretence for war. But now on the contrary, that neither the sword nor the pen should be allowed any cessation; that the knowledge of the law of nature should lose its growth, not advancing a whit beyond its ancient stature; that there should still be such siding with the several factions of philosophers, that the very same action should be decried by some, and as much elevated by others; that the very same man should at several times embrace his several opinions, and esteem his own actions far otherwise in himself than he does in others: these, I say, are so many signs, so many manifest arguments, that what hath hitherto been written by moral philosophers, hath not made any progress in the knowledge of the truth; but yet hath took with the world, not so much by giving any light to the understanding as entertainment to the affections, whilst by the successful rhetorications of their speech they have confirmed them in their rashly received opinions. So that this part of philosophy hath suffered the same destiny with the *public ways*, which lie open to all passengers to traverse up and down: or the same lot *with highways and open streets*, some for divertisement, and some for business; so that what with the impertinences of some and the altercations of others, those ways have never a seed time, and therefore yield never a harvest. The only reason of which unluckiness should seem to be this; that amongst all the writers of that part of philosophy there is not one that hath used an idoneous principle of tractation. For we may not, as in a circle, begin the handling of a science from what point we please. There is a certain clue of reason, whose beginning is in the dark; but by the benefit of whose conduct, we are led as it were by the hand into the clearest light. So that the principle of tractation is to be taken from that darkness; and then the light to be carried thither for irradiating its doubts. As often therefore as any writer doth either weakly forsake that clue, or wilfully cut it asunder; he describes the footsteps, not of his progress in science, but of his wanderings from it. And from this it was, that when I applied my thoughts to the investigation of natural justice, I was presently advertised from the very word *justice* (which signifies a steady will of giving every one his *own*), that my first enquiry was to be, from whence it proceeded that any man should call anything rather his *own*, than *another man's*. And when I found that this proceeded not from nature, but consent (for what nature at first laid forth in common, men did afterwards distribute into several *impropriations*); I was conducted from thence to another inquiry; namely, to what end and upon what impulsives, when all was equally every man's in common, men did rather think it fitting that every man should have his inclosure. And I found the reason was, that from a community of goods there must needs arise contention, whose enjoyment should be greatest. And from that contention all kind of calamities must unavoidably ensue, which by the instinct of nature every man is taught to shun. Having therefore thus arrived at two maxims of human nature; the one arising from the *concupiscible* part, which desires to appropriate to itself the use of those things in which all others have a joint interest; the other proceeding from the *rational*, which teaches every man to fly a contra-natural dissolution, as the greatest mischief that can arrive to nature: which principles being laid down, I seem from them to have demonstrated by a most evident connexion, in this little work of mine, first, the absolute necessity of leagues and contracts, and thence the rudiments both of moral and of civil prudence. That appendage which is added concerning the regiment of God, hath been done with this intent; that the dictates of God Almighty in the law of nature, might not seem repugnant to the written law, revealed to us in his word. I have also been very wary in the whole tenour of my discourse, not to meddle with the civil laws of any particular nation whatsoever: that is to say, I have avoided coming ashore, which those times have so infested both with

shelves and tempests. At what expense of time and industry I have been in this scrutiny after truth, I am not
ignorant; but to what purpose, I know not. For being
partial judges of ourselves, we lay a partial estimate upon
our own productions. I therefore offer up this book to
your Lordship's, not favour, but censure first; as having
found by many experiments, that it is not the credit of
the author, nor the newness of the work, nor yet the orna-
ment of the style, but only the weight of reason, which
recommends any *opinion* to your Lordship's favour and
approbation. If it fortune to please, that is to say, if it be
sound, if it be useful, if it be not vulgar; I humbly offer
it to your Lordship, as both my glory and my protection.
But if in anything I have erred, your Lordship will yet
accept it as a testimony of my gratitude; for that the
means of study, which I enjoyed by your Lordship's goodness, I have employed to the procurement of your Lordship's favour. The God of heaven crown your Lordship
with length of days, in this earthly station; and in the
heavenly Jerusalem with a crown of glory.

Your Honour's most humble,
and most devoted Servant,
THOMAS HOBBES.

THE AUTHOR'S PREFACE TO THE READER.

Reader, I promise thee here such things, which ordinarily promised do seem to challenge the greatest attention, (whether thou regard the dignity or profit of the matter treated, or the right method of handling it, or the honest motive and good advice to undertake it, or lastly the moderation of the author,) and I lay them here before thine eyes. In this book thou shalt find briefly described the duties of men: first, as men; then as subjects; lastly, as Christians. Under which duties are contained, not only the elements of the laws of nature and of nations, together with the true original and power of justice; but also the very essence of Christian religion itself, so far forth as the measure of this my purpose could well bear it.

Which kind of doctrine, excepting what relates to Christian religion, the most ancient sages did judge fittest to be delivered to posterity, either curiously adorned with verse, or clouded with allegories, as a most beautiful and hallowed mystery of royal authority; lest by the disputations of private men it might be defiled. Other philosophers in the meantime, to the advantage of mankind, did contemplate the faces and motions of things; others, without disadvantage, their natures and causes. But in aftertimes, Socrates is said to have been the first who truly loved this civil science; although hitherto not thoroughly understood, yet glimmering forth as through a cloud in the government of the commonweal: and that he set so great a value on this, that utterly abandoning and despising all other parts of philosophy, he wholly embraced this, as judging it only worthy the labour of his mind. After him come Plato, Aristotle, Cicero, and other philosophers, as well Greek as Latin. And now at length all men of all nations, not only philosophers but even the vulgar, have and do still deal with this as a matter of ease, exposed and prostitute to every mother-wit, and to be attained without any great care or study. And, which makes mainly for its dignity, those who suppose themselves to have it, or are in such employment as they ought to have it, do so wonderfully please themselves in its *idea*, as they easily brook the followers of other arts to be esteemed and styled ingenuous, learned, skilful, what you will, except prudent: for this name, in regard of civil knowledge, they presume to be due to themselves only. Whether therefore the worth of arts is to be weighed by the worthiness of the persons who entertain them, or by the number of those who have written of them, or by the judgment of the wisest; certainly this must carry it, which so nearly relates to princes, and others engaged in the government of mankind; in whose adulterate species also the most part of men do delight themselves, and in which the most excellent wits of philosophers have been conversant. The benefit of it, when rightly delivered, that is, when derived from true principles by evident connexion, we shall then best discern, when we shall but well have considered the mischiefs that have befallen mankind from its counterfeit and babbling form. For in such matters as are speculated for the exercise of our wits, if any error escape us, it is without hurt; neither is there any loss, but of time only. But in those things which every man ought to meditate for the steerage of his life, it necessarily happens that not only from errors, but even from ignorance itself, there arise offences, contentions, nay, even slaughter itself. Look now, how great a prejudice these are; such and so great is the benefit arising from this doctrine of morality truly declared. How many kings, and those good men too, hath this one error, that a tyrant king might lawfully be put to death, been the slaughter of! How many throats hath this false position cut, that a prince for some causes may by some certain men be deposed! And what bloodshed hath not this erroneous doctrine caused, that kings are not superiors to, but administrators for the multitude! Lastly, how many rebellions hath this opinion been the cause of, which teacheth that the knowledge whether the commands of kings be just or unjust, belongs to private men; and that before they yield obedience, they not only may, but ought to dispute them! Besides, in the moral philosophy now commonly received, there are many things no less dangerous than those, which it matters not now to recite. I suppose those ancients foresaw this, who rather chose to have the science of justice wrapped up in fables, than openly exposed to disputations. For before such questions began to be moved, princes did not sue for, but already exercised the supreme power. They kept their empire entire, not by arguments, but by punishing the wicked and protecting the good. Likewise subjects did not measure what was just by the sayings and judgments of private men, but by the laws of the realm; nor were they kept in peace by disputations, but by power and authority. Yea, they reverenced the supreme power, whether residing in one man or in a council, as a certain visible divinity. Therefore they little used, as in our days, to join themselves with ambitious and hellish spirits, to the utter ruin of their state. For they could not entertain so strange a fancy, as not to desire the preservation of that by which they were preserved. In truth, the simplicity of those times was not yet capable of so learned a piece of folly. Wherefore it was peace and a golden age, which ended not before that, Saturn being expelled, it was taught lawful to take up arms against kings. This, I say, the ancients not only themselves saw, but in one of their fables they seem very aptly to have signified it to us. For they say, that when Ixion was invited by Jupiter to a banquet, he fell in love, and began to court Juno herself. Offering to embrace her, he clasped a cloud; from whence the Centaurs proceeded, by nature half men, half horses, a fierce, a fighting, and unquiet generation. Which changing the names only, is as much as if they should have said, that private men being called to councils of state, desired to prostitute justice, the only sister and wife of the supreme, to their own judgments and apprehensions; but embracing a false and empty shadow instead of it, they have begotten those hermaphrodite opinions of moral philosophers, partly right and comely, partly brutal and wild; the causes of all contentions and bloodsheds. Since therefore such opinions are daily seen to arise, if any man now shall dispel those clouds, and by most firm reasons demonstrate that there are no authentical doctrines concerning right and wrong, good and evil, besides the constituted laws in each realm and government; and that the question whether any future action will prove just or unjust, good or ill, is to be demanded of none but those to whom the supreme hath committed the interpretation of his laws: surely he will not only show us the highway to peace, but will also teach us how to avoid the close, dark, and dangerous by-paths of faction and sedition; than which I know not what can be thought more profitable.

Concerning my method, I thought it not sufficient to use a plain and evident style in what I have to deliver, except I took my beginning from the very matter of civil government, and thence proceeded to its generation and form, and the first beginning of justice. For everything is best understood by its constitutive causes. For as in a watch, or some such small engine, the matter, figure, and motion of the wheels cannot well be known, except it be taken insunder and viewed in parts; so to make a more curious search into the rights of states and duties of subjects, it is necessary, I say, not to take them insunder, but yet that they be so considered as if they were dissolved; that is, that we rightly understand what the quality of human nature is, in what matters it is, in what not, fit to make up a civil government, and how men must be agreed amongst themselves that intend to grow up into a well-grounded state. Having therefore followed this kind of method, in the first place I set down for a principle, by experience known to all men and denied by none, to wit, that the dispositions of men are naturally such, that except they be restrained through fear of some coercive power, every man will distrust and dread each other; and as by natural right he may, so by necessity he will be forced to make use of the strength he hath, toward the preservation of himself. You will object perhaps, that there are some who deny this. Truly so it happens, that very many do deny it. But shall I therefore seem to fight against myself, because I affirm that the same men confess and deny the same thing? In truth I do not; but they do, whose actions disavow what their discourses approve of. We see all countries, though they be at peace with their neighbours, yet guarding their frontiers with armed men, their towns with walls and ports, and keeping constant watches. To what purpose is all this, if there be no fear of the neighbouring power? We see even in well-governed states, where there are laws and punishments appointed for offenders, yet particular men travel not without their sword by their sides for their defences; neither sleep they without shutting not only their doors against their fellow subjects, but also their trunks and coffers for fear of domestics. Can men give a clearer testimony of the distrust they have each of other, and all of all? How, since they do thus, and even countries as well as men, they publicly profess their mutual fear and diffidence. But in disputing they deny it; that is as much as to say, that out of a desire they have to contradict others, they gainsay themselves. Some object that this principle being admitted, it would needs follow, not only that all men were wicked (which perhaps though it seem hard, yet we must yield to, since it is so clearly declared by holy writ), but also wicked by nature, which cannot be granted without impiety. But this, that men are evil by nature, follows not from this principle. For though the wicked were fewer than the righteous, yet because we cannot distinguish them, there is a necessity of suspecting, heeding, anticipating, subjugating, self-defending, ever incident to the most honest and fairest conditioned. Much less does it follow, that those who are wicked, are so by nature. For though from nature, that is, from their first birth, as they are merely sensible creatures, they have this disposition, that immediately as much as in them lies they desire and do whatsoever is best pleasing to them, and that either through fear they fly from, or through hardness repel those dangers which approach them; yet are they not for this reason to be accounted wicked. For the affections of the mind, which arise only from the lower parts of the soul, are not wicked themselves; but the actions thence proceeding may be so sometimes, as when they are either offensive or against duty. Unless you give children all they ask for, they are peevish and cry, aye, and strike their parents sometimes; and all this they have from nature. Yet are they free from guilt, neither may we properly call them wicked; first, because they cannot hurt; next, because wanting the free use of reason they are exempted from all duty. These when they come to riper years, having acquired power whereby they may do hurt, if they shall continue to do the same things, then truly they both begin to be, and are properly accounted wicked. Insomuch as a wicked man is almost the same thing with a child grown strong and sturdy, or a man of a childish disposition; and malice the same with a defect of reason in that age when nature ought to be better governed through good education and experience.

Unless therefore we will say that men are naturally evil, because they receive not their education and use of reason from nature, we must needs acknowledge that men may derive desire, fear, anger, and other passions from nature, and yet not impute the evil effects of those unto nature. The foundation therefore which I have laid, standing firm, I demonstrate, in the first place, that the state of men without civil society, which state we may properly call the state of nature, is nothing else but a mere war of all against all; and in that war all men have equal right unto all things. Next, that all men as soon as they arrive to understanding of this hateful condition, do desire, even nature itself compelling them, to be freed from this misery. But that this cannot be done, except by compact, they all quit that right they have to all things. Furthermore, I declare and confirm what the nature of compact is; how and by what means the right of one might be transferred unto another to make their compacts valid; also what rights, and to whom they must necessarily be granted, for the establishing of peace; I mean, what those dictates of reason are, which may properly be termed the laws of nature. And all these are contained in that part of this book which I entitle *Liberty*.

These grounds thus laid, I show further what civil government, and the supreme power in it, and the divers kinds of it are; by what means it becomes so; and what rights particular men, who intend to constitute this civil government, must so necessarily transfer from themselves on the supreme power, whether it be one man or an assembly of men, that, except they do so, it will evidently appear to be no civil government, but the rights which all men have to all things, that is, the rights of war will still remain. Next I distinguish the divers kinds of it, to wit, monarchy, aristocracy, democracy; and paternal dominion, and that of masters over their servants. I declare how they are constituted, and I compare their several conveniences and inconveniences, each with other. Furthermore, I unfold what those things are which destroy it, and what his or their duty is, who rule in chief. Last of all, I explicate the natures of law and of sin; and I distinguish law from counsel, from compact, from that which I call right. All which I comprehend under the title of *Dominion*.

In the last part of it, which is entitled *Religion*, lest that right, which by strong reason I had confirmed the sovereign powers in the preceding discourse, have over their subjects, might seem to be repugnant to the sacred Scriptures; I show, in the first place, how it repugns not the divine right, for as much as God overrules all rulers by nature, that is, by the dictates of natural reason. In the second, forasmuch as God himself had a peculiar dominion over the Jews, by virtue of that ancient covenant of circumcision. In the third, because God doth now rule over us Christians, by virtue of our covenant of baptism. And therefore the authority of rulers in chief, or of civil government, is not at all, we see, contrary to religion.

In the last place, I declare what duties are necessarily required from us, to enter into the *kingdom of heaven*. And of those I plainly demonstrate, and conclude out of evident testimonies of holy writ according to the interpretation made by all, that the obedience, which I have affirmed to be due from particular Christian subjects unto their Christian princes, cannot possibly in the least sort be repugnant unto Christian religion.

You have seen my method: receive now the reason which moved me to write this. I was studying philosophy for my mind sake, and I had gathered together its first elements in all kinds; and having digested them into three sections by degrees, I thought to have written them, so as in the first I would have treated of *body* and its general properties; in the second of *man* and his special faculties and affections; in the third, of *civil government* and the duties of subjects. Wherefore the first section would have contained *the first philosophy*, and certain elements of physic; in it we would have considered the reasons of *time, place, cause, power, relation, proportion, quantity, figure,* and *motion.* In the second, we would have been conversant about *imagination, memory, intellect, ratiocination, appetite, will, good* and *evil, honest* and *dishonest,* and the like. What this last section handles, I have now already showed you. Whilst I contrive, order, pensively and slowly compose these matters; (for I only do reason, I dispute not); it so happened in the interim, that my country, some few years before the civil wars did rage, was boiling hot with questions concerning the rights of dominion and the obedience due from subjects, the true forerunners of an approaching war; and was the cause which, all those other matters deferred, ripened and plucked from me this third part. Therefore it happens, that what was last in order, is yet come forth first in time. And the rather, because I saw that, grounded on its own principles sufficiently known by experience, it would not stand in need of the former sections. Yet I have not made it out of a desire of praise: although if I had, I might have defended myself with this fair excuse, that very few do things laudably, who are not affected with commendation: but for your sakes, readers, who I persuaded myself, when you should rightly apprehend and thoroughly understand this doctrine I here present you with, would rather choose to brook with patience some inconveniences under government, (because human affairs cannot possibly be without some), than self-opiniatedly disturb the quiet of the public; that, weighing the justice of those things you are about, not by the persuasion and advice of private men, but by the laws of the realm, you will no longer suffer ambitious men through the streams of your blood to wade to their own power; that you will esteem

it better to enjoy yourselves in the present state, though
perhaps not the best, than by waging war endeavour to
procure a reformation for other men in another age, yourselves in the meanwhile either killed or consumed with
age. Furthermore, for those who will not acknowledge
themselves subject to the civil magistrate, and will be exempt from all public burthens, and yet will live under his
jurisdiction, and look for protection from the violence
and injuries of others, that you would not look on them
as fellow-subjects, but esteem them for enemies and spies;
and that ye rashly admit not for God's word all which,
either openly or privately, they shall pretend to be so. I
say more plainly, if any preacher, confessor, or casuist,
shall but say that this doctrine is agreeable with God's
word, namely, that the chief ruler, nay, any private man
may lawfully be put to death without the chief's command, or that subjects may resist, conspire, or covenant
against the supreme power; that ye by no means believe
them, but instantly declare their names. He who ap-
proves of these reasons, will also like my intentions in
writing this book.

Last of all, I have propounded to myself this rule
through this whole discourse. First, not to define aught
which concerns the justice of single actions, but leave
them to be determined by the laws. Next, not to dispute
the laws of any government in special, that is, not to point
which are the laws of any country, but to declare what
the laws of all countries are. Thirdly, not to seem of opinion, that there is a less proportion of obedience due to
an *aristocracy* or *democracy* than a *monarchy*. For though
I have endeavoured, by arguments in my tenth chapter,
to gain a belief in men, that monarchy is the most commodious government; which one thing alone I confess
in this whole book not to be demonstrated, but only probably stated; yet every where I expressly say, that in all

kind of government whatsoever there ought to be a supreme and equal power. Fourthly, not in anywise to dispute the positions of divines, except those which strip
subjects of their obedience, and shake the foundations of
civil government. Lastly, lest I might imprudently set
forth somewhat of which there would be no need, what
I had thus written I would not presently expose to public
interest. Wherefore I got some few copies privately
dispersed among some of my friends; that discrying the
opinions of others, if any things appeared erroneous,
hard, or obscure, I might correct, soften and explain
them.

These things I found most bitterly excepted against.
That I had made the civil powers too large; but this by
ecclesiastical persons. That I had utterly taken away liberty of conscience; but this by sectaries. That I had set
princes above the civil laws; but this by lawyers. Wherefore I was not much moved by these men's reprehensions,
as who in doing this, did but do their own business; except it were to tie those knots somewhat faster.

But for their sakes who have a little been staggered at
the principles themselves, to wit, the nature of men, the
authority or right of nature, the nature of compacts and
contracts, and the original of civil government; because
in finding fault they have not so much followed their passions, as their common sense, I have therefore in some
places added some annotations, whereby I presumed I
might give some satisfaction to their differing thoughts.
Lastly, I have endeavoured to offend none, beside those
whose principles these contradict, and whose tender
minds are lightly offended by every difference of opinions.

Wherefore, if ye shall meet with some things which
have more of sharpness, and less of certainty than they
ought to have, since they are not so much spoken for the
maintenance of parties as the establishment of peace, and

by one whose just grief for the present calamities of his country may very charitably be allowed some liberty; it is his only request to ye, readers, ye will deign to receive them with an equal mind.

THE INDEX.

OF LIBERTY.

I. Of the state of men without civil society — 109

II. Of the law of nature concerning contracts — 121

III. Of the other laws of nature — 135

IV. That the law of nature is a divine law — 153

OF DOMINION.

V. Of the causes and first original of civil government — 165

VI. Of the right, whether we consider it in an assembly or in one person, which he hath who is endued with supreme authority — 173

VII. Of the three kinds of government, Democracy, Aristocracy, and Monarchy — 191

VIII. Of the right which lords and masters have over their servants — 205

IX. Of the right which parents have over their children, and of a kingdom paternal — 211

X. A comparison of the three kinds of government, each with other, according to the inconveniences of each one — 221

XI. The places and examples of Scripture concerning the right of government, which make for proof of the foresaid doctrines — 237

XII. Of the inward causes which dissolve all civil government — 243

XIII. Of the duties of those men who sit at the helm of state — 257

XIV. Of laws and sins — 271

OF RELIGION.

XV. Of God's government by nature — 289

XVI. *Of his government by the old covenant*   309

XVII. *Of his government by the new covenant*   329

XVIII. *Of those things which are necessary for our entrance
        into the kingdom of heaven*   369

LIBERTY

I

Of the State of Men Without Civil Society

1. The Introduction. 2. That the beginning of civil society is from mutual fear. 3. That men by nature are all equal. 4. Whence the will of mischieving each other ariseth. 5. The discord arising from comparison of wits. 6. From the appetite many have to the same thing. 7. The definition of *right*. 8. A right to the end, gives a right to the means necessary to that end. 9. By the right of nature, every man is judge of the means which tend to his own preservation. 10. By nature all men have equal right to all things. 11. This right which all men have to all things, is unprofitable. 12. The state of men without civil society, is a mere state of war: the definitions of *peace* and *war*. 13. War is an adversary to man's preservation. 14. It is lawful for any man, by natural right, to compel another whom he hath gotten in his power, to give caution of his future obedience. 15. Nature dictates the seeking after peace.

1. The faculties of human nature may be reduced unto four kinds: bodily strength, experience, reason, passion. Taking the beginning of this following doctrine from these, we will declare, in the first place, what manner of inclinations men who are endued with these faculties bear towards each other, and whether, and by what fac-

ulty they are born apt for society, and |to| preserve themselves against mutual violence; then proceeding, we will show what advice was necessary to be taken for this business, and what are the conditions of society, or of human peace; that is to say (changing the words only), what are the fundamental *laws of nature*.

2. The greatest part of those men who have written aught concerning commonwealths, either suppose, or require us or beg of us to believe, that man is a creature born fit* for society. The Greeks call him ζῶον πολιτικον; and on this foundation they so build up the doctrine of civil society, as if for the preservation of peace, and the government of mankind, there were nothing else necessary than that men should agree to make certain

---

* *Born fit*. Since we now see actually a constituted society among men, and none living out of it, since we discern all desirous of congress and mutual correspondence, it may seem a wonderful kind of stupidity, to lay in the very threshold of this doctrine such a stumbling block before the reader, as to deny *man to be born fit for society*. Therefore I must more plainly say, that it is true indeed, that to man by nature, or as man, that is, as soon as he is born, solitude is an enemy; for infants have need of others to help them to live, and those of riper years to help them to live well. Wherefore I deny not that men (even nature compelling) desire to come together. But civil societies are not mere meetings, but bonds, to the making whereof faith and compacts are necessary; the virtue whereof to children and fools, and the profit whereof to those who have not yet tasted the miseries which accompany its defects, is altogether unknown; whence it happens, that those, because they know not what society is, cannot enter into it; these, because ignorant of the benefit it brings, care not for it. Manifest therefore it is, that all men, because they are born in infancy, are born unapt for society. Many also, perhaps most men, either through defect of mind or want of education, remain unfit during the whole course of their lives; yet have they, infants as well as those of riper years, a human nature. Wherefore man is made fit for society not by nature, but by education. Furthermore, although man were born in such a condition as to desire it, it follows not, that he therefore were born fit to enter into it. For it is one thing to desire, another to be in capacity fit for what we desire; for even they, who through their pride, will not stoop to equal conditions, without which there can be no society, do yet desire it.

covenants and conditions together, which themselves should then call laws. Which axiom, though received by most, is yet certainly false; and an error proceeding from our too slight contemplation of human nature. For they who shall more narrowly look into the causes for which men come together, and delight in each other's company, shall easily find that this happens not because naturally it could happen no otherwise, but by accident. For if by nature one man should love another, that is, as man, there could no reason be returned why every man should not equally love every man, as being equally man; or why he should rather frequent those, whose society affords him honour or profit. We do not therefore by nature seek society for its own sake, but that we may receive some honour or profit from it; these we desire primarily, that secondarily. How, by what advice, men do meet, will be best known by observing those things which they do when they are met. For if they meet for traffic, it is plain every man regards not his fellow, but his business; if to discharge some office, a certain market-friendship is begotten, which hath more of jealousy in it than true love, and whence factions sometimes may arise, but good will never; if for pleasure and recreation of mind, every man is wont to please himself most with those things which stir up laughter, whence he may, according to the nature of that which is ridiculous, by comparison of another man's defects and infirmities, pass the more current in his own opinion. And although this be sometimes innocent and without offence, yet it is manifest they are not so much delighted with the society, as their own vain glory. But for the most part, in these kind of meetings we wound the absent; their whole life, sayings, actions are examined, judged, condemned. Nay, it is very rare but some present receive a fling|as soon as|they part; so as his reason was not ill, who was wont always at parting to go out last. And these are indeed the true delights of society, unto which we are carried by nature, that is, by those passions which are incident to all creatures, until either by sad experience or good precepts it so fall out, which in many never happens, that the appetite of present matters be dulled with the memory of things past: without which the discourse of most quick and nimble men on this subject, is but cold and hungry.

But if it so happen, that being met they pass their time in relating some stories, and one of them begins to tell one which concerns himself; instantly every one of the rest most greedily desires to speak of himself too; if one relate some wonder, the rest will tell you miracles, if they have them; if not, they will feign them. Lastly, that I may say somewhat of them who pretend to be wiser than others: if they meet to talk of philosophy, look, how many men, so many would be esteemed masters, or else they not only love not their fellows, but even persecute them with hatred. So clear is it by experience to all men who a little more narrowly consider human affairs, that all free congress ariseth either from mutual poverty, or from vain glory, whence the parties met endeavour to carry with them either some benefit, or to leave behind them that same ἐυδοκιμεῖν, some esteem and honour with those, with whom they have been conversant. The same is also collected by reason out of the definitions themselves of *will, good, honour, profitable.* For when we voluntarily contract society, in all manner of society we look after the object of the will, that is, that which every one of those who gather together, propounds to himself for good. Now whatsoever seems good, is pleasant, and relates either to the senses, or the mind. But all the mind's pleasure is either glory, (or to have a good opinion of one's self), or refers to glory in the end; the rest are sensual, or conducing to sensuality, which may be all comprehended under the word *conveniences.* All society therefore is either for gain, or for glory; that is, not so much for love of our fellows, as for the love of ourselves. But no society can be great or lasting, which begins from vain glory. Because that glory is like honour; if all men have it no man hath it, for they consist in comparison and precellence. Neither doth the society of others advance any whit the cause of my glorying in myself; for every man must account himself, such as he can make himself without the help of others. But though the benefits of this life may be much furthered by mutual help; since yet those may be better attained to by dominion than by the society of others, I hope no body will doubt, but that men would much more greedily be carried by nature, if all fear were removed, to obtain dominion, than to gain society. We must therefore resolve, that the original of all great and lasting societies consisted not in the mutual good will men had towards each other, but in the mutual fear† they had of each other.

3. The cause of mutual fear consists partly in the natural equality of men, partly in their mutual will of hurting: whence it comes to pass, that we can neither expect from others, nor promise to ourselves the least security.

† *The mutual fear.* It is objected: it is so improbable that men should grow into civil societies out of fear, that if they had been afraid, they would not have endured each other's looks. They presume, I believe, that to fear is nothing else than to be affrighted. I comprehend in this word *fear*, a certain foresight of future evil; neither do I conceive flight the sole property of fear, but to distrust, suspect, take heed, provide so that they may not fear, is also incident to the fearful. They who go to sleep, shut their doors; they who travel, carry their swords with them, because they fear thieves. Kingdoms guard their coasts and frontiers with forts and castles; cities are compact with walls; and all for fear of neighbouring kingdoms and towns. Even the strongest armies, and most accomplished for fight, yet sometimes parley for peace, as fearing each other's power, and lest they might be overcome. It is through fear that men secure themselves by flight indeed, and in corners, if they think they cannot escape otherwise; but for the most part, by arms and defensive weapons; whence it happens, that daring to come forth they know each other's spirits. But then if they fight, civil society ariseth from the victory; if they agree, from their agreement.

For if we look on men full grown, and consider how brittle the frame of our human body is, which perishing, all its strength, vigour, and wisdom itself perisheth with it; and how easy a matter it is, even for the weakest man to kill the strongest: there is no reason why any man, trusting to his own strength, should conceive himself made by nature above others. They are equals, who can do equal things one against the other; but they who can do the greatest things, namely, kill, can do equal things. All men therefore among themselves are by nature equal; the inequality we now discern, hath its spring from the civil law.

4. All men in the state of nature have a desire and will to hurt, but not proceeding from the same cause, neither equally to be condemned. For one man, according to that natural equality which is among us, permits as much to others as he assumes to himself; which is an argument of a temperate man, and one that rightly values his power. Another, supposing himself above others, will have a license to do what he lists, and challenges respect and honour, as due to him before others; which is an argument of a fiery spirit. This man's will to hurt ariseth from vain glory, and the false esteem he hath of his own strength; the other's from the necessity of defending himself, his liberty, and his goods, against this man's violence.

5. Furthermore, since the combat of wits is the fiercest, the greatest discords which are, must necessarily arise from this contention. For in this case it is not only odious to contend against, but also not to consent. For not to approve of what a man saith, is no less than tacitly to accuse him of an error in that thing which he speaketh: as in very many things to dissent, is as much as if you accounted him a fool whom you dissent from. Which may appear hence, that there are no wars so sharply waged as between sects of the same religion, and factions of the

same commonweal, where the contestation is either concerning doctrines or politic prudence. And since all the pleasure and jollity of the mind consists in this, even to get some, with whom comparing, it may find somewhat wherein to triumph and vaunt itself; it is impossible but men must declare sometimes some mutual scorn and contempt, either by laughter, or by words, or by gesture, or some sign or other; than which there is no greater vexation of mind, and than from which there cannot possibly arise a greater desire to do hurt.

6. But the most frequent reason why men desire to hurt each other, ariseth hence, that many men at the same time have an appetite to the same thing; which yet very often they can neither enjoy in common, nor yet divide it; whence it follows that the strongest must have it, and who is strongest must be decided by the sword.

7. Among so many dangers therefore, as the natural lusts of men do daily threaten each other withal, to have a care of one's self | is not a matter so scornfully to be looked upon, as if so be there had not been a power and will left in one | to have done otherwise. For every man is desirous of what is good for him, and shuns what is evil, but chiefly the chiefest of natural evils, which is death; and this he doth by a certain impulsion of nature, no less than that whereby a stone moves downward. It is therefore neither absurd nor reprehensible, neither against the dictates of true reason, for a man to use all his endeavours to preserve and defend his body and the members thereof from death and sorrows. But that which is not contrary to right reason, that all men account to be done justly, and with right. Neither by the word *right* is anything else signified, than that liberty which every man hath to make use of his natural faculties according to right reason. Therefore the first foundation of natural right is this, that *every man as much as in him lies endeavour to protect his life and members.*

8. But because it is in vain for a man to have a right
to the end, if the right to the necessary means be denied
him, it follows, that since every man hath a right to preserve himself, he must also be allowed a right *to use all
the means, and do all the actions, without which he cannot preserve himself.*

9. Now whether the means which he is about to use,
and the action he is performing, be necessary to the preservation of his life and members or not, he himself, by
the right of nature, must be judge.|For say, another man
judge that it is contrary to right reason that I should
judge of mine own peril.|Why now, because he judgeth of
what concerns me, by the same reason, because we are
equal by nature, will I judge also of things which do belong to him. Therefore it agrees with right reason, that
is, it is the right of nature that I judge of his opinion, that
is, whether it conduce to my preservation or not.

10. Nature hath given to *every one a right to all*; that
is, it was lawful for every man, in the bare state of nature,‡ or before such time as men had engaged them-

‡ *In the|bare|state of nature.* This is thus to be understood: what
any man does in the bare state of nature, is injurious to no man;
not that in such a state he cannot offend God, or break the laws of
nature; for injustice against men presupposeth human laws, such as
in the state of nature there are none. Now the truth of this proposition thus conceived, is sufficiently demonstrated to the mindful
reader in the articles immediately foregoing; but because in certain
cases the difficulty of the conclusion makes us forget the premises,
I will contract this argument, and make it most evident to a single
view. Every man hath right to protect himself, as appears by the
seventh article. The same man therefore hath a right to use all the
means which necessarily conduce to this end, by the eighth article.
But those are the necessary means which he shall judge to be such,
by the ninth article. He therefore hath a right to make use of, and
to do all whatsoever he shall judge requisite for his preservation;
wherefore by the judgment of him that doth it, the thing done is
either right or wrong, and therefore right. True it is therefore in the
bare state of nature, &c. But if any man pretend somewhat to tend
necessarily to his preservation, which yet he himself doth not confi-
dently believe so, he may offend against the laws of nature, as in the

selves by any covenants or bonds, to do what he would, and against whom he thought fit, and to possess, use, and enjoy all what he would, or could get. Now because whatsoever a man would, it therefore seems good to him because he wills it, and either it really doth, or at least seems to him to contribute towards his preservation (but we have already allowed him to be judge, in the foregoing article, whether it doth or not, insomuch as we are to hold all for necessary whatsoever he shall esteem so), and by the 7th article it appears that by the right of nature those things may be done, and must be had, which necessarily conduce to the protection of life and members, it follows, that in the state of nature, to have all, and do all, is lawful for all. And this is that which is meant by that common saying, *nature hath given all to all*. From whence we understand likewise, that in the state of nature profit is the measure of right.

11. But it was the least benefit for men thus to have a common right to all things. For the effects of this right are the same, almost, as if there had been no right at all. For although any man might say of every thing, *this is mine*, yet could he not enjoy it, by reason of his neighbour, who having equal right and equal power, would pretend the same thing to be his.

12. If now to this natural proclivity of men, to hurt each other, which they derive from their passions, but chiefly from a vain esteem of themselves, you add, the right of all to all, wherewith one by right invades, the other by right resists, and whence arise perpetual jealousies and suspicions on all hands, and how hard a thing it

third chapter of this book is more at large declared. It hath been objected by some: if a son kill his father, doth he him no injury? I have answered, that a son cannot be understood to be at any time in the state of nature, as being under the power and command of them to whom he|owes|his protection as soon as ever he is born, namely, either his father's or his mother's, or his that nourished him; as is demonstrated in the ninth chapter.

is to provide against an enemy invading us with an intention to oppress and ruin, though he come with a small number, and no great provision; it cannot be denied but that the natural state of men, before they entered into society, was a mere war, and that not simply, but a war of all men against all men. For what is WAR, but that same time in which the will of contesting by force is fully declared, either by words or deeds? The time remaining is termed PEACE.

13. But it is easily judged how disagreeable a thing to the preservation either of mankind, or of each single man, a perpetual war is. But it is perpetual in its own nature; because in regard of the equality of those that strive, it cannot be ended by victory. For in this state the conqueror is subject to so much danger, as it were to be accounted a miracle, if any, even the most strong, should close up his life with many years and old age. They of America are examples hereof, even in this present age: other nations have been in former ages; which now indeed are become civil and flourishing, but were then few, fierce, short-lived, poor, nasty, and |deprived| of all that pleasure and beauty of life, which peace and society are wont to bring with them. Whosoever therefore holds, that it had been best to have continued in that state in which all things were lawful for all men, he contradicts himself. For every man by natural necessity desires that which is good for him; nor is there any that esteems a war of all against all, which necessarily adheres to such a state, to be good for him. And so it happens, that through fear of each other we think it fit to rid ourselves of this condition, and to get some fellows; that if there needs must be war, it may not yet be against all men, nor without some helps.

14. Fellows are gotten either by constraint, or by consent; by constraint, when after fight the conqueror makes the conquered serve him, either through fear of

death, or by laying fetters on him; by consent, when men enter into society to help each other, both parties consenting without any constraint. But the conqueror may by right compel the conquered, or the strongest the weaker (as a man in health may one that is sick, or he that is of riper years a child), unless he will choose to die, to give caution of his future obedience. For since the right of protecting ourselves according to our own wills, proceeded from our danger, and our danger from our equality, it is more consonant to reason, and more certain for our conservation, using the present advantage to secure ourselves by taking caution, than when they shall be full grown and strong, and got out of our power, to endeavour to recover that power again by doubtful fight. And on the other side, nothing can be thought more absurd, than by discharging whom you already have weak in your power, to make him at once both an enemy and a strong one. From whence we may understand likewise as a corollary in the natural state of men, that *a sure and irresistible power confers the right of dominion and ruling over those who cannot resist*; insomuch, as the right of all things that can be done, adheres essentially and immediately unto this omnipotence hence arising.

15. Yet cannot men expect any lasting preservation, continuing thus in the state of nature, that is, of war, by reason of that equality of power, and other human faculties they are endued withal. Wherefore to seek peace, where there is any hopes of obtaining it, and where there is none, to enquire out for auxiliaries of war, is the dictate of right reason, that is, the law of nature; as shall be showed in the next chapter.

II

Of the Law of Nature Concerning Contracts

1. That the law of nature is not an agreement of men, but the dictate of reason. 2. That the fundamental law of nature, is to seek peace, where it may be had, and where not, to defend ourselves. 3. That the first special law of nature, is not to retain our right to all things. 4. What it is to quit our right: what to transfer it. 5. That in the transferring of our right, the will of him that receives it is necessarily required. 6. No words but those of the present tense, transfer any right. 7. Words of the future, if there be some other tokens to signify the will, are valid in the translation of right. 8. In matters of free gift, our right passeth not from us through any words of the future. 9. The definition of contract and compact. 10. In compacts, our right passeth from us through words of the future. 11. Compacts of mutual faith, in the state of nature are of no effect and vain; but not so in civil government. 12. That no man can make compacts with beasts, nor yet with God without revelation. 13. Nor yet make a vow to God. 14. That compacts oblige not beyond our utmost endeavour. 15. By what means we are freed from our compacts. 16. That promises extorted through fear of death, in the state of nature are valid. 17. A later compact contradicting the former, is invalid. 18. A compact not to resist him that shall prejudice my body, is invalid. 19. A compact to accuse one's self, is invalid. 20. The definition of swearing. 21. That swearing is to be conceived in that form which he useth that takes the oath. 22. An oath superadds nothing to the obligation which is made by compact. 23. An oath ought not to be pressed, but where the breach of compacts may be kept private, or cannot be punished but from God himself.

1. All authors agree not concerning the definition of *the natural law,* who notwithstanding do very often make

use of this term in their writings. The method therefore wherein we begin from definitions and exclusion of all equivocation, is only proper to them who leave no place for contrary disputes. For the rest, if any man say that somewhat is done against the law of nature, one proves it hence; because it was done against the general agreement of all the most wise and learned nations: but this declares not who shall be the judge of the wisdom and learning of all nations. Another hence, that it was done against the general consent of all mankind; which definition is by no means to be admitted. For then it were impossible for any but children and fools, to offend against such a law; for sure, under the notion of mankind, they comprehend all men actually endued with reason. These therefore either do nought against it, or if they do aught, it is without their|joint accord,|and therefore ought to be excused. But to receive the laws of nature from the consents of them who oftener break than observe them, is in truth unreasonable. Besides, men condemn the same things in others, which they approve in themselves; on the other side, they publicly commend what they privately condemn; and they deliver their opinions more by hearsay, than any speculation of their own; and they accord more through hatred of some object, through fear, hope, love, or some other perturbation of mind, than true reason. And therefore it comes to pass, that whole bodies of people often do those things|by general accord, or contention,|which those writers most willingly acknowledge to be against the law of nature. But since all do grant, that is done by *right*, which is not done against reason, we ought to judge those actions only *wrong*, which are repugnant to right reason, that is, which contradict some certain truth collected by right reasoning from true principles. But that|*wrong* which is done,|we say it is done against some law. Therefore *true reason* is a certain *law*; which, since it is no less a part of human nature than any other faculty or affection of the mind, is also termed natural. Therefore the *law of nature*, that I may define it, is the dictate of right reason,* conversant about those things which are either to be done or omitted for the constant preservation of life and members, as much as in us lies.

2. But the first and fundamental law of nature is, *that peace is to be sought after, where it may be found; and where not, there to provide ourselves for helps of war.* For we showed in the last article of the foregoing chapter, that this precept is the dictate of right reason; but that the dictates of right reason are natural laws, that hath been newly proved above. But this is the first, because the rest are derived from this, and they direct the ways either to peace or self-defence.

3. But one of the natural laws derived from this fundamental one is this: *that the right of all men to all things ought not to be retained; but that some certain rights ought to be transferred or relinquished.* For if everyone should retain his right to all things, it must necessarily follow that some by right might invade, and others, by

---

* *Right reason.* By right reason in the natural state of men, I understand not, as many do, an infallible faculty, but the act of reasoning, that is, the peculiar and true ratiocination of every man concerning those actions of his, which may either redound to the damage or benefit of his neighbours. I call it peculiar, because although in a civil government the reason of the supreme, that is, the civil law, is to be received by each single subject for the right; yet being without this civil government, in which state no man can know right reason from false, but by comparing it with his own, every man's own reason is to be accounted, not only the rule of his own actions, which are done at his own peril, but also for the measure of another man's reason, in such things as do concern him. I call it true, that is, concluding from true principles rightly framed, because that the whole breach of the laws of nature consists in the false reasoning, or rather folly of those men, who see not those duties they are necessarily to perform towards others in order to their own conservation. But the principles of right reasoning about such like duties, are those which are explained in the second, third, fourth, fifth, sixth, and seventh articles of the first chapter.

the same right, might defend themselves against them. For every man by natural necessity endeavours to defend his body, and the things which he judgeth necessary towards the protection of his body. Therefore war would follow. He therefore acts against the reason of peace, that is, against the law of nature, whosoever he be, that doth not part with his right to all things.

4. But he is said to part with his right, who either absolutely renounceth it, or conveys it to another. He absolutely renounceth it, who by some sufficient sign or meet tokens declares, that he is willing that it shall never be lawful for him to do that again, which before *by right* he might have done. But he conveys it to another, who by some sufficient sign or meet tokens declares to that other, that he is willing it should be unlawful for him to resist him, in going about to do somewhat in the performance whereof he might before *with right* have resisted him. But that the conveyance of right consists merely in not resisting, is understood by this, that before it was conveyed, he to whom he conveyed it, had even then also a right to all; whence he could not give any new right; but the resisting right he had before he gave it, by reason whereof the other could not freely enjoy his rights, is utterly abolished. Whosoever therefore acquires some right in the natural state of men, he only procures himself security and freedom from just molestation in the enjoyment of his primitive right. As for example, if any man shall sell or give away a farm, he utterly deprives himself only from all right to this farm; but he does not so from others also.

5. But in the conveyance of right, the will is requisite not only of him that conveys, but of him also that accepts it. If either be wanting, the right remains. For if I would have given what was mine to one who refused to accept of it, I have not therefore either simply renounced my right, or conveyed it to any man. For the cause which

moved me to part with it to this man, was in him only, not in others too.

6. But if there be no other token extant of our will either to quit or convey our right, but only words; those words must either relate to the present or time past; for if they be of the future only, they convey nothing. For example, he that speaks thus of the time to come, *I will give tomorrow*, declares openly that yet he hath not given it. So that all this day his right remains, and abides tomorrow too, unless in the interim he actually bestows it: for what is mine, remains mine till I have parted with it. But if I shall speak of the time present, suppose thus; *I do give or have given you this to be received tomorrow.* By these words is signified that I have already given it, and that his right to receive it tomorrow is conveyed to him by me today.

7. Nevertheless, although words alone are not sufficient tokens to declare the will; if yet to words relating to the future there shall some other signs be added, they may become as valid as if they had been spoken of the present. If therefore, as by reason of those other signs, it appear that he that speaks of the future, intends those words should be effectual toward the perfect transferring of his right, they ought to be valid. For the conveyance of right depends not on words, but, as hath been instanced in the fourth article, on the declaration of the will.

8. If any man convey some part of his right to another, and doth not this for some certain benefit received, or for some compact, a conveyance in this kind is called a gift or free donation. But in free donation, those words only oblige us, which signify the present or the time past; for if they respect the future, they oblige not as *words*, for the reason given in the foregoing article. It must needs therefore be, that the obligation arise from some other tokens of the will. But, because whatsoever is voluntarily done, is done for some good to him that wills it; there

can no other token be assigned of the will to give it, except some benefit either already received, or to be acquired. But it is supposed that no such benefit is acquired, nor any compact in being; for if so, it would cease to be a free gift. It remains therefore, that a mutual good turn without agreement be expected. But no sign can be given, that he, who used future words toward him who was in no sort engaged to return a benefit, should desire to have his words so understood as to oblige himself thereby. Nor is it suitable to reason, that those who are easily inclined to do well to others, should be obliged by every promise, testifying their present good affection. And for this cause, a promiser in this kind must be understood to have time to deliberate, and power to change that affection, as well as he to whom he made that promise, may alter his desert. But he that deliberates, is so far forth free, nor can be said to have already given. But if he promise often, and yet give seldom, he ought to be condemned of levity, and be called not a donor, but doson.

9. But the act of two, or more, mutually conveying their rights, is called a *contract*. But in every contract, either both parties instantly perform what they contract for, insomuch as there is no trust had from either to other; or the one performs, the other is trusted; or neither perform. Where both parties perform presently, there the contract is ended as soon as it is performed. But where there is credit given, either to one or both, there the party trusted promiseth after-performance; and this kind of promise is called a *covenant*.

10. But the covenant made by the party trusted with him who hath already performed, although the promise be made by words pointing at the future, doth no less transfer the right of future time, than if it had been made by words signifying the present or time past. For the other's performance is a most manifest sign that he so understood the speech of him whom he trusted, as that

he would certainly make performance also at the appointed time; and by this sign the party trusted knew himself to be thus understood; which because he hindered not, was an evident token of his will to perform. The promises therefore which are made for some benefit received, which are also covenants, are tokens of the will; that is, as in the foregoing section hath been declared, of the last act of deliberating, whereby the liberty of non-performance is abolished, and by consequence are obligatory. For where liberty ceaseth, there beginneth obligation.

11. But the covenants which are made in contract of mutual trust, neither party performing out of hand, if there ariset a just suspicion in either of them, are in the state of nature invalid. For he that first performs, by reason of the wicked disposition of the greatest part of men studying their own advantage either by right or wrong, exposeth himself to the perverse will of him with whom he hath contracted. For it suits not with reason, that any man should perform first, if it be not likely that the other will make good his promise after; which, whether it be probable or not, he that doubts it must be judge of, as hath been showed in the foregoing chapter in the ninth article. Thus, I say, things stand in the state of nature. But in a civil state, when there is a power which can compel both parties, he that hath contracted to perform first, must first perform; because, that since the other may be compelled, the cause which made him fear the other's non-performance, ceaseth.

12. But from this reason, that in all free gifts and compacts there is an acceptance of the conveyance of right

† *Arise.* For, except there appear some new cause of fear, either from somewhat done, or some other token of the will not to perform from the other part, it cannot be judged to be a just fear; for the cause which was not sufficient to keep him from making compact, must not suffice to authorize the breach of it, being made.

required, it follows that no man can compact with him who doth not declare his acceptance. And therefore we cannot compact with beasts, neither can we give or take from them any manner of right, by reason of their want of speech and understanding. Neither can any man covenant with God, or be obliged to him by vow; except so far forth as it appears to him by Holy Scriptures, that he hath substituted certain men who have authority to accept of such-like vows and covenants, as being in God's stead.

13. Those therefore do vow in vain, who are in the state of nature, where they are not tied by any civil law, except, by most certain revelation, the will of God to accept their vow or pact, be made known to them. For if what they vow be contrary to the law of nature, they are not tied by their vow; for no man is tied to perform an unlawful act. But if what is vowed be commanded by some law of nature, it is not their vow, but the law itself which ties them. But if he were free, before his vow, either to do it or not do it, his liberty remains; because that the openly declared will of the obliger is requisite to make an obligation by vow; which, in the case propounded, is supposed not to be. Now I call him the obliger, to whom any one is tied; and the obliged, him who is tied.

14. Covenants are made of such things only as fall under our deliberation. For it can be no covenant without the will of the contractor. But the will is the last act of him who deliberates; wherefore they only concern things *possible* and *to come*. No man, therefore, by his compact obligeth himself to an impossibility. But yet, though we often covenant to do such things as then seemed possible when we promised them, which yet afterward appear to be impossible, are we therefore freed from all obligation? The reason whereof is, that he who promiseth a future,| in certainty |receives a present benefit, on condition that he return another for it. For his will,

who performs the present benefit, hath simply before it
for its object a certain good, [equally] valuable with the
thing promised; but the thing itself not simply, but with
condition if it could be done. But if it should so happen,
that even this should prove impossible, why then he must
perform as much as he can. Covenants, therefore, oblige
us not to perform just the thing itself covenanted for,
but our utmost endeavour; for this only is, the things
themselves are not in our power.

15. We are freed from covenants two ways, either by
performing, or by being forgiven. By performing, for beyond that we obliged not ourselves. By being forgiven,
because he whom we obliged ourselves to, by forgiving is
conceived to return to us that right which we passed over
to him. For forgiving implies giving, that is, by the fourth
article of this chapter, a conveyance of right to him to
whom the gift is made.

16. It is a usual question, whether compacts extorted
from us through fear, do oblige or not. For example, if,
to redeem my life from the power of a robber, I promise
to pay him 100*l.* next day, and that I will do no act
whereby to apprehend and bring him to justice: whether
I am tied to keep promise or not. But though such a
promise must sometimes be judged to be of no effect, yet
it is not to be accounted so because it proceedeth from
fear. For then it would follow, that those promises which
reduced men to a civil life, and by which laws were made,
might likewise be of none effect (for it proceeds from
fear of mutual slaughter, that one man submits himself
to the dominion of another); and he should play the fool
finely, who should trust his captive covenanting with the
price of his redemption. It holds universally true, that
promises do oblige when there is some benefit received,
and that to promise, and the thing promised, be lawful.
But it is lawful, for the redemption of my life, both to
promise and to give what I will of mine own to any man,

even to a thief. We are obliged, therefore, by promises proceeding from fear, except the civil law forbid them; by virtue whereof, that which is promised becomes unlawful.

17. Whosoever shall contract with one to do or omit somewhat, and shall after covenant the contrary with another, he maketh not the former, but the latter contract unlawful. For he hath no longer right to do or to omit aught, who by former contracts hath conveyed it to another. Wherefore he can convey no right by latter contracts, and what is promised is promised without right. He is therefore tied only to his first contract, to break which is unlawful.

18. No man is obliged by any contracts whatsoever not to resist him who shall offer to kill, wound, or any other way hurt his body. For there is in every man a certain high degree of fear, through which he apprehends that evil which is done to him to be the greatest; and therefore by natural necessity he shuns it all he can, and it is supposed he can do no otherwise. When a man is arrived to this degree of fear, we cannot expect but he will provide for himself either by flight or fight. Since therefore no man is tied to impossibilities, they who are threatened either with death (which is the greatest evil to nature), or wounds, or some other bodily hurts, and are not stout enough to bear them, are not obliged to endure them. Furthermore, he that is tied by contract is trusted; for faith only is the bond of contracts; but they who are brought to punishment, either capital or more gentle, are fettered or strongly guarded; which is a most certain sign that they seemed not sufficiently bound from nonresistance by their contracts. It is one thing, if I promise thus: if I do it not at the day appointed, kill me. Another thing, if thus: if I do it not, though you should offer to kill me, I will not resist. All men, if need be, contract the first way, but there is need sometimes. This second way,

none; neither is it ever needful. For in the mere state of nature, if you have a mind to kill, that state itself affords you a right; insomuch as you need not first trust him, if for breach of trust you will afterwards kill him. But in a civil state, where the right of life and death and of all corporal punishment is with the supreme, that same right of killing cannot be granted to any private person. Neither need the supreme himself contract with any man patiently to yield to his punishment; but only this, that no man offer to defend others from him. If in the state of nature, as between two realms, there should a contract be made on condition of killing if it were not performed, we must presuppose another contract of not killing before the appointed day. Wherefore on that day, if there be no performance, the right of war returns, that is an hostile state, in which all things are lawful, and therefore resistance also. Lastly, by the contract of not resisting, we are obliged, of two evils to make choice of that which seems the greater. For certain death is a greater evil than fighting. But of two evils it is impossible not to choose the least. By such a compact, therefore, we should be tied to impossibilities; which is contrary to the very nature of compacts.

19. Likewise no man is tied by any compacts whatsoever to accuse himself, or any other, by whose damage he is like to procure himself a bitter life. Wherefore neither is a father obliged to bear witness against his son, nor a husband against his wife, nor a son against his father, nor any man against any one by whose means he hath his subsistence; for in vain is that testimony which is presumed to be corrupted from nature. But although no man be tied to accuse himself by any compact, yet in a public trial he may by torture be forced to make answer. But such answers are no testimony of the fact, but helps for the searching out of truth; insomuch as whether the party

tortured his answer be true or false, or whether he answer not at all, whatsoever he doth, he doth it by right.

20. Swearing is a speech joined to a promise, whereby the promiser declares his renouncing of God's mercy, unless he perform his word. Which definition is contained in the words themselves, which have in them the very essence of an oath, to wit, *so God help me*, or other equivalent, as with the Romans, *do thou Jupiter so destroy the deceiver, as I slay this same beast*. Neither is this any let, but that an oath may as well sometimes be affirmatory as promissory; for he that confirms his affirmation with an oath, promiseth that he speaks truth. But though in some places it was the fashion for subjects to swear by their kings, that custom took its original hence, that those kings took upon them divine honour. For oaths were therefore introduced, that by religion and consideration of the divine power, men might have a greater dread of breaking their faiths, than that wherewith they fear men, from whose eyes their actions may lie hid.

21. Whence it follows that an oath must be conceived in that form, which he useth who takes it; for in vain is any man brought to swear by a God whom he believes not, and therefore neither fears him. For though by the light of nature it may be known that there is a God, yet no man thinks he is to swear by him in any other fashion, or by any other name, than what is contained in the precepts of his own proper, that is (as he who swears imagines) the true religion.

22. By the definition of an oath, we may understand that a bare contract obligeth no less, than that to which we are sworn. For it is the contract which binds us; the oath relates to the divine punishment, which it could not provoke, if the breach of contract were not in itself unlawful; but it could not be unlawful, if the contract were not obligatory. Furthermore, he that renounceth the mercy of God, obligeth himself not to any punishment;

because it is ever lawful to deprecate the punishment, howsoever provoked, and to enjoy God's pardon if it be granted. The only effect therefore of an oath is this: to cause men, who are naturally inclined to break all manner of faith, through fear of punishment to make the more conscience of their words and actions.

23. To exact an oath where the breach of contract, if any be made, cannot but be known, and where the party compacted withal wants not power to punish, is to do somewhat more than is necessary unto self-defence, and shows a mind desirous not so much to benefit itself, as to prejudice another. For an oath, out of the very form of swearing, is taken in order to the provocation of God's anger, that is to say, of him that is omnipotent, against those who therefore violate their faith, because they think that by their own strength they can escape the punishment of men; and of him that is omniscient, against those who therefore usually break their trust, because they hope that no man shall see them.

III

Of the Other Laws of Nature

1. The second law of nature, is to perform contracts.
2. That trust is to be held with all men without exception. 3. What injury is. 4. Injury can be done to none
but those with whom we contract. 5. The distinction of
justice into that of men, and that of actions. 6. The distinction of commutative and distributive justice examined.
7. No injury can be done to him that is willing. 8. The
third law of nature, concerning ingratitude. 9. The fourth
law of nature, that every man render himself useful. 10.
The fifth law, of mercy. 11. The sixth law, that punishments regard the future only. 12. The seventh law, against
reproach. 13. The eighth law, against pride. 14. The
ninth law, of humility. 15. The tenth, of equity, or
against acceptance of persons. 16. The eleventh, of
things to be had in common. 17. The twelfth, of things
to be divided by lot. 18. The thirteenth, of birthright
and first possession. 19. The fourteenth, of the safeguard
of them who are mediators for peace. 20. The fifteenth,
of constituting an umpire. 21. The sixteenth, that no
man is judge in his own cause. 22. The seventeenth,
that umpires must be without all hope of reward from those
whose cause is to be judged. 23. The eighteenth, of witnesses. 24. The nineteenth, that there can no contract
be made with the umpire. 25. The twentieth, against
gluttony, and all such things as hinder the use of reason.
26. The rule by which we may presently know, whether
what we are doing be against the law of nature or not.
27. The laws of nature oblige only in the court of conscience. 28. The laws of nature are sometimes broke by
doing things|agreeable|to those laws. 29. The laws of
nature are unchangeable. 30. Whosoever endeavours to
fulfil the laws of nature, is a just man. 31. The natural
and moral law are one. 32. How it comes to pass, that
what hath been said of the laws of nature, is not the same

with what philosophers have delivered concerning the virtues. 33. The law of nature is not properly a law, but as it is delivered in Holy Writ.

1. Another of the laws of nature is to *perform contracts*, or *to keep trust*. For it hath been showed in the foregoing chapter, that the law of nature commands every man, as a thing necessary, to obtain peace, to convey certain rights from each to other; and that this, as often as it shall happen to be done, is called a contract. But this is so far forth only conducible to peace, as we shall perform ourselves what we contract with others shall be done or omitted; and in vain would|contacts|be made, unless we stood to them. Because therefore to stand to our covenants, or to keep faith, is a thing necessary for the obtaining of peace; it will prove, by the second article of the second chapter, to be a precept of the natural law.

2. Neither is there in this matter any exception of the persons with whom we contract; as if they keep no faith with others, or hold that none ought to be kept, or are guilty of any other kind of vice. For he that contracts, in that he doth contract, denies that action to be in vain; and it is against reason for a knowing man to do a thing in vain; and if he think himself not bound to keep it, in thinking so he affirms the contract to be made in vain. He therefore who contracts with one with whom he thinks he is not bound to keep faith, he doth at once think a contract to be a thing done in vain, and not in vain; which is absurd. Either therefore we must hold trust with all men, or else not bargain with them; that is, either there must be a declared war, or a sure and faithful peace.

3. The breaking of a bargain, as also the taking back of a gift (whichever consists in some action or omission), is called an injury. But that action or omission is called unjust; insomuch as an injury, and an unjust action or

omission, signify the same thing, and both are the same with breach of contract and trust. And it seems the word *injury* came to be given to any action or omission, because they were *without right*; he that acted or omitted, having before conveyed his right to some other. And there iş some likeness between that which in the common course of life we call *injury*, and that which in the Schools is usually called *absurd*. For even as he who by arguments is driven to deny the assertion which he first maintained, is said to be brought to an absurdity; in like manner, he who through weakness of mind does or omits that which before he had by contract promised not to do or omit, commits an injury, and falls into no less contradiction than he who in the Schools is reduced to an absurdity. For by contracting for some future action, he wills it done; by not doing it, he wills it not done: which is to will a thing done and not done at the same time, which is a contradiction. An injury therefore is a kind of absurdity in conversation, as an absurdity is a kind of injury in disputation.

4. From these grounds it follows, that an injury can be done to no man* but him with whom we enter covenant, or to whom somewhat is made over by deed of gift, or to whom somewhat is promised by way of bargain. And therefore damaging and ihjuring are often

---

* *Injury can be done to no man, &c.* The word *injustice* relates to some law; *injury*, to some person, as well as some law. For what is unjust, is unjust to all; but there may an injury be done, and yet not against me, nor thee, but some other; and sometimes against no private person, but the magistrate only; sometimes also neither against the magistrate, not any private man, but only against God. For through contract and conveyance of right, we say, that an injury is done against this or that man. Hence it is, which we see in all kind of government, that what private men contract between themselves by word or writing, is released again at the will of the obliger. But those mischiefs which are done against the laws of the land, as theft, homicide, and the like, are punished, not as he wills to whom the hurt is done, but according to the will of the magistrate; that is, the constituted laws.

disjoined. For if a master command his servant, who hath promised to obey him, to pay a sum of money, or carry some present to a third man; the servant, if he do it not, hath indeed damaged this third party, but he injured his master only. So also in a civil government, if any man offend another with whom he hath made no contract, he damages him to whom the evil is done; but he injures none but him to whom the power of government belongs. For if he who receives the hurt should expostulate the mischief, he that did it should answer thus: *what art thou to me; why should I rather do according to your than mine own will, since I do not hinder but you may do your own, and not my mind?* In which speech, where there hath no manner of pre-contract passed, I see not, I confess, what is reprehensible.

5. These words, *just* and *unjust*, as also *justice* and *injustice*, are equivocal; for they signify one thing when they are attributed to persons, another when to actions. When they are attributed to actions, *just* signifies as much as what is done with right, and *unjust*, as what is done with injury. He who hath done some just thing, is not therefore said to be a *just* person, but *guiltless*; and he that hath done some unjust thing, we do not therefore say he is an *unjust*, but *guilty* man. But when the words are applied to persons, *to be just* signifies as much as to be delighted in just dealing, to study how to do righteousness, or to endeavour in all things to do that which is just; and *to be unjust* is to neglect righteous dealing, or to think it is to be measured not according to my contract, but some present benefit. So as the justice or injustice of the mind, the intention, or the man, is one thing, that of an action or omission another; and innumerable actions of a just man may be unjust, and of an unjust man, just. But that man is to be accounted just, who doth just things because the law commands it, unjust things only by reason of his infirmity; and he is properly said to be unjust, who

doth righteousness for fear of the punishment annexed unto the law, and unrighteousness by reason of the iniquity of his mind.

6. The justice of actions is commonly distinguished into two kinds, commutative and distributive; the former whereof, they say, consists in arithmetical, the latter in geometrical proportion; and that is conversant in exchanging, in buying, selling, borrowing, lending, location and conduction, and other acts whatsoever belonging to contractors; where, if there be an equal return made, hence, they say, springs a commutative justice: but this is busied about the dignity and merits of men; so as if there be rendered to every man κατὰ τὴν ἀξίαν, more to him who is more worthy, and less to him that deserves less, and that proportionably; hence, they say, ariseth distributive justice. I acknowledge here some certain distinction of equality: to wit, that one is an equality simply so called; as when two things of equal value are compared together, as a pound of silver with twelve ounces of the same silver: the other is an equality *secundum quod*; as when a thousand pounds is to be divided to a hundred men, six hundred pounds are given to sixty men, and four hundred to forty, where there is no equality between six hundred and four hundred; but when it happens that there is the same inequality in the number of them to whom it is distributed, every one of them shall take an equal part, whence it is called an equal distribution. But such like equality is the same thing with geometrical proportion. But what is all this to justice? For neither if I sell my goods for as much as I can get for them, do I injure the buyer, who sought and desired them of me; neither if I divide more of what is mine to him who deserves less, so long as I give the other what I have agreed for, do I wrong to either. Which truth our Saviour himself, being God, testifies in the Gospel. This therefore is no distinction of justice, but of equality. Yet perhaps it can-

not be denied but that justice is a certain equality, as consisting in this only; that since we are all equal by nature, one should not arrogate more right to himself than he grants to another, unless he have fairly gotten it by compact. And let this suffice to be spoken against this distinction of justice, although now almost generally received by all; lest any man should conceive an injury to be somewhat else than the breach of faith or contract, as hath been defined above.

7. It is an old saying, *volenti non fit injuria,* the willing man receives no injury; yet the truth of it may be derived from our principles. For grant that a man be willing that that should be done which he conceives to be an injury to him; why then, that is done by his will, which by contract was not lawful to be done. But he being willing that should be done which was not lawful by contract, the contract itself (by the fifteenth article of the foregoing chapter) becomes void. The right therefore of doing it returns; therefore it is done by right; wherefore it is no injury.

8. The third precept of the natural law is, *that you suffer not him to be the worse for you, who, out of the confidence he had in you, first did you a good turn; or that you accept not a gift, but with a mind to endeavour that the giver shall have no just occasion to repent him of his gift.* For without this, he should act without reason, that would confer a benefit where he sees it would be lost; and by this means all beneficence and trust, together with all kind of benevolence, would be taken from among men, neither would there be aught of mutual assistance among them, nor any commencement of gaining grace and favour; by reason whereof the state of war would necessarily remain, contrary to the fundamental law of nature. But because the breach of this law is not a breach of trust or contract (for we suppose no contracts to have passed among them), therefore is it not usually termed an in-

jury; but because good turns and thanks have a mutual eye to each other, it is called *ingratitude*.

9. The fourth precept of nature is, *that every man render himself useful unto others:* which that we may rightly understand, we must remember that there is in men a diversity of dispositions to enter into society, arising from the diversity of their affections, not unlike that which is found in stones, brought together in the building, by reason of the diversity of their matter and figure. For as a stone, which in regard of its sharp and angular form takes up more room from other stones than it fills up itself, neither because of the hardness of its matter cannot well be pressed together, or easily cut, and would hinder the building from being fitly compacted, is cast away, as not fit for use; so a man, for the harshness of his disposition in retaining superfluities for himself, and detaining of necessaries from others, and being incorrigible by reason of the stubbornness of his affections, is commonly said to be useless and troublesome unto others. Now, because each one not by right only, but even by natural necessity, is supposed with all his main might to intend the procurement of those things which are necessary to his own preservation; if any man will contend on the other side for superfluities, by his default there will arise a war; because that on him alone there lay no necessity of contending; he therefore acts against the fundamental law of nature. Whence it follows (which we were to show), that it is a precept of nature, that every man accommodate himself to others. But he who breaks this law may be called *useless* and troublesome. Yet Cicero opposeth *inhumanity* to this *usefulness*, as having regard to this very law.

10. The fifth precept of the law of nature is, *that we must forgive him who repents and asks pardon for what is past, having first taken caution for the time to come.* The pardon of what is past, or the remission of an offence,

is nothing else but the granting of peace to him that
asketh it, after he hath warred against us, and now is become penitent. But peace granted to him that repents
not, that is, to him that retains an hostile mind, or that
gives not caution for the future, that is, seeks not peace,
but opportunity; is not properly peace, but fear, and
therefore is not commanded by nature. Now to him that
will not pardon the penitent and that gives future
caution, peace itself it seems is not pleasing: which is contrary to the natural law.

11. The sixth precept of the natural law is, *that in revenge and punishments we must have our eye not at the
evil past, but the future good:* that is, it is not lawful to
inflict punishment for any other end, but that the
offender may be corrected, or that others warned by his
punishment may become better. But this is confirmed
chiefly from hence, that each man is bound by the law of
nature to forgive one another, provided he give caution
for the future, as hath been showed in the foregoing
article. Furthermore, because revenge, if the time past be
only considered, is nothing else but a certain triumph
and glory of mind, which points at no end; for it contemplates only what is past, but the end is a thing to
come; but that which is directed to no end, is vain: that
revenge therefore which regards not the future, proceeds
from vain glory, and is therefore without reason. But to
hurt another without reason introduces a war, and is contrary to the fundamental law of nature. It is therefore a
precept of the law of nature, that in revenge we look not
backwards, but forward. Now the breach of this law is
commonly called *cruelty.*

12. But because all signs of hatred and contempt provoke most of all to brawling and fighting, insomuch as
most men would rather lose their lives (that I say not,
their peace) than suffer slander; it follows in the seventh
place, that it is prescribed by the law of nature, *that no*

man, either by deeds or words, countenance or laughter, do declare himself to hate or scorn another. The breach of which law is called *reproach.* But although nothing be more frequent than the scoffs and jeers of the powerful against the weak, and namely, of judges against guilty persons, which neither relate to the offence of the guilty, nor the duty of the judges; yet these kind of men do act against the law of nature, and are to be esteemed for contumelious.

13. The question whether of two men be the more worthy, belongs not to the natural, but civil state. For it hath been showed before (Chap. 1. Art. 3) that all men by nature are equal; and therefore the inequality which now is, suppose from riches, power, nobility of kindred, is come from the civil law. I know that Aristotle, in his first book of Politics, affirms as a foundation of the whole political science, that some men by nature are made worthy to command, others only to serve; as if lord and |servant| were distinguished not by consent of men, but by an aptness, that is, a certain kind of natural knowledge or ignorance. Which foundation is not only against reason (as but now hath been showed), but also against experience. For neither almost is any man so dull of understanding as not to judge it better to be ruled by himself, than to yield himself to the government of another; neither if the wiser and stronger do contest, have these |ever or after| the upper hand of those. Whether therefore men be equal by nature, the equality is to be acknowledged; or whether unequal, because they are like to contest for dominion, it is necessary for the obtaining of peace, *that they be esteemed as equal*; and therefore it is in the eighth place a precept of the law of nature, *that every man be accounted by nature equal to another*; the contrary to which law is *pride.*

14. As it was necessary to the conservation of each man that he should part with some of his rights, so it is no less

necessary to the same conservation that he retain some others, to wit, the right of bodily protection, of free enjoyment of air, water, and all necessaries for life. Since therefore many common rights are retained by those who enter into a peaceable state, and that many peculiar ones are also acquired, hence ariseth this ninth dictate of the natural law, to wit, that *what rights soever any man challenges to himself, he also grant the same as due to all the rest*; otherwise he frustrates the equality acknowledged in the former article. For what is it else to acknowledge an equality of persons in the making up of society, but to attribute equal right and power to those whom no reason would else engage to enter into society? But to ascribe *equal things* to *equals*, is the same with giving things *proportional* to *proportionals*. The observation of this law is called *meekness*, the violation πλεονεξία; the breakers by the Latins are styled *immodici et immodesti*.

15. In the tenth place it is commanded by the law of nature, *that every man in dividing right to others, show himself equal to either party*. By the foregoing law we are forbidden to assume more right by nature to ourselves, than we grant to others. We may take less if we will; for that sometimes is an argument of modesty. But if at any time matter of right be to be divided by us unto others, we are forbidden by this law to favour one more or less than another. For he that by favouring one before another observes not this natural equality, reproaches him whom he thus undervalues; but it is declared above, that a reproach is against the laws of nature. The observance of this precept is called *equity*; the breach, *respect of persons*. The Greeks in one word term it προσωποληψία.

16. From the foregoing law is collected this eleventh, *those things which cannot be divided, must be used in common if they can, and that the quantity of the matter permit, every man as much as he lists; but if the quantity permit not, then with limitation, and proportionally to*

the number of the users. For otherwise that equality can by no means be observed, which we have showed in the foregoing article to be commanded by the law of nature.

17. Also what cannot be divided nor had in common, it is provided by the law of nature, which may be the twelfth precept, *that the use of that thing be either by turns, or adjudged to one only by lot; and that in the using it by turns, it be also decided by lot, who shall have the first use of it*. For here also regard is to be had unto equality: but no other can be found but that of lot.

18. But all lot is twofold, *arbitrary* or *natural*.

Arbitrary is that which is cast by the consent of the contenders, and it consists in mere chance, as they say, or fortune. *Natural* is primogeniture, in Greek κληρονομία, as it were, given by lot; or first possession. Therefore the things which can neither be divided nor had in common, must be granted to the first possessor; as also those things which belonged to the father are due to the son, unless the father himself have formerly conveyed away that right to some other. Let this therefore stand for the thirteenth law of nature.

19. The fourteenth precept of the law of nature is, *that safety must be assured to the mediators for peace*. For the reason which commands the end, commands also the means necessary to the end. But the first dictate of reason is peace; all the rest are means to obtain it, and without which peace cannot be had. But neither can peace be had without mediation, nor mediation without safety. It is therefore a dictate of reason, that is, a law of nature, that we must give all security to the mediators for peace.

20. Furthermore because, although men should agree to make all these and whatsoever other laws of nature, and should endeavour to keep them, yet doubts and controversies would daily arise concerning the application of them unto their actions, to wit, whether what was done were against the law or not, which we call the question of

right; whence will follow a fight between parties, either sides supposing themselves wronged: it is therefore necessary to the preservation of peace, because in this case no other fit remedy can possibly be thought on, that both the disagreeing parties refer the matter unto some third, and oblige themselves by mutual compacts to stand to his judgment in deciding the controversy. And he to whom they thus refer themselves, is called an arbiter. It is therefore the fifteenth precept of the natural law, *that both parties disputing concerning the matter of right, submit themselves unto the opinion and judgment of some third.*

21. But from this ground, that an arbiter or judge is chosen by the differing parties to determine the controversy, we gather that the arbiter must not be one of the parties. For every man is presumed to seek what is good for himself naturally, and what is just only for peace's sake and accidentally; and therefore cannot observe that same equality commanded by the law of nature, so exactly as a third man would do. It is therefore in the sixteenth place contained in the law of nature, *that no man must be judge or arbiter in his own cause.*

22. From the same ground follows in the seventeenth place, *that no man must be judge, who propounds unto himself any hope of profit or glory from the victory of either part:* for the like reason sways here, as in the foregoing law.

23. But when there is some controversy of the fact itself, to wit, whether that be done or not which is said to be done, the natural law wills that the arbiter trust both parties alike, that is, because they affirm contradictories, that he believe neither. He must therefore give credit to a third, or a third and fourth, or more, that he may be able to give judgment of the fact, as often as by other signs he cannot come to the knowledge of it. The eighteenth law of nature therefore enjoins arbiters and judges

of fact, *that where firm and certain signs of the fact appear not, there they rule their sentence by such witnesses as seem to be indifferent to both parts.*

24. From the above declared definition of an arbiter may be furthermore understood, *that no contract or promise must pass between him and the parties whose judge he is appointed, by virtue whereof he may be engaged to speak in favour of either part, nay, or be obliged to judge according to equity, or to pronounce such sentence as he shall truly judge to be equal.* The judge is indeed bound to give such sentence as he shall judge to be equal, by the law of nature recounted in the 15th article: to the obligation of which law nothing can be added by way of compact. Such compact therefore would be in vain. Besides, if giving wrong judgment he should contend for the equity of it, except such compact be of no force, the controversy would remain after judgment given: which is contrary to the constitution of an arbiter, who is so chosen, as both parties have obliged themselves to stand to the judgment which he should pronounce. The law of nature therefore commands the judge to be disengaged, which is its nineteenth precept.

25. Furthermore, forasmuch as the laws of nature are nought else but the dictates of reason; so as, unless a man endeavour to preserve the faculty of right reasoning, he cannot observe the laws of nature; it is manifest, that he who knowingly or willingly doth aught whereby the rational faculty may be destroyed or weakened, he knowingly and willingly breaks the law of nature. For there is no difference between a man who performs not his duty, and him who does such things willingly as make it impossible for him to do it. But they destroy and weaken the reasoning faculty, who do that which disturbs the mind from its natural state; that which most manifestly happens to drunkards, and gluttons. We therefore

sin, in the twentieth place, against the law of nature by
drunkenness.

26. Perhaps some man, who sees all these precepts of
nature derived by a certain artifice from the single dictate
of reason advising us to look to the preservation and safeguard of ourselves, will say that the deduction of these
laws is so hard, that it is not to be expected they will be
vulgarly known, and therefore neither will they prove
obliging: for laws, if they be not known, oblige not, nay
indeed, are not laws. To this I answer, it is true, that hope,
fear, anger, ambition, covetousness, vain glory, and other
perturbations of mind, do hinder a man, so as he cannot
attain to the knowledge of these laws whilst those passions prevail in him: but there is no man who is not sometimes in a quiet mind. At that time therefore there is
nothing easier for him to know, though he be never so
rude and unlearned, than this only rule, that when he
doubts whether what he is now doing to another may be
done by the law of nature or not, he conceive himself to
be in that other's stead. Here instantly those perturbations which persuaded him to the fact, being now cast
into the other scale, dissuade him as much. And this rule
is not only easy, but is anciently celebrated in these words,
*quod tibi fieri non vis, alteri ne feceris: do not that
to others, you would not have done to yourself.*

27. But because most men, by reason of their perverse
desire of present profit, are very unapt to observe these
laws, although acknowledged by them; if perhaps some,
more humble than the rest, should exercise that equity
and usefulness which reason dictates, those not practis-
ing the same, surely they would not follow reason in so
doing; nor would they hereby procure themselves peace,
but a more certain quick destruction, and the keepers of
the law become a mere prey to the breakers of it. It is not
therefore to be imagined, that by nature, that is, by rea-

son, men are obliged to the exercise of all these laws† in
that state of men wherein they are not practised by others.
We are obliged yet, in the interim, to a readiness of mind
to observe them, whensoever their observation shall seem
to conduce to the end for which they were ordained. We
must therefore conclude, that the law of nature doth always and everywhere oblige in the internal court, or that
of conscience; but not always in the external court, but
then only when it may be done with safety.

28. But the laws which oblige conscience may be
broken by an act not only contrary to them, but also
agreeable with them; if so be that he who does it, be of
another opinion. For though the act itself be answerable
to the laws, yet his conscience is against them.

29. *The laws of nature are immutable and eternal:*
what they forbid, can never be lawful; what they command, can never be unlawful. For *pride, ingratitude,
breach of contracts* (or *injury*), *inhumanity, contumely,*
will never be lawful, nor the contrary virtues to these ever
unlawful, as we take them for dispositions of the mind,
that is, as they are considered in the court of conscience,
where only they oblige and are laws. Yet actions may be

---

† *The exercise of all these laws.* Nay, among these laws some
things there are, the omission whereof, provided it be done for peace
or self-preservation, seems rather to be the fulfilling, than breach of
the natural law. For he that doth all things against those that do
all things, and plunders plunderers, doth equity. But on the other
side, to do that which in peace is a handsome action, and becoming
an honest man, is dejectedness and poorness of spirit, and a be-
traying of one's self, in the time of war. But there are certain natural
laws, whose exercise ceaseth not even in the time of war itself. For
I cannot understand what drunkenness or cruelty, that is, revenge
which respects not the future good, can advance toward peace, or
the preservation of any man. Briefly, in the state of nature, what is
just and unjust, is not to be esteemed by the actions but by the
counsel and conscience of the actor. That which is done out of
necessity, out of endeavour for peace, for the preservation of ourselves, is done with right, otherwise every damage done to a man
would be a breach of the natural law, and an injury against God.

so diversified by circumstances and the civil law, that what
is done with equity at one time, is guilty of iniquity at
another; and what suits with reason at one time, is contrary to it another. Yet reason is still the same, and
changeth not her end, which is peace and defence, nor
the means to attain them, to wit, those virtues of the
mind which we have declared above, and which cannot
be abrogated by any custom or law whatsoever.

30. It is evident by what hath hitherto been said, how
easily the laws of nature are to be observed, because they
require the endeavour only (but that must be true and
constant); which whoso shall perform, we may rightly call
him *just*. For he who tends to this with his whole might,
namely, that his actions be squared according to the precepts of nature, he shows clearly that he hath a mind to
fulfil all those laws; which is all we are obliged to by
rational nature. Now he that hath done all he is obliged
to, is a just man.

31. All writers do agree, that the natural law is the
same with the moral. Let us see wherefore this is true.
We must know, therefore, that good and evil are names
given to things to signify the inclination or aversion of
them, by whom they were given. But the inclinations of
men are diverse, according to their diverse constitutions,
customs, opinions; as we may see in those things we apprehend by sense, as by tasting, touching, smelling; but
much more in those which pertain to the common actions
of life, where what this man commends, that is to say,
calls *good*, the other undervalues, as being evil. Nay, very
often the same man at diverse times praises and dispraises
the same thing. Whilst thus they do, necessary it is there
should be discord and strife. They are, therefore, so long
in the state of war, as by reason of the diversity of the
present appetites, they mete good and evil by diverse
measures. All men easily acknowledge this state, as long
as they are in it, to be evil, and by consequence that peace

is good. They therefore who could not agree concerning a present, do agree concerning a future good; which indeed is a work of reason; for things present are obvious to the sense, things to come to our reason only. Reason declaring peace to be good, it follows by the same reason, that all the necessary means to peace be good also; and therefore that modesty, equity, trust, humanity, mercy (which we have demonstrated to be necessary to peace), are good manners or habits, that is, virtues. The law therefore, in the means to peace, commands also good manners, or the practice of virtue; and therefore it is called *moral*.

32. But because men cannot put off this same irrational appetite, whereby they greedily prefer the present good (to which, by strict consequence, many unforeseen evils do adhere) before the future; it happens, that though all men do agree in the commendation of the foresaid virtues, yet they disagree still concerning their nature, to wit, in what each of them doth consist. For as oft as another's good action displeaseth any man, that action hath the name given of some neighbouring vice; likewise the bad actions which please them, are ever intituled to some virtue. Whence it comes to pass that the same action is praised by these, and called virtue, and dispraised by those, and termed vice. Neither is there as yet any remedy found by philosophers for this matter. For since they could not observe the goodness of actions to consist in this, that it was in order to peace, and the evil in this, that it related to discord, they built a moral philosophy wholly estranged from the moral law, and unconstant to itself. For they would have the nature of virtues seated in a certain kind of mediocrity between two extremes, and the vices in the extremes themselves; which is apparently false. For *to dare* is commended, and, under the name of *fortitude* is taken for a virtue, although it be an extreme, if the cause be approved. Also the quantity of a

thing given, whether it be great or little, or between both, makes not liberality, but the cause of giving it. Neither is it injustice, if I give any man more of what is mine own than I owe him. The laws of nature, therefore, are the sum of *moral* philosophy; whereof I have only delivered such precepts in this place, as appertain to the preservation of ourselves against those dangers which arise from discord. But there are other precepts of *rational* nature, from whence spring other virtues; for temperance, also, is a precept of reason, because intemperance tends to sickness and death. And so fortitude too, that is, that same faculty of resisting stoutly in present dangers, and which are more hardly declined than overcome; because it is a means tending to the preservation of him that resists.

33. But those which we call the laws of nature (since they are nothing else but certain conclusions, understood by reason, of things to be done and omitted; but a law, to speak properly and accurately, is the speech of him who by right commands somewhat to others to be done or omitted), are not in propriety of speech laws, as they proceed from nature. Yet, as they are delivered by God in holy Scriptures, as we shall see in the chapter following, they are most properly called by the name of laws. For the sacred Scripture is the speech of God commanding over all things by greatest right.

IV

That the Law of Nature Is a Divine Law

1. The natural and moral law is divine. 2. Which is confirmed in Scripture, in general. 3. Specially, in regard of the fundamental law of nature in seeking of peace. 4. Also in regard of the first law of nature in abolishing all things to be had in common. 5. Also of the second law of nature, concerning faith to be kept. 6. Also of the third law, of thankfulness. 7. Also of the fourth law, of rendering ourselves useful. 8. Also of the fifth law, concerning mercy. 9. Also of the sixth law, that punishment only looks at the future. 10. Also of the seventh law, concerning slander. 11. Also of the eighth law, against pride. 12. Also of the ninth law, of equity. 13. Also of the tenth law, against respect of persons. 14. Also of the eleventh law, of having those things in common which cannot be divided. 15. Also of the twelfth law, of things to be divided by lot. 16. Also of appointing a judge. 17. Also of the seventeenth law, that the arbiters must receive no reward for their sentence. 18. Also of the eighteenth law, concerning witnesses. 19. Also of the twentieth law, against drunkenness. 20. Also in respect of that which hath been said, that the law of nature is eternal. 21. Also that the laws of nature do pertain to conscience. 22. Also that the laws of nature are easily observed. 23. Lastly, in respect of the rule by which a man may presently know, whether what he is about to act, be against the law of nature, or not. 24. The law of Christ is the law of nature.

1. The same law which is *natural* and *moral*, is also wont to be called *divine*, nor undeservedly; as well because reason, which is the law of nature, is given by God to every man for the rule of his actions; as because the precepts of living which are thence derived, are the same

with those which have been delivered from the divine Majesty for the *laws* of his heavenly kingdom, by our Lord Jesus Christ, and his holy prophets and apostles. What therefore by reasoning we have understood above concerning the law of nature, we will endeavour to confirm the same in this chapter by holy writ.

2. But first we will show those places in which it is declared, that the divine law is seated in right reason. Psalm xxxvii. 30, 31: *The mouth of the righteous will be exercised in wisdom, and his tongue will be talking of judgment: the law of God is in his heart.* Jeremiah xxxi. 33: *I will put my law in their inward parts, and write it in their hearts.* Psalm xix. 7: *The law of the Lord is an undefiled law, converting the soul.* Verse 8: *The commandment of the Lord is pure, and giveth light unto the eyes.* Deuteron. xxx. 11: *This commandment, which I command thee this day, it is not hidden from thee, neither is it far off,* &c. Verse. 14: *But the word is very nigh unto thee in thy mouth, and in thine heart, that thou mayest do it.* Psalm cxix. 34: *Give me understanding, and I shall keep thy law.* Verse 105: *Thy word is a lamp unto my feet, and a light unto my paths.* Prov. ix. 10: *The knowledge of the holy is understanding.* Christ the law-giver, himself is called (John i. 1): *the word.* The same Christ is called (verse 9): *the true light, that lighteth every man that cometh in the world.* All which are descriptions of right reason, whose dictates, we have showed before, are the laws of nature.

3. But that that which we set down for the fundamental law of nature, namely, that peace was to be sought for, is also the sum of the Divine law, will be manifest by these places. Rom. iii. 17: *Righteousness*, which is the sum of the law, is called *the way of peace.* Psalm lxxxv. 10: *Righteousness and peace have kissed each other.* Matth. v. 9: *Blessed are the peace-makers, for they shall be called the children of God.* And after St. Paul, in his sixth

chapter to the Hebrews, and the last verse, had called Christ (the legislator of that law we treat of), *an High-priest for ever after the order of Melchisedec*: he adds in the following chapter, the first verse: *This Melchisedec was king of Salem, priest of the most high God*, &c. (Verse 2): *First being by interpretation king of righteousness, and after that also king of Salem, which is, king of peace*. Whence it is clear, that Christ, the King, in his kingdom placeth righteousness and peace together. Psalm xxxiv. 14: *Eschew evil and do good; seek peace and pursue it*. Isaiah ix. 6, 7: *Unto us a child is born, unto us a son is given, and the government shall be upon his shoulder, and his name shall be called Wonderful, Counsellor, the Mighty God, the everlasting Father, the Prince of Peace*. Isaiah lii. 7: *How beautiful upon the mountains are the feet of him that bringeth good tidings, that publisheth peace, that bringeth good tidings of good, that publisheth salvation, that saith unto Sion, thy God reigneth!* Luke ii. 14: In the nativity of Christ, the voice of them that praised God, saying, *Glory be to God on high, and in earth peace, good-will towards men*. And Isaiah liii. 5: the Gospel is called the *chastisement of our peace*. Isaiah lix. 8: Righteousness is called the *way of peace. The way of peace they know not, and there is no judgment in their goings*. Micah v. 4, 5, speaking of the Messias, he saith thus: *He shall stand and feed in the strength of the Lord, in the majesty of the name of the Lord his God, and they shall abide, for now shall he be great unto the end of the earth; and this man shall be your peace*, &c. Prov. iii. 1, 2: *My son, forget not my law, but let thine heart keep my commandments; for length of days, and long life, and peace, shall they add to thee.*

4. What appertains to the first law of abolishing the community of all things, or concerning the introduction of *meum* and *tuum*; we perceive in the first place, how great an adversary this same community is to peace, by

those words of Abraham to Lot (Gen. xiii. 8, 9): *Let there be no strife, I pray thee, between thee and me, and between thy herdmen and my herdmen; for we be brethren. Is not the whole land before thee? Separate thyself, I pray thee from me.* And all those places of Scripture by which we are forbidden to trespass upon our neighbours: as, *Thou shalt not kill, thou shalt not commit adultery, thou shalt not steal,* &c. do confirm the law of distinction between *mine* and *thine;* for they suppose *the right of all men to all things* to be taken away.

5. The same precepts establish the second law of nature, of keeping trust. For what doth, *Thou shalt not invade another's right,* import, but this? *Thou shalt not take possession of that, which by thy contract ceaseth to be thine:* but expressly set down? Psalm xv. 1: to him that asked, *Lord who shall dwell in thy tabernacle?* it is answered (verse 4): *He that sweareth unto his neighbour, and disappointeth him not.* And Prov. vi. 1, 2: *My son, if thou be surety for thy friend, if thou have stricken thy hand with a stranger, thou art snared with the words of thy mouth.*

6. The third law concerning gratitude, is proved by these places. Deut. xxv. 4: *Thou shalt not muzzle the ox, when he treadeth out the corn:* which St. Paul (1 Cor. ix. 9) interprets to be spoken of men, not oxen only. Prov. xvii. 13: *Whoso rewardeth evil for good, evil shall not depart from his house.* And Deut. xx. 10, 11: *When thou comest nigh unto a city to fight against it, then proclaim peace unto it. And it shall be, if it make thee answer of peace, and open unto thee, then it shall be that all the people that is found therein, shall be tributaries unto thee, and they shall serve thee.* Prov. iii. 29: *Devise not evil against thy neighbour, seeing he dwelleth securely by thee.*

7. To the fourth law of accommodating ourselves, these precepts are conformable: Exod. xxiii. 4, 5: *If thou meet*

*thine enemy's ox, or his ass going astray, thou shalt surely
bring it back to him again. If thou see the ass of him that
hateth thee, lying under his burden, and wouldst forbear
to help him, thou shalt surely help with him.* Also (verse
9): *Thou shalt not oppress a stranger.* Prov. iii. 30: *Strive
not with a man without a cause, if he have done thee no
harm.* Prov. xv. 18: *A wrathful man stirreth up strife; but
he that is slow to anger, appeaseth strife.* Prov. xviii. 24:
There is a friend that sticketh closer than a brother. The
same is confirmed, Luke x, by the parable of the Samari-
tan, who had compassion on the Jew that was wounded by
thieves; and by Christ's precept (Matth. v. 39): *But I
say unto you that ye resist not evil; but whosoever shall
smite thee on the right cheek, turn to him the other
also* &c.

8. Among infinite other places which prove the fifth
law, these are some: Matth. vi. 14, 15: *If you forgive men
their trespasses, your heavenly Father will also forgive
you: but if you forgive not men their trespasses, neither
will your Father forgive your trespasses.* Matth. xviii. 21,
22: *Lord how oft shall my brother sin against me, and I
forgive him? Till seven times? Jesus saith unto him; I say
not till seven times, but till seventy times seven times;*
that is, *toties quoties.*

9. For the confirmation of the sixth law, all those places
are pertinent which command us to show mercy, such as
Matth. v. 7: *Blessed are the merciful, for they shall obtain mercy.* Levit. xix. 18: *Thou shalt not avenge, nor bear
any grudge against the children of thy people.* But there
are, who not only think this law is not proved by Scripture, but plainly disproved from hence; that there is an
eternal punishment reserved for the wicked after death,
where there is no place either for amendment or example.
Some resolve this objection by answering, that God,
whom no law restrains, refers all to his glory, but that
man must not do so; as if God sought his glory, that is to

say, pleased himself in the death of a sinner. It is more rightly answered, that the institution of eternal punishment was before sin, and had regard to this only, that men might dread to commit sin for the time to come.

10. The words of Christ prove this seventh (Matth. v. 22): *But I say unto you, that whosoever is angry with his brother without a cause, shall be in danger of the judgment; and whosoever shall say unto his brother* Racha, *shall be in danger of the council; but whosoever shall say, thou fool, shall be in danger of hell-fire.* Prov. x. 18: *He that uttereth a slander, is a fool.* Prov. xiv. 21: *He that despiseth his neighbour, sinneth.* Prov. xv. 1: *Grievous words stir up anger.* Prov. xxii. 10: *Cast out the scorner, and contention shall go out, and reproach shall cease.*

11. The eighth law of acknowledging equality of nature, that is, of humility, is established by these places: Matth. v. 3: *Blessed are the poor in spirit, for theirs is the kingdom of heaven.* Prov. vi. 16–19: *These six things doth the Lord hate, yea, seven are an abomination unto him. A proud look, &c.* Prov. xvi. 5: *Every one that is proud, is an abomination unto the Lord; though hand join in hand, he shall not be unpunished.* Prov. xi. 2: *When pride cometh, then cometh shame; but with the lowly is wisdom.* Thus Isaiah xl. 3 (where the coming of the Messias is showed forth, for preparation towards his kingdom): *The voice of him that cried in the wilderness, was this: Prepare ye the way of the Lord, make straight in the desert a highway for our God. Every valley shall be exalted, and every mountain and hill shall be made low:* which doubtless is spoken to men, and not to mountains.

12. But that same equity, which we proved in the ninth place to be a law of nature, which commands every man to allow the same rights to others they would be allowed themselves, and which contains in it all the other laws besides, is the same which Moses sets down (Levit. xix.

18): *Thou shalt love thy neighbour as thyself.* And our Saviour calls it *the sum of the moral law:* Matth. xxii. 36–40: *Master, which is the great commandment in the law? Jesus said unto him, Thou shalt love the Lord thy God with all thine heart, and with all thy soul, and with all thy mind; this is the first and great commandment; and the second is like unto it, Thou shalt love thy neighbour as thyself. On these two commandments hang all the law and the prophets.* But to love our neighbour as ourselves, is nothing else but to grant him all we desire to have granted to ourselves.

13. By the tenth law respect of persons is forbid; as also by these places following: Matth. v. 45: *That ye may be children of your Father which is in heaven; for he maketh the sun to rise on the evil, and on the good,* &c. Coloss. iii. 11: *There is neither Greek nor Jew, circumcision nor uncircumcision, barbarian or Scythian, bond or free, but Christ is all, and in all.* Acts x. 34: *Of a truth I perceive that God is no respecter of persons.* 2 Chron. xix. 7: *There is no iniquity with the Lord our God, nor respect of persons, nor taking of gifts.* Ecclesiasticus xxxv. 12: *The Lord is Judge, and with him is no respect of persons.* Rom. ii. 11: *For there is no respect of persons with God.*

14. The eleventh law, which commands those things to be held in common which cannot be divided, I know not whether there be any express place in Scripture for it or not; but the practice appears every where, in the common use of wells, ways, rivers, sacred things, &c.; for else men could not live.

15. We said in the twelfth place, that it was a law of nature, that where things could neither be divided nor possessed in common, they should be disposed by lot. Which is confirmed, as by the example of Moses who, by God's command (Numb. xxvi. 55), divided the several parts of the land of promise unto the tribes by lot: so (Acts i. 24) by the example of the Apostles, who re-

ceived Matthias before Justus into their number, by
casting lots, and saying, *Thou, Lord, who knowest the
hearts of all men, show whether of these two thou hast
chosen, &c.* Prov. xvi. 33: *The lot is cast into the lap, but
the whole disposing thereof is of the Lord.* And, which
is the thirteenth law, the succession was due unto Esau,
as being the first born of Isaac; if himself had not sold it
(Gen. xxv. 33), or that the father had not otherwise appointed.

16. St. Paul, writing to the Corinthians (1 Epist. vi),
reprehends the Corinthians of that city for going to law
one with another before infidel judges, who were their
enemies: calling it a fault, that they would not rather take
wrong, and suffer themselves to be defrauded; for that is
against that law, whereby we are commanded to be help-
ful to each other. But if it happen the controversy be concerning things necessary, what is to be done? Therefore
the Apostle (verse 5) speaks thus: *I speak to your shame.
Is it so, that there is not one wise man among you, no,
not one that shall be able to judge between his brethren?*
He therefore, by those words, confirms that law of nature which we called the fifteenth, to wit, where controversies cannot be avoided; there by the consent of parties
to appoint some arbiter, and him some third man; so as
(which is the sixteenth law) neither of the parties may be
judge in his own cause.

17. But that the judge or arbiter must receive no reward for his sentence, which is the seventeenth law appears, Exod. xxiii. 8: *Thou shalt take no gift; for the gift
blindeth the wise, and perverteth the words of the
righteous.* Ecclesiasticus xx. 29: *Presents and gifts blind
the eyes of the wise.* Whence it follows, that he must not
be more obliged to one part than the other; which is the
nineteenth law; and is also confirmed, Deut. i. 17: *Ye
shall not respect persons in judgment, ye shall hear the*

small as well as the great; and in all those places which are brought against respect of persons.

18. That in the judgment of fact witnesses must be had, which is the eighteenth law, the Scripture not only confirms, but requires more than one. Deut. xvii. 6: *At the mouth of two witnesses, or three witnesses, shall he that is worthy of death be put to death.* The same is repeated Deut. xix. 15.

19. Drunkenness, which we have therefore in the last place numbered among the breaches of the natural law, because it hinders the use of right reason, is also forbid in Sacred Scripture for the same reason. Prov. xx. 1: *Wine is a mocker, strong drink is raging, whosoever is deceived thereby is not wise.* And Prov. xxxi. 4, 5: *It is not for kings to drink wine, lest they drink and forget the law, and pervert the judgment of any of the afflicted.* But that we might know that the malice of this vice consisted not formally in the quantity of the drink, but in that it destroys judgment and reason, it follows in the next verse: *Give strong drink to him that is ready to perish, and wine to those that be heavy of heart. Let him drink and forget his poverty, and remember his misery no more.* Christ useth the same reason in prohibiting drunkenness (Luke xxi. 34): *Take heed to yourselves, lest at any time your hearts be overcharged with surfeiting and drunkenness.*

20. That we said in the foregoing chapter, the law of nature is eternal, is also proved out of Matth. v. 18: *Verily I say unto you, till heaven and earth pass, one jot or one tittle shall in no wise pass from the law;* and Psalm cxix. 160: *Every one of thy righteous judgments endureth for ever.*

21. We also said, that the laws of nature had regard chiefly unto conscience; that is, that he is just, who by all possible endeavour strives to fulfil them. And although a man should order all his actions so much as belongs to external obedience just as the law commands, but not

for the law's sake, but by reason of some punishment annexed unto it, or out of vain glory; yet he is unjust. Both
these are proved by the Holy Scriptures. The first (Isaiah
lv. 7): *Let the wicked forsake his way, and the unright-
eous man his thoughts, and let him return unto the Lord,
and he will have mercy upon him; and to our God, for
he will abundantly pardon.* Ezek. xviii. 31: *Cast away from
you all your transgressions whereby you have transgressed,
and make you a new heart and a new spirit; for why will
you die, O House of Israel?* By which, and the like places,
we may sufficiently understand that God will not punish
their deeds whose heart is right. The second, out of Isaiah
xxix. 13, 14: *The Lord said, forasmuch as this people
draw near me with their mouth, and with their lips do
honour me, but have removed their heart far from me,
therefore I will proceed, &c.* Matth. v. 20: *Except your
righteousness shall exceed the righteousness of the
Scribes and Pharisees, ye shall in no case enter into the
kingdom of heaven.* And in the following verses, our
Saviour explains to them how that the commands of God
are broken, not by deeds only, but also by the will. For
the Scribes and Pharisees did in outward act observe the
law most exactly, but for glory's sake only; else they
would as readily have broken it. There are innumerable
places of Scripture in which is most manifestly declared,
that God accepts the will for the deed, and that as well
in good as in evil actions.

22. That the law of nature is easily kept, Christ himself
declares (Matth. xi. 28, 29, 30): *Come unto me, &c. Take
my yoke upon you, and learn of me, &c.; for my yoke is
easy, and my burden light.*

23. Lastly, the rule by which I said any man might
know, whether what he was doing were contrary to the
law or not, to wit, what thou wouldst not be done to, do
not that to another; is almost in the self-same words delivered by our Saviour (Matth. vii. 12): *Therefore all*

things whatsoever ye would that men should do unto you, do you even so to them.

24. As the law of nature is all of it divine, so the law of Christ by conversion (which is wholly explained in the v. vi. and vii. chapters of St. Matthew's Gospel), is all of it also (except that one commandment, of not marrying her who is put away for adultery; which Christ brought for explication of the divine positive law, against the Jews, who did not rightly interpret the Mosaical law) the doctrine of nature. I say, the whole law of Christ is explained in the fore-named chapters, not the whole doctrine of Christ; for faith is a part of Christian doctrine, which is not comprehended under the title of a law. For laws are made and given in reference to such actions as follow our will; not in order to our opinions and belief, which being out of our power, follow not the will.

DOMINION

V

Of the Causes and First Beginning of Civil Government

1. That the laws of nature are not sufficient to preserve peace. 2. That the laws of nature, in the state of nature, are silent. 3. That the security of living according to the laws of nature, consists in the concord of many persons. 4. That the concord of many persons is not constant enough for a lasting peace. 5. The reason why the government of certain brute creatures stands firm in concord only, and why not of men. 6. That not only consent, but union also, is required to establish the peace of men. 7. What union is. 8. In union, the right of all men is conveyed to one. 9. What civil society is. 10. What a civil person is. 11. What it is to have the supreme power, and what to be a subject. 12. Two kinds of cities, natural, and by institution.

1. It is of itself manifest that the actions of men proceed from the will, and the will from hope and fear, insomuch as when they shall see a greater good or less evil likely to happen to them by the breach than observation of the laws, they will wittingly violate them. The hope therefore which each man hath of his security and self-preservation, consists in this, that by force or craft he may disappoint his neighbour, either openly or by stratagem. Whence we

may understand, that the natural laws, though well understood, do not instantly secure any man in their practice; and consequently, that as long as there is no caution had from the invasion of others, there remains to every man that same primitive right of self-defence by such means as either he can or will make use of, that is, a right to all things, or the right of war. And it is sufficient for the fulfilling of the natural law, that a man be prepared in mind to embrace peace when it may be had.

2. It is a|fond|saying, that all laws are silent in the time of war, and it is a true one, not only if we speak of the civil, but also of the natural laws, provided they be referred not to the mind, but to the actions of men, by chap. iii. art. 27. And we mean such a war, as is of all men against all men; such as is the mere state of nature; although in the war of nation against nation, a certain mean was wont to be observed. And therefore in old time, there was a manner of living, and as it were a certain economy, which they called ληστρικὴν, living by rapine; which was neither against the law of nature (things then so standing), nor void of glory to those who exercised it with valour, not with cruelty. Their custom was, taking away the rest, to spare life, and abstain from oxen fit for plough, and every instrument serviceable to husbandry. Which yet is not so to be taken, as if they were bound to do thus by the law of nature; but that they had regard to their own glory herein, lest by too much cruelty they might be suspected guilty of fear.

3. Since therefore the exercise of the natural law is necessary for the preservation of peace, and that for the exercise of the natural law security is no less necessary; it is worth the considering what that is which affords such a security. For this matter nothing else can be imagined, but that each man provide himself of such meet helps, as the invasion of one on the other may be rendered so dangerous, as either of them may think it better to refrain

than to meddle. But first, it is plain that the consent of two or three cannot make good such a security; because that the addition but of one, or some few on the other side, is sufficient to make the victory undoubtedly sure, and heartens the enemy to attack us. It is therefore necessary, to the end the security sought for may be obtained, that the number of them who conspire in a mutual assistance be so great, that the accession of some few to the enemy's party may not prove to them a matter of moment sufficient to assure the victory.

4. Furthermore, how great soever the number of them is who meet on self-defence, if yet they agree not among themselves of some excellent means whereby to compass this, but every man after his own manner shall make use of his endeavours, nothing will be done; because that, divided in their opinions, they will be a hinderance to each other; or if they agree well enough to some one action, through hope of victory, spoil, or revenge, yet afterward, through diversity of wits and counsels, or emulation and envy, with which men naturally contend, they will be so torn and rent, as they will neither give mutual help nor desire peace, except they be constrained to it by some common fear. Whence it follows that the consent of many (which consists in this only, as we have already defined in the foregoing section, that they direct all their actions to the same end and the common good), that is to say, that the society proceeding from mutual help only, yields not that security which they seek for, who meet and agree in the exercise of the above-named laws of nature; but that somewhat else must be done, that those who have once consented for the common good to peace and mutual help, may by fear be restrained lest afterwards they again dissent, when their private interest shall appear discrepant from the common good.

5. Aristotle reckons among those animals which he calls politic, not man only, but divers others, as the ant, the

bee, &c.; which, though they be destitute of reason, by
which they may contract and submit to government, notwithstanding by consenting, that is to say, ensuing or
eschewing the same things, they so direct their actions
to a common end, that their meetings are not obnoxious
unto any seditions. Yet is not their gathering together a
civil government, and therefore those animals not to be
termed political; because their government is only a consent, or many wills concurring in one object, not (as is
necessary in civil government) one will. It is very true,
that in those creatures living only by sense and appetite,
their consent of minds is so durable, as there is no need
of anything more to secure it, and by consequence to preserve peace among them, than barely their natural inclination. But among men the case is otherwise. For, first,
among them there is a contestation of honour and preferment; among beasts there is none: whence hatred and
envy, out of which arise sedition and war, is among men;
among beasts no such matter. Next, the natural appetite
of bees, and the like creatures, is conformable; and they
desire the common good, which among them differs not
from their private. But man scarce esteems anything
good, which hath not somewhat of eminence in the enjoyment, more than that which others do possess.
Thirdly, those creatures which are void of reason, see no
defect, or think they see none, in the administration of
their commonweals; but in a multitude of men there are
many who, supposing themselves wiser than others, endeavour to innovate, and divers innovators innovate
divers ways; which is a mere distraction and civil war.
Fourthly, these brute creatures, howsoever they may have
the use of their voice to signify their affections to each
other, yet want they that same art of words which is necessarily required to those motions in the mind, whereby
good is represented to it as being better, and evil as worse
than in truth it is. But the tongue of man is a trumpet

of war and sedition: and it is reported of Pericles, that he sometimes by his elegant speeches thundered and lightened, and confounded whole Greece itself. Fifthly, they cannot distinguish between *injury* and *harm*; thence it happens that as long as it is well with them, they blame not their fellows. But those men are of most trouble to the republic, who have most leisure to be idle; for they use not to contend for public places, before they have gotten the victory over hunger and cold. Last of all, the consent of those brutal creatures is natural; that of men by compact only, that is to say, artificial. It is therefore no matter of wonder, if somewhat more be needful for men to the end they may live in peace. Wherefore consent or contracted society, without some common power whereby particular men may be ruled through fear of punishment, doth not suffice to make up that security, which is requisite to the exercise of natural justice.

6. Since therefore the conspiring of many wills to the same end doth not suffice to preserve peace, and to make a lasting defence, it is requisite that, in those necessary matters which concern peace and self-defence, there be but one will of all men. But this cannot be done, unless every man will so subject his will to some other one, to wit, either man or council, that whatsoever his will is in those things which are necessary to the common peace, it be received for the wills of all men in general, and of every one in particular. Now the gathering together of many men, who deliberate of what is to be done or not to be done for the common good of all men, is that which I call a *council*.

7. This submission of the wills of all those men to the will of one man or one council, is then made, when each one of them obligeth himself by contract to every one of the rest, not to resist the will of that one man or council, to which he hath submitted himself; that is, that he refuse him not the use of his wealth and strength against

any others whatsoever; for he is supposed still to retain a right of defending himself against violence: and this is called *union*. But we understand that to be the will of the council, which is the will of the major part of those men of whom the council consists.

8. But though the will itself be not voluntary, but only the beginning of voluntary actions (for we will not to will, but to act); and therefore falls least of all under deliberation and compact; yet he who submits his will to the will of another, conveys to that other the right of his strength and faculties. Insomuch as when the rest have done the same, he to whom they have submitted, hath so much power, as by the terror of it he can conform the wills of particular men unto unity and concord.

9. Now union thus made is called a city or civil society; and also a civil person. For when there is one will of all men, it is to be esteemed for one person; and by the word *one*, it is to be known and distinguished from all particular men, as having its own rights and properties. Insomuch as neither any one citizen, nor all of them together (if we except him, whose will stands for the will of all), is to be accounted the city. A *city* therefore (that we may define it), is *one person*, whose will, by the compact of many men, is to be received for the will of them all; so as he may use all the power and faculties of each particular person to the maintenance of peace, and for common defence.

10. But although every city be a civil person, yet every civil person is not a city; for it may happen that many citizens, by the permission of the city, may join together in one person, for the doing of certain things. These now will be civil persons; as the companies of merchants, and many other convents. But cities they are not, because they have not submitted themselves to the will of the company simply and in all things, but in certain things only determined by the city, and on such terms as it is

lawful for any one of them to contend in judgment against the body itself of the sodality; which is by no means allowable to a citizen against the city. Such like societies, therefore, are civil persons subordinate to the city.

11. In every city, that man or council to whose will each particular man hath subjected his will so as hath been declared, is said to have the *supreme power*, or *chief command*, or *dominion*. Which power and right of commanding consists in this, that each citizen hath conveyed all his strength and power to that man or council; which to have done, because no man can transfer his power in a natural manner, is nothing else than to have parted with his right of resisting. Each citizen, as also every subordinate civil person, is called the *subject* of him who hath the chief command.

12. By what hath been said, it is sufficiently showed in what manner and by what degrees many natural persons, through desire of preserving themselves and by mutual fear, have grown together into a civil person, whom we have called a *city*. But they who submit themselves to another for fear, either submit to him whom they fear, or some other whom they confide in for protection. They act according to the first manner, who are vanquished in war, that they may not be slain; they according to the second, who are not yet overcome, that they may not be overcome. The first manner receives its beginning from natural power, and may be called the natural beginning of a city; the latter from the council and constitution of those who meet together, which is a beginning by institution. Hence it is that there are two kinds of cities: the one natural, such as is the paternal and despotical; the other institutive, which may be also called political. In the first, the lord acquires to himself such citizens as he will; in the other, the citizens by their own wills appoint

a lord over themselves, whether he be one man or one company of men, endued with the command in chief. But we will speak, in the first place, of a city political or by institution; and next, of a city natural.

VI

Of the Right of Him, Whether Council or One Man Only, Who Hath the Supreme Power in the City

1. There can no right be attributed to a multitude out of civil society, nor any action to which they have not under seal consented. 2. The right of the greater number consenting, is the beginning of a city. 3. That every man retains a right to protect himself according to his own free will, so long as there is no sufficient regard had to his security. 4. That a coercive power is necessary to secure us. 5. What the sword of justice is. 6. That the sword of justice belongs to him, who hath the chief command. 7. That the sword of war belongs to him also. 8. All judicature belongs to him too. 9. The legislative power is his only. 10. The naming of magistrates and other officers of the city belongs to him. 11. Also the examination of all doctrines. 12. Whatsoever he doth is unpunishable. 13. That the command his citizens have granted is absolute, and what proportion of obedience is due to him. 14. That the laws of the city bind him not. 15. That no man can challenge a propriety to anything against his will. 16. By the laws of the city only we come to know what theft, murder, adultery, and injury is. 17. The opinion of those who would constitute a city, where there | should not be any one endued with | an absolute power. 18. The marks of supreme authority. 19. If a city be compared with a man, he that hath the supreme power is in order to the city, as the human soul is in relation to the man. 20. That the supreme command cannot by right be dissolved through their consents, by whose compacts it was first constituted.

1. We must consider, first of all, what a multitude* of men, gathering themselves of their own free wills into society, is; namely, that it is not any one body, but many men, whereof each one hath his own will and his peculiar judgment concerning all things that may be proposed. And though by particular contracts each single man may have his own right and propriety, so as one may say *this is mine*, the other, *that is his*; yet will there not be any-

---

* *Multitude, &c.* The doctrine of the power of a city over its citizens almost wholly depends on the understanding of the difference which is between a multitude of men ruling, and a multitude ruled. For such is the nature of a city, that a multitude or company of citizens not only may have command, but may also be subject to command; but in diverse senses. Which difference I did believe was clearly enough explained in the first article; but by the objections of many against those things which follow, I discern otherwise. Wherefore it seemed good to me, to the end I might make a fuller explication, to add these few things.

By multitude, because it is a collective word, we understand more than one: so as a multitude of men is the same with many men. The same word, because it is of the singular number, signifies one thing; namely, one multitude. But in neither sense can a multitude be understood to have one will given to it by nature, but to|either|a several; and therefore neither is any one action whatsoever to be attributed to it. Wherefore a multitude cannot promise, contract, acquire right, convey right, act, have, possess, and the like, unless it be every one apart, and man by man; so as there must be as many promises, compacts, rights, and actions, as men. Wherefore a multitude is no natural person. But if the same multitude do contract one with another, that the will of one man, or the agreeing wills of the major part of them, shall be received for the will of all; then it becomes one person. For it is endued with a will, and therefore can do voluntary actions, such as are commanding, making laws, acquiring and transferring of right, and so forth; and it is oftener called the people, than the multitude. We must therefore distinguish thus. When we say the people or multitude wills, commands, or doth anything, it is understood that the city which commands, wills and acts by the will of one, or the concurring wills of more; which cannot be done but in an assembly. But as oft as anything is said to be done by a multitude of men, whether great or small, without the will of that man or assembly of men, that is understood to be done by a subjected people; that is, by many single citizens together; and not proceeding from one will, but from diverse wills of diverse men, who are citizens and subjects, but not a city.

thing of which the whole multitude, as a person distinct from a single man, can rightly say, this is *mine*, more than another's. Neither must we ascribe any action to the multitude, as its|own;|but if all or more of them do agree, it will not be an action, but as many actions as men. For although in some great sedition, it is commonly said, that the people of that city have taken up arms; yet is it true of those only who are in arms, or who consent to them. For the city, which is one person, cannot take up arms against itself. Whatsoever, therefore, is done by the multitude, must be understood to be done by every one of those by whom it is made up; and that he, who being in the multitude, and yet consented not, nor gave any help to the things that were done by it, must be judged to have done nothing. Besides, in a multitude not yet reduced into one person, in that manner as hath been said, there remains that same state of nature in which all things belong to all men; and there is no place for *meum* and *tuum*, which is called dominion and propriety, by reason that that security is not yet extant, which we have declared above to be necessarily requisite for the practice of the natural laws.

2. Next, we must consider that every one of the multitude, by whose means there may be a beginning to make up the city, must agree with the rest, that in those matters which shall be propounded by any one in the assembly, that be received for the will of all, which the major part shall approve of; for otherwise there will be no will at all of a multitude of men, whose wills and votes differ so variously. Now, if any one will not consent, the rest, notwithstanding, shall among themselves constitute the city without him. Whence it will come to pass, that the city retains its primitive right against the dissenter; that is, the right of war, as against an enemy.

3. But because we said in the foregoing chapter, the sixth article, that there was required to the security of

men, not only their consent, but also the subjection of their wills in such things as were necessary to peace and defence; and that in that union and subjection the nature of a city consisted; we must discern now in this place, out of those things which may be propounded, discussed, and stated in an assembly of men, all whose wills are contained in the will of the major part, what things are necessary to peace and common defence. But first of all, it is necessary to peace, that a man be so far forth protected against the violence of others, that he may live securely; that is, that he may have no just cause to fear others, so long as he doth them no injury. Indeed, to make men altogether safe from mutual harms, so as they cannot be hurt or injuriously killed, is impossible; and, therefore, comes not within deliberation. But care may be had, there be no just cause of fear; for security is the end wherefore men submit themselves to others; which if it be not had, no man is supposed to have submitted himself to aught, or to have quitted his right to all things, before that there was a care had of his security.

4. It is not enough to obtain this security, that every one of those who are now growing up into a city, do covenant with the rest, either by words or writing, *not to steal, not to kill,* and to observe the like laws; for the pravity of human disposition is manifest to all, and by experience too well known how little (removing the punishment) men are kept to their duties through conscience of their promises. We must therefore provide for our security, not by compacts, but by punishments; and there is then sufficient provision made, when there are so great punishments appointed for every injury, as apparently it prove a greater evil to have done it, than not to have done it. For all men, by a necessity of nature, choose that which to them appears to be the less evil.

5. Now, the right of punishing is then understood to be given to any one, when every man contracts not to

assist him who is to be punished. But I will call this right, *the sword of justice*. But these kind of contracts men observe well enough, for the most part, till either themselves or their near friends are to suffer.

6. Because, therefore, for the security of particular men, and, by consequence, for the common peace, it is necessary that the right of using the sword for punishment be transferred to some man or council; that man or council is necessarily understood by right to have the supreme power in the city. For he that by right punisheth at his own discretion, by right compels all men to all things which he himself wills; than which a greater command cannot be imagined.

7. But in vain do they worship peace at home, who cannot defend themselves against foreigners; neither is it possible for them to protect themselves against foreigners, whose forces are not united. And therefore it is necessary for the preservation of particulars, that there be some one council or one man, who hath the right to arm, to gather together, to unite so many citizens, in all dangers and on all occasions, as shall be needful for common defence against the certain number and strength of the enemy; and again, as often as he shall find it expedient, to make peace with them. We must understand, therefore, that particular citizens have conveyed their whole right of war and peace unto some one man or council; and that this right, which we may call *the sword of war*, belongs to the same man or council, to whom the sword of justice belongs. For no man can by right compel citizens to take up arms and be at the expenses of war, but he who by right can punish him who doth not obey. Both swords therefore, as well this of war as that of justice, even by the constitution itself of a city and essentially do belong to the chief command.

8. But because the right of the sword, is nothing else but to have power by right to use the sword at his own

will, it follows, that the judgment of its right use pertains
to the same party; for if the power of judging were in one,
and the power of executing in another, nothing would
be done. For in vain would he give judgment, who could
not execute his commands; or, if he executed them by
the power of another, he himself is not said to have the
power of the sword, but that other, to whom he is only
an officer. All judgment therefore, in a city, belongs to
him who hath the swords; that is, to him who hath the
supreme authority.

9. Furthermore, since it no less, nay, it much more conduceth to peace, to prevent brawls from arising than to
appease them being risen; and that all controversies are
bred from hence, that the opinions of men differ concerning *meum* and *tuum, just* and *unjust, profitable* and
unprofitable, good and *evil, honest* and *dishonest,* and
the like; which every man esteems according to his own
judgment: it belongs to the same chief power to make
some common rules for all men, and to declare them publicly, by which every man may know what may be called
his, what another's, what just, what unjust, what honest,
what dishonest, what good, what evil; that is summarily,
what is to be done, what to be avoided in our common
course of life. But those rules and measures are usually
called the civil laws, or the laws of the city, as being the
commands of him who hath the supreme power in the
city. And the *civil laws* (that we may define them) are
nothing else but *the commands of him who hath the chief
authority in the city, for direction of the future actions
of his citizens.*

10. Furthermore, since the affairs of the city, both those
of war and peace, cannot possibly be all administered by
one man or one council without officers and subordinate
magistrates; and that it appertaineth to peace and common defence, that they to whom it belongs justly to judge
of controversies, to search into neighbouring councils,

prudently to wage war, and on all hands warily to attend the benefit of the city, should also rightly exercise their offices; it is consonant to reason that they depend on, and be chosen by him who hath the chief command both in war and in peace.

11. It is also manifest, that all voluntary actions have their beginning from, and necessarily depend on the will; and that the will of doing or omitting aught, depends on the opinion of the good and evil, of the reward or punishment which a man conceives he shall receive by the act or omission: so as the actions of all men are ruled by the opinions of each. Wherefore, by evident and necessary inference, we may understand that it very much concerns the interest of peace, that no opinions or doctrines be delivered to citizens, by which they may imagine that either by right they may not obey the laws of the city, that is, the commands of that man or council to whom the supreme power is committed, or that it is lawful to resist him, or that a less punishment remains for him that denies, than him that yields obedience. For if one command somewhat to be done under penalty of natural death, another forbid it under pain of eternal death, and both by their own right, it will follow that the citizens, although innocent, are not only by right punishable, but that the city itself is altogether dissolved. For no man can serve two masters; nor is he less, but rather more a master, whom we believe we are to obey for fear of damnation, than he whom we obey for fear of temporal death. It follows therefore that this one, whether man or court, to whom the city hath committed the supreme power, have also this right; that he both judge what opinions† and

† *Judge what opinions, &c.* There is scarce any principle, neither in the worship of God nor human sciences, from whence there may not spring dissensions, discords, reproaches, and by degrees war itself. Neither doth this happen by reason of the falsehood of the principle, but of the disposition of men, who, seeming wise to them-

doctrines are enemies unto peace, and also that he forbid them to be taught.

12. Last of all, from this consideration, that each citizen hath submitted his will to his who hath the supreme command in the city, so as he may not employ his strength against him; it follows manifestly, that whatsoever shall be done by him who commands, must not be punished. For as he who hath not power enough, cannot punish him naturally, so neither can he punish him by right, who by right hath not sufficient power.

13. It is most manifest by what hath been said, that in every perfect city, that is, where no citizen hath right to use his faculties at his own discretion for the preservation of himself, or where the right of the private sword is excluded; there is a supreme power in some one, greater than which cannot by right be conferred by men, or

---

selves, will needs appear such to all others. But though such dissensions cannot be hindered from arising, yet may they be restrained by the exercise of the supreme power, that they prove no hindrance to the public peace. Of these kinds of opinions, therefore, I have not spoken in this place. There are certain doctrines wherewith subjects being tainted, they verily believe that obedience may be refused to the city, and that by right they may, nay ought, to oppose and fight against chief princes and dignities. Such are those which, whether directly and openly, or more obscurely and by consequence, require obedience to be given to others beside them to whom the supreme authority is committed. I deny not but this reflects on that power which many, living under other government, ascribe to the chief head of the Church of Rome, and also on that which elsewhere, out of that Church, bishops require in their's to be given to them; and last of all, on that liberty which the lower sort of citizens, under pretence of religion, do challenge to themselves. For what civil war was there ever in the Christian world, which did not either grow from, or was nourished by this root? The judgment therefore of doctrines, whether they be repugnant to civil obedience or not, and if they be repugnant, the power of prohibiting them to be taught, I do here attribute to the civil authority. For since there is no man who grants not to the city the judgment of those things which belong to its peace and defence, and it is manifest that the opinions which I have already recited do relate to its peace; it follows necessarily, that the examination of those opinions, whether they be such or not, must be referred to the city; that is, to him who hath the supreme authority.

greater than which no mortal man can have over himself. But that power, greater than which cannot by men be conveyed on a man, we call *absolute.*‡ For whosoever hath so submitted his will to the will of the city, that he can,

‡ *Absolute.* A popular state openly challengeth absolute dominion, and the citizens oppose it not. For, in the gathering together of many men, they acknowledge the face of a city; and even the unskilful understand, that matters there are ruled by council. Yet monarchy is no less a city than democracy; and absolute kings have their counsellors, from whom they will take advice, and suffer their power, in matters of greater consequence, to be guided but not recalled. But it appears not to most men, how a city is contained in the person of a king. And therefore they object against absolute command: first, that if any man had such a right, the condition of the citizens would be miserable. For thus they think; he will take all, spoil all, kill all; and every man counts it his only happiness, that he is not already spoiled and killed. But why should he do thus? Not because he can; for unless he have a mind to it, he will not do it. Will he, to please one or some few, spoil all the rest? First, though by right, that is, without injury to them, he may do it, yet can he not do it justly, that is, without breach of the natural laws and injury against God. And therefore there is some security for subjects in the oaths which princes take. Next, if he could justly do it, or that he made no account of his oath, yet appears there no reason why he should desire it, since he finds no good in it. But it cannot be denied, but a prince may sometimes have an inclination to do wickedly. But grant then, that thou hadst given him a power which were not absolute, but so much only as sufficed to defend thee from the injuries of others; which, if thou wilt be safe, is necessary for thee to give; are not all the same things to be feared? For he that hath strength enough to protect all, wants not sufficiency to oppress all. Here is no other difficulty then, but that human affairs cannot be without some inconvenience. And this inconvenience itself is in the citizens, not in the government. For if men could rule themselves, every man by his own command, that is to say, could they live according to the laws of nature, there would be no need at all of a city, nor of a common coercive power. Secondly, they object, that there is no dominion in the Christian world absolute. Which, indeed, is not true; for all monarchies, and all other states, are so. For although they who have the chief command, do not all those things they would, and what they know profitable to the city; the reason of that is, not the defect of right in them, but the consideration of their citizens, who busied about their private interest, and careless of what tends to the public, cannot sometimes be drawn to perform their duties without the hazard of the city. Wherefore princes sometimes forbear the exercise of their right; and prudently remit somewhat of the act, but nothing of their right.

unpunished, do any thing, make laws, judge controversies, set penalties, make use at his own pleasure of the strength and wealth of men, and all this by right; truly he hath given him the greatest dominion that can be granted. This same may be confirmed by experience, in all the cities which are or ever have been. For though it be sometimes in doubt what man or council hath the chief command, yet ever there is such a command and always exercised, except in the time of sedition and civil war; and then there are two chief commands made out of one. Now, those seditious persons who dispute against absolute authority, do not so much care to destroy it, as to convey it on others: for removing this power, they together take away civil society, and a confusion of all things returns. There is so much obedience joined to this absolute right of the chief ruler, as is necessarily required for the government of the city, that is to say, so much as that right of his may not be granted in vain. Now this kind of obedience, although for some reasons it may sometimes by right be denied, yet because a greater cannot be performed, we will call it *simple*. But the obligation to perform this grows not immediately from that contract, by which we have conveyed all our right on the city; but | immediately | from hence, that without obedience the city's right would be frustrate, and by consequence there would be no city constituted. For it is one thing if I say, *I give you right to command what you will*; another, if I say, *I will do whatsoever you command*. And the command may be such, as I would rather die than do it. Forasmuch, therefore, as no man can be bound to will being killed, much less is he tied to that which to him is worse than death. If therefore I be commanded to kill myself, I am not bound to do it. For though I deny to do it, yet the right of dominion is not frustrated; since others may be found, who being commanded will not refuse to do it; neither do I refuse to do that, which I have contracted to do. In like manner, if the chief ruler command any man to kill him, he is not tied to do it; because it cannot be conceived that he made any such covenant. Nor if he command to execute a parent, whether he be innocent or guilty and condemned by the law; since there are others who being commanded will do that, and a son will rather die than live infamous and hated of all the world. There are many other cases in which, since the commands are shameful to be done by some and not by others, obedience may by right be performed by these, and refused by those; and this without breach of that absolute right which was given to the chief ruler. For in no case is the right taken away from him, of slaying those who shall refuse to obey him. But they who thus kill men, although by right given them from him that hath it, yet if they use that right otherwise than right reason requires, they sin against the laws of nature, that is, against God.

14. Neither can any man give somewhat to himself; for he is already supposed to have what he can give himself. Nor can he be obliged to himself; for the same party being both *the obliged* and *the obliger*, and the obliger having power to release the obliged, it were merely in vain for a man to be obliged to himself; because he can release himself at his own pleasure, and he that can do this is already actually free. Whence it is plain, that the city is not tied to the civil laws; for the civil laws are the laws of the city, by which, if she were engaged, she should be engaged to herself. Neither can the city be obliged to her citizen; because, if he will, he can free her from her obligation; and he will, as oft as she wills; for the will of every citizen is in all things comprehended in the will of the city; the city therefore is free when she pleaseth, that is, she is now actually free. But the will of a council, or one who hath the supreme authority given him, is the will of the city: he therefore contains the wills of all particular citizens. Therefore neither is he bound to the civil laws,

for this is to be bound to himself; nor to any of his citizens.

15. Now because, as hath been shown above, before the constitution of a city all things belonged to all men; nor is there that thing which any man can so call his, as any other may not, by the same right, claim as his own; for where all things are *common*, there can be nothing *proper* to any man; it follows, that *propriety* received its beginning** when cities received their's, and that that only is *proper* to each man, which he can keep by the laws and the power of the whole city, that is, of him on whom its chief command is conferred. Whence we understand, that each particular citizen hath a *propriety* to which none of his fellow-citizens hath right, because they are tied to the same laws; but he hath no propriety in which the chief ruler (whose commands are the laws, whose will contains the will of each man, and who by every single person is constituted the supreme judge) hath not a right. But although there be many things which the city permits to its citizens, and therefore they may sometimes go to law against their chief; yet is not that action belonging to civil right, but to natural equity. Neither is it concerning what by right he may do†† who hath the supreme

** *Propriety received its beginning, &c.* What is objected by some, that the propriety of goods, even before the constitution of cities, was found in fathers of families, that objection is vain; because I have already declared that a family is a little city. For the sons of a family have a propriety of their goods granted them by their father, distinguished indeed from the rest of the sons of the same family, but not from the propriety of the father himself. But the fathers of divers families, who are subject neither to any common father nor lord, have a common right in all things.

†† *What by right he may do, &c.* As often as a citizen is granted to have an action of law against the supreme, that is, against the city, the question is not in that action, whether the city may by right keep possession of the thing in controversy, but whether by the laws formerly made she would keep it; for the law is the declared will of the supreme. Since then the city may raise money from the citizens under two titles, either as tribute, or as debt; in the former

power, but what he hath been willing should be done; and therefore he shall be judge himself, as though (the equity of the cause being well understood) he could not give wrong judgment.

16. Theft, murder, adultery, and all injuries, are forbid by the laws of nature; but what is to be called *theft*, what *murder*, what *adultery*, what *injury* in a citizen, this is not to be determined by the natural, but by the civil law. For not every taking away of the thing which another possesseth, but only another man's goods, is theft; but what is our's, and what another's, is a question belonging to the civil law. In like manner, not every killing of a man is murder, but only that which the civil law forbids; neither is all encounter with women adultery, but only that which the civil law prohibits. Lastly, all breach of promise is an injury, where the promise itself is lawful; but where there is no right to make any compact, there can be no conveyance of it, and therefore there can no injury follow, as hath been said in the second chapter, Article 17. Now what we may contract for, and what not, depends wholly upon the civil laws. The city of Lacedæmon therefore rightly ordered, that those young men who could so take away certain goods from others as not to be caught, should go unpunished; for it was nothing else but to make a law, that what was so acquired should be their own, and not another's. Rightly also is that man everywhere slain, whom we kill in war or by the necessity of self-defence. So also that copulation which in one city is matrimony, in another will be judged adultery. Also those contracts which make up marriage in one citizen, do not

___

case there is no action of law allowed, for there can be no question whether the city have right to require tribute; in the latter it is allowed, because the city will take nothing from its citizens by fraud or cunning, and yet if need require, all they have, openly. And therefore he that condemns this place, saying, that by this doctrine it is easy for princes to free themselves from their debts, he does it impertinently.

so in another, although of the same city; because that he who is forbidden by the city, that is, by that one man or council whose the supreme power is, to contract aught, hath no right to make any contract, and therefore having made any, it is not valid, and by consequence no marriage. But his contract which received no prohibition, was therefore of force, and so was matrimony. Neither adds it any force to any unlawful contracts, that they were made by an oath or sacrament;‡‡ for those add nothing to the strengthening of the contract, as hath been said above, Chap. ii. Art. 22. What therefore theft, what murder, what adultery, and in general what injury is, must be known by the civil laws; that is, the commands of him who hath the supreme authority.

17. This same supreme command and absolute power seems so harsh to the greatest part of men, as they hate the very naming of them; which happens chiefly through want of knowledge, what human nature and the civil laws are; and partly also through their default, who, when they are invested with so great authority, abuse their power to their own lust. That they may therefore avoid this kind of supreme authority, some of them will have

‡‡ *That they were made by an oath or sacrament, &c.* Whether matrimony be a sacrament (in which sense that word is used by some divines), or not, it is not my purpose to dispute. Only I say, that the legitimate contract of a man and woman to live together, that is, granted by the civil law, whether it be a sacrament or not, is surely a legitimate marriage; but that copulation which the city hath prohibited is no marriage, since it is of the essence of marriage to be a legitimate contract. There were legitimate marriages in many places, as among the Jews, the Grecians, the Romans, which yet might be dissolved. But with those who permit no such contracts but by a law that they shall never be broke, wedlock cannot be dissolved; and the reason is, because the city hath commanded it to be indissoluble, not because matrimony is a sacrament. Wherefore the ceremonies which at weddings are to be performed in the temple, to bless, or, if I may say so, to consecrate the husband and wife, will perhaps belong only to the office of clergymen; all the rest, namely, who, when, and by what contracts marriages may be made, pertains to the laws of the city.

a city well enough constituted, if they who shall be the citizens' convening, do agree concerning certain articles propounded, and in that convent agitated and approved, and do command them to be observed, and punishments prescribed to be inflicted on them who shall break them. To which purpose, and also to the repelling of a foreign enemy, they appoint a certain and limited return, with this condition, that if that suffice not, they may call a new convention of estates. Who sees not in a city thus constituted, that the assembly who prescribed those things had an absolute power? If therefore the assembly continue, or from time to time have a certain day and place of meeting, that power will be perpetual. But if they wholly dissolve, either the city dissolves with them, and so all is returned to the state of war; or else there is somewhere a power left to punish those who shall transgress the laws, whosoever or how many soever they be that have it; which cannot possibly be without an absolute power. For he that by right hath this might given, by punishments to restrain what citizens he pleaseth, hath such a power as a greater cannot possibly be given by any citizens.

18. It is therefore manifest, that in every city there is some one man, or council, or court, who by right hath as great a power over each single citizen, as each man hath over himself considered out of that civil state; that is, supreme and absolute, to be limited only by the strength and forces of the city itself, and by nothing else in the world. For if his power were limited, that limitation must necessarily proceed from some greater power. For he that prescribes limits, must have a greater power than he who is confined by them. Now that confining power is either without limit, or is again restrained by some other greater than itself; and so we shall at length arrive to a power which hath no other limit but that which is the *terminus ultimus* of the forces of all the citizens together. That same is called the supreme command; and if it be com-

mitted to a council, a supreme council, but if to one man, the supreme lord of the city. Now the notes of supreme command are these: to make and abrogate laws, to determine war and peace, to know and judge of all controversies, either by himself, or by judges appointed by him; to elect all magistrates, ministers, and counsellors. Lastly, if there be any man who by right can do some one action, which is not lawful for any citizen or citizens to do beside himself, that man hath obtained the supreme power. For those things which by right may not be done by any one or many citizens, the city itself can only do. He therefore that doth those things, useth the city's right; which is the supreme power.

19. They who compare a city and its citizens with a man and his members, almost all say, that he who hath the supreme power in the city is in relation to the whole city, such as the head is to the whole man. But it appears by what hath been already said, that he who is endued with such a power, whether it be a man or a court, hath a relation to the city, not as that of the head, but of the soul to the body. For it is the soul by which a man hath a will, that is, can either will or nill; so by him who hath the supreme power, and no otherwise, the city hath a will, and can either will or nill. A court of counsellors is rather to be compared with the head, or one counsellor, whose only counsel (if of any one alone) the chief ruler makes use of in matters of greatest moment: for the office of the head is to counsel, as the soul's is to command.

20. Forasmuch as the supreme command is constituted by virtue of the compacts which each single citizen or subject mutually makes with the other; but all contracts, as they receive their force from the contractors, so by their consent they lose it again and are broken: perhaps some may infer hence, that by the consent of all the subjects together the supreme authority may be wholly taken away. Which inference, if it were true, I cannot discern what

danger would thence by right arise to the supreme commanders. For since it is supposed that each one hath
obliged himself to each other; if any one of them shall
refuse, whatsoever the rest shall agree to do, he is bound
notwithstanding. Neither can any man without injury to
me, do that which by contract made with me he hath
obliged himself not to do. But it is not to be imagined
that ever it will happen, that all the subjects together, not
so much as one excepted, will combine against the supreme power. Wherefore there is no fear for rulers in
chief, that by any right they can be despoiled of their authority. If, notwithstanding, it were granted that their
right depended only on that contract which each man
makes with his fellow citizen, it might very easily happen
that they might be robbed of that dominion under pretence of right. For subjects being called either by the command of the city, or seditiously flocking together, most
men think that the consents of all are contained in the
votes of the greater part; which in truth is false. For it is
not from nature that the consent of the major part should
be received for the consent of all, neither is it true in
tumults; but it proceeds from civil institution: and is then
only true, when that man or court which hath the supreme
power, assembling his subjects, by reason of the greatness
of their number allows those that are elected a power of
speaking for those who elected them; and will have the
major part of voices, in such matters as are by him propounded to be discussed, to be as effectual as the whole.
But we cannot imagine that he who is chief, ever convened his subjects with intention that they should dispute
his right; unless weary of the burthen of his charge, he
declared in plain terms that he renounces and abandons
his government. Now, because most men through ignorance esteem not the consent of the major part of citizens
only, but even of a very few, provided they be of their
opinion, for the consent of the whole city; it may very

well seem to them, that the supreme authority may by right be abrogated, so it be done in some great assembly of citizens by the votes of the greater number. But though a government be constituted by the contracts of particular men with particulars, yet its right depends not on that obligation only; there is another tie also towards him who commands. For each citizen compacting with his fellow, says thus: *I convey my right on this party, upon condition that you pass yours to the same:* by which means, that right which every man had before to use his faculties to his own advantage, is now wholly translated on some certain man or council for the common benefit. Wherefore what by the mutual contracts each one hath made with the other, what by the donation of right which every man is bound to ratify to him that commands, the government is upheld by a double obligation from the citizens; first, that which is due to their fellow-citizens; next, that which they owe to their prince. Wherefore no subjects, how many soever they be, can with any right despoil him who bears the chief rule of his authority, even without his own consent.

VII

Of the Three Kinds of Government, Democracy, Aristocracy, Monarchy

1. That there are three kinds of government only, democracy, aristocracy, monarchy. 2. That oligarchy is not a diverse form of government distinct from aristocracy, nor anarchy any form at all. 3. That a tyranny is not a diverse state from a legitimate monarchy. 4. That there cannot be a mixed state, fashioned out of these several species. 5. That democracy, except there be certain times and places of meeting prefixed, is dissolved. 6. In a democracy the intervals of the times of meeting must be short, or the administration of government during the interval committed to some one. 7. In a democracy, particulars contract with particulars to obey the people: the people is obliged to no man. 8. By what acts aristocracy is constituted. 9. In an aristocracy the nobles make no compact, neither are they obliged to any citizen or to the whole people. 10. The nobles must necessarily have their set meetings. 11. By what acts monarchy is constituted. 12. Monarchy is by compact obliged to none for the authority it hath received. 13. Monarchy is ever in the readiest capacity to exercise all those acts which are requisite to good government. 14. What kind of sin that is, and what sort of men are guilty of it, when the city performs not its office towards the citizens, nor the citizens towards the city. 15. A monarch made without limitation of time hath power to elect his successor. 16. Of limited monarchs. 17. A monarch, retaining his right of government, cannot by any promise whatsoever be conceived to have parted with his right to the means necessary to the exercise of his authority. 18. How a citizen is freed from subjection.

1. We have already spoken of a city by institution in its genus; we will now say somewhat of its species. As for

the difference of cities, it is taken from the difference of the persons to whom the supreme power is committed. This power is committed either to *one man*, or *council*, or some *one court* consisting of many men. Furthermore, a council of many men consists either of all the citizens, insomuch as every man of them hath a right to vote, and an interest in the ordering of the greatest affairs, if he will himself; or of a part only. From whence there arise three sorts of government; the one, when the power is in a council where every citizen hath a right to vote; and it is called a *democracy*. The other, when it is in a council, where not all, but some part only have their suffrages; and we call it an *aristocracy*. The third is that, when the supreme authority rests only in one; and it is styled a *monarchy*. In the first, he that governs is called δῆμος, the *people*; in the second, the *nobles*; in the third, the *monarch*.

2. Now, although ancient writers of politics have introduced three other kinds of government opposite to these; to wit, *anarchy* or confusion to *democracy*; *oligarchy*, that is, the command of some few, to *aristocracy*; and *tyranny* to *monarchy*; yet are not these three distinct forms of government, but three diverse titles given by those who were either displeased with that present government or those that bear rule. For men, by giving names, do usually not only signify the things themselves, but also their own affections, as love, hatred, anger, and the like. Whence it happens that what one man calls a *democracy*, another calls an *anarchy*; what one counts an *aristocracy*, another esteems an *oligarchy*; and whom one titles a *king*, another styles him a *tyrant*. So as we see, these names betoken not a diverse kind of government, but the *diverse opinions* of the subjects concerning him who hath the supreme power. For first, who sees not that *anarchy* is equally opposite to all the aforenamed forms? For that word signifies that there is no government at all,

that is, not any city. But how is it possible that *no city* should be the species of *a city?* Furthermore, what difference is there between an *oligarchy,* which signifies the command of a *few* or *grandees,* or an *aristocracy,* which is that of the *prime* or *chief heads,* more than that men differ so among themselves, that the same things seem not good to all men? Whence it happens that those persons, who by some are looked on as the *best,* are by others esteemed to be the *worst* of all men.

3. But men, by reason of their passions, will very hardly be persuaded that a *kingdom* and *tyranny* are not diverse kinds of cities; who though they would rather have the city subject to one than many, yet do they not believe it to be well governed unless it accord with their judgments. But we must discover by reason, and not by passion, what the difference is between a king and a tyrant. But first, they differ not in this, that a tyrant hath the greater power; for greater than the supreme cannot be granted; nor in this, that one hath a limited power, the other not; for he whose authority is limited, is no king, but his subject that limits him. Lastly, neither differ they in their manner of acquisition; for if in a democratical or aristocratical government some one citizen should, by force, possess himself of the supreme power, if he gain the consent of all the citizens, he becomes a legitimate monarch; if not, he is an enemy, not a tyrant. They differ therefore in the sole exercise of their command, insomuch as he is said to be a king who governs well, and he a tyrant that doth otherwise. The case therefore is brought to this pass: that *a king,* legitimately constituted in his government, if he seem to his subjects to rule well and to their liking, they afford him the appellation of a *king;* if not, they count him a *tyrant.* Wherefore we see a *kingdom* and *tyranny* are not diverse forms of government, but one and the self-same monarch hath the name of a *king* given him in point of honour and reverence to him, and of a

tyrant in way of contumely and reproach. But what we frequently find in books said against tyrants, took its original from Greek and Roman writers, whose government was partly democratical, and partly aristocratical, and therefore not tyrants only, but even kings were odious to them.

4. There are, who indeed do think it necessary that a supreme command should be somewhere extant in a city; but if it should be in any one, either man or council, it would follow, they say, that all the citizens must be slaves. Avoiding this condition, they imagine that there may be a certain form of government compounded of those three kinds we have spoken of, yet different from each particular; which they call a *mixed monarchy*, or *mixed aristocracy*, or *mixed democracy*, according as any one of these three sorts shall be more eminent than the rest. For example, if the naming of magistrates and the arbitration of war and peace should belong to the King, judicature to the Lords, and contribution of monies to the People, and the power of making laws to all together, this kind of state would they call a *mixed monarchy* forsooth. But if it were possible that there could be such a state, it would no whit advantage the liberty of the subject. For as long as they all agree, each single citizen is as much subject as possibly he can be: but if they disagree, the state returns to a civil war and the right of the private sword; which certainly is much worse than any subjection whatsoever. But that there can be no such kind of government,* hath been sufficiently demonstrated in the foregoing chapter, art. 6–12.

* *But that there can be no such kind of government.* Most men grant, that a government ought not to be divided; but they would have it moderated and bounded by some limits. Truly it is very reasonable it should be so; but if these men, when they speak of moderating and limiting, do understand dividing it, they make a very fond distinction. Truly, for my part, I wish that not only kings, but all other persons endued with supreme authority, would so temper themselves as to commit no wrong, and only minding their

5. Let us see a little now, in the constituting of each form of government what the constitutors do. Those who met together with intention to erect a city, were almost in the very act of meeting, a democracy. For in that they willingly met, they are supposed obliged to the observation of what shall be determined by the major part; which, while that convent lasts, or is adjourned to some certain days and places, is a clear democracy. For that convent, whose will is the will of all the citizens, hath the supreme authority; and because in this convent every man is supposed to have a right to give his voice, it follows that it is a democracy, by the definition given in the first article of this chapter. But if they depart and break up the convent, and appoint no time or place where and when they shall meet again, the public weal returns to anarchy and the same state it stood in before their meeting, that is, to the state of all men warring against all. The people, therefore, retains the supreme power, no longer than there is a certain day and place publicly appointed and known, to which whosoever will may resort. For except that be known and determined, they may either meet at divers times and places, that is, in factions, or not at all; and then it is no longer δῆμος, *the people*, but a dissolute multitude, to whom we can neither attribute any action or right. Two things therefore frame a democracy; whereof one, to wit, the perpetual prescription of convents, makes δῆμον, *the people*; the other, which is a plurality of voices, τὸ κράτος, or *the power*.

6. Furthermore, it will not be sufficient for the people, so as to maintain its supremacy, to have some certain known times and places of meeting, unless that either the

charges, contain themselves within the limits of the natural and divine laws. But they who distinguish thus, they would have the chief power bounded and restrained by others: which, because it cannot be done but they who do set the limits must needs have some part of the power, whereby they may be enabled to do it, the government is properly divided, not moderated.

intervals of the times be of less distance, than that anything may in the meantime happen whereby, by reason of the defect of power, the city may be brought into some danger; or at least that the exercise of the supreme authority be, during the interval, granted to some one man or council. For unless this be done, there is not that wary care and heed taken for the defence and peace of single men, which ought to be; and therefore will not deserve the name of a city, because that in it, for want of security, every man's right of defending himself at his own pleasure returns to him again.

7. Democracy is not framed by contract of particular persons with the *people*, but by mutual compacts of single men each with other. But hence it appears, in the first place, that the persons contracting must be in being before the contract itself. But the *people* is not in being before the constitution of government, as not being any person, but a multitude of single persons; wherefore there could then no contract pass between the people and the subject. Now, if after that government is framed, the subject make any contract with the people, it is in vain; because the people contains within its will the will of that subject, to whom it is supposed to be obliged; and therefore may at its own will and pleasure disengage itself, and by consequence is now actually free. But in the second place, that single persons do contract each with other, may be inferred from hence; that in vain sure would the city have been constituted, if the citizens had been engaged by no contracts to do or omit what the city should command to be done or omitted. Because, therefore, such kind of compacts must be understood to pass as necessary to the making up of a city, but none can be made (as is already showed) between the subject and the people; it follows, that they must be made between single citizens, namely, that each man contract to submit his will to the will of the major part, on condition that

the rest also do the like. As if every one should say thus: I give up my right unto the people for your sake, on condition that you also deliver up yours for mine.

8. An *aristocracy* or council of nobles endowed with supreme authority, receives its original from a democracy, which gives up its right unto it. Where we must understand that certain men distinguished from others, either by eminence of title, blood, or some other character, are propounded to the people, and by plurality of voices are elected; and being elected, the whole right of the people or city is conveyed on them, insomuch as whatsoever the people might do before, the same by right may this court of elected nobles now do. Which being done, it is clear that the people, considered as one person, its supreme authority being already transferred on these, is no longer now in being.

9. As in democracy the people, so in an aristocracy the court of nobles is free from all manner of obligation. For seeing subjects not contracting with the people, but by mutual compacts among themselves, were tied to all that the people did; hence also they were tied to that act of the people, in resigning up its right of government into the hands of nobles. Neither could this court, although elected by the people, be by it obliged to anything. For being erected, the people is at once dissolved, as was declared above, and the authority it had as being a person, utterly vanisheth. Wherefore the obligation which was due to the *person* must also vanish, and perish together with it.

10. *Aristocracy* hath these considerations, together with *democracy*. First, that without an appointment of some certain times and places, at which the court of nobles may meet, it is no longer a court, or one person, but a dissolute multitude without any supreme power. Secondly, that the times of their assembling cannot be disjoined by long intervals without prejudice to the supreme power,

unless its administration be transferred to some one man.
Now the reasons why this happens are the same which
we set down in the fifth article.

11. As an *aristocracy*, so also a *monarchy* is derived from
the power of the *people*, transferring its right, that is, its
authority on one man. Here also we must understand,
that some *one* man, either by name or some other token,
is propounded to be taken notice of above all the rest;
and that by a plurality of voices the whole right of the
people is conveyed on him; insomuch as whatsoever the
people could do before he were elected, the same in every
respect may he by right now do, being elected. Which
being done, the people is no longer one *person*, but a rude
multitude, as being only one before by virtue of the supreme command, whereof they now have made a conveyance from themselves on this one man.

12. And therefore neither doth the monarch oblige
himself to any for the command he receives. For he receives it from the people; but as hath been showed above,
the people, as soon as that act is done, ceaseth to be a *person*; but the *person* vanishing, all obligation to the *person*
vanisheth. The subjects therefore are tied to perform
obedience to the monarch, by those compacts only by
which they mutually obliged themselves to the observation of all that the people should command them, that
is, to obey that *monarch*, if he were made by the *people*.

13. But a *monarchy* differs as well from an *aristocracy*
as a *democracy*, in this chiefly; that in those there must
be certain set times and places for deliberation and consultation of affairs, that is, for the actual exercise of it in
all times and places. For the people or the nobles not being *one natural person*, must necessarily have their meetings. The *monarch*, who is one by nature, is always in a
present capacity to execute his authority.

14. Because we have declared above (in art. 7, 9, 12),
that they who have gotten the *supreme command*, are by

no compacts obliged to any man, it necessarily follows, that they can do no *injury* to the subjects. For *injury*, according to the definition made in chap. III. art. 3, is nothing else but a breach of contract; and therefore where no contracts have part, there can be no injury. Yet the people, the nobles, and the monarch may diverse ways transgress against the other laws of nature, as by cruelty, iniquity, contumely, and other like vices, which come not under this strict and exact notion of *injury*. But if the subject yield not obedience to the supreme, he will in propriety of speech be said to be *injurious*, as well to his fellow subjects, because each man hath compacted with the other to obey; as to his *chief ruler*, in resuming that right which he hath given him, without his consent. And in a *democracy* or *aristocracy*, if anything be decreed against any *law of nature*, the city itself, that is, the civil person, sins not, but those subjects only by whose votes it was decreed; for sin is a consequence of the natural express will, not of the political, which is artificial. For if it were otherwise, they would be guilty by whom the decree was absolutely disliked. But in a *monarchy*, if the *monarch* make any decree against the *laws of nature*, he sins himself; because in him the civil will and the natural are all one.

15. The people who are about to make a *monarch*, may give him the *supremacy* either simply without limitation of time, or for a certain season and time determined. If simply, we must understand that he who receives it, hath the self-same power which they had who gave it. On the same grounds, therefore, that the *people* by right could make him a monarch, may he make another monarch. Insomuch as the *monarch* to whom the command is simply given receives a right not of *possession* only, but of *succession* also; so as he may declare whom he pleaseth for his successor.

16. But if the power be given for a time limited,

we must have regard to somewhat more than the bare gift only. First, whether the *people* conveying its authority, left itself any right to meet at certain times and places, or not. Next, if it have reserved this power, whether it were done so as they might meet before that time were expired, which they prescribed to the monarch. Thirdly, whether they were contented to meet only at the will of that temporary monarch, and not otherwise. Suppose now the *people* had delivered up its power to some one man for term of life only; which being done, let us suppose in the first place, that every man departed from the council without making any order at all concerning the place, where after his death they should meet again to make a new election. In this case, it is manifest by the fifth article of this chapter, that the *people* ceaseth to be a *person*, and is become a dissolute multitude; every one whereof hath an equal, to wit, a natural right to meet with whom he lists at divers times, and in what places shall best please him; nay, and if he can, engross the supreme power to himself, and settle it on his own head. What monarch soever, therefore, hath a command in such a condition, he is bound by the *law of nature*, set down in chap. III. art. 8, *of not returning evil for good*, prudently to provide that by his death the city suffer not a dissolution; either by appointing a certain day and place, in which those subjects of his, who have a mind to it, may assemble themselves, or else by nominating a successor; whether of these shall to him seem most conducible to their common benefit. He therefore, who on this foresaid manner hath received his command during life, hath an absolute power, and may at his discretion dispose of the succession. In the next place, if we grant that the *people* departed not from the election of the *temporary monarch*, before they decreed a certain time and place of meeting after his death; then the monarch being dead, the authority is confirmed in the people, not by any new acts of the subjects, but by virtue of the former right. For all the supreme command, as *dominion,* was in the people; but the use and exercise of it was only in the temporary monarch, as in one that takes the benefit, but hath not the right. But if the *people* after the election of a *temporary monarch,* depart not from the court before they have appointed certain times and places to convene during the time prescribed him; as the dictators in ancient times were made by the people of Rome; such an one is not to be accounted a monarch, but the prime officer of the people. And if it shall seem good, the people may deprive him of his office even before that time; as the people of Rome did, when they conferred an equal power on Minutius, master of the horse, with Quintus Fabius Maximus, whom before they had made dictator. The reason whereof is, that it is not to be imagined, that he, whether man or council, who hath the readiest and most immediate power to act, should hold his command on such terms, as not to be able actually to execute it; for command is nothing else but a right of commanding, as oft as nature allows it possible. Lastly, if the *people* having declared a *temporary monarch,* depart from the court on such terms, as it shall not be lawful for them to meet without the command of the monarch, we must understand the people to be immediately dissolved, and that his authority, who is thus declared, is absolute; forasmuch as it is not in the power of all the subjects to frame the city anew, unless he give consent who hath now alone the authority. Nor matters it, that he hath perhaps made any promise to assemble his subjects on some certain times; since there remains no *person* now in being, but at his discretion, to whom the promise was made. What we have spoken of these four cases of a *people* electing a *temporary monarch,* will be more clearly explained by comparing them with an *absolute monarch* who hath no heir-apparent. For the people is lord of the subject in such a manner, as there can be no heir but whom itself doth appoint. Besides, the spaces between the times of the subjects' meeting, may be fitly compared to those times wherein the monarch sleeps; for in either the *acts* of commanding cease, the *power* remains. Furthermore, to dissolve the convent, so as it cannot meet again, is the death of the *people*; just as sleeping, so as he can never wake more, is the death of a man. As therefore a king who hath no heir, going to his rest so as never to rise again, that is, dying, if he commit the exercise of his regal authority to any one till he awake, does by consequence give him the succession; the *people* also electing a *temporary monarch*, and not reserving a power to convene, delivers up to him the whole dominion of the country. Furthermore, as a king going to sleep for some season entrusts the administration of his kingdom to some other, and waking takes it again; so the people having elected a *temporary monarch*, and withal retaining a right to meet at a certain day and place, at that day receives its supremacy again. And as a king who hath committed the execution of his authority to another, himself in the meanwhile waking, can recall this commission again when he pleaseth; so the *people*, who during the time prescribed to the *temporary monarch* doth by right convene, may if they please deprive the monarch of his authority. Lastly, the king, who commits his authority to another while himself sleeps, not being able to wake again till he whom he entrusted give consent, loses at once both his power and his life; so the people, who hath given the supreme power to a temporary monarch in such sort as they cannot assemble without his command, is absolutely dissolved, and the power remains with him whom they have chosen.

17. If the monarch *promise* aught to any one or many subjects together, by consequence whereof the exercise of his power may suffer prejudice, that *promise* or *compact*, whether made by oath or without it, is null. For all

compact is a conveyance of right, which by what hath
been said in the fourth article of the second chapter, requires meet and proper signs of the will in the conveyer.
But he who sufficiently signifies his will of retaining the
end, doth also sufficiently declare that he quits not his
right to the means necessary to that end. Now he who
hath promised to part with somewhat necessary to the
supreme power, and yet retains the power itself, gives
sufficient tokens that he no otherwise promised it, than
so far forth as the power might be retained without it.
Whensoever therefore it shall appear, that what is promised cannot be performed without prejudice to the power,
the promise must be valued as not made, that is, of no
effect.

18. We have seen how subjects, nature dictating, have
obliged themselves by mutual compacts to obey the supreme power. We will see now by what means it comes
to pass, that they are released from these bonds of obedience. And first of all, this happens by *rejection*, namely,
if a man cast off or forsake, but convey not the *right of
his command* on some other. For what is thus rejected,
is openly exposed to all alike, catch who catch can;
whence again, by the right of nature, every subject may
heed the preservation of himself according to his own
judgment. In the second place, if the kingdom fall into
the power of the enemy, so as there can no more opposition be made against them, we must understand that he
who before had the supreme authority, hath now lost it:
for when the subjects have done their full endeavour to
prevent their falling into the enemy's hands, they have
fulfilled those contracts of obedience which they made
each with other; and what, being conquered, they promise afterwards to avoid death, they must with no less endeavour labour to perform. Thirdly, in a monarchy (for a
democracy and aristocracy cannot fail), if there be no
successor, all the subjects are discharged from their obliga-

tions; for no man is supposed to be tied he knows not to whom; for in such a case it were impossible to perform aught. And by these three ways, all subjects are restored from their civil subjection to that liberty which all men have to all things; to wit, natural and savage; for the natural state hath the same proportion to the civil (I mean, liberty to subjection), which passion hath to reason, or a beast to a man. Furthermore, each subject may lawfully be freed from his subjection by the will of him who hath the supreme power, namely, if he change his soil; which may be done two ways, either by permission, as he who gets license to dwell in another country; or command, as he who is banished. In both cases, he is free from the laws of his former country because he is tied to observe those of the latter.

VIII

Of the Rights of Lords over Their Servants

1. What lord and servant signify. 2. The distinction of
servants, into such as upon trust enjoy their natural liberty,
|and slaves, or|such as serve being imprisoned or bound in
fetters. 3. The obligation of a servant arises from the
liberty of body allowed him by his lord. 4. Servants that
are bound, are not by any compacts tied to their lords.
5. Servants have no propriety in their goods against their
lord. 6. The lord may sell his servant, or alienate him by
testament. 7. The lord cannot injure his servant. 8. He
that is lord of the lord, is lord also of his servants. 9. By
what means servants are freed. 10. Dominion over beasts
belongs to the right of nature.

1. In the two foregoing chapters we have treated of an
institutive or *framed* government, as being that which
receives its original from the consent of many, who by
contract and faith mutually given have obliged each
other. Now follows what may be said concerning a *natural* government; which may also be called *acquired,* because it is that which is gotten by power and natural
force. But we must know in the first place, by what means
the right of dominion may be gotten over the persons of
men. Where such a right is gotten, there is a kind of a
little kingdom; for to be a *king,* is nothing else but to have
dominion over many persons; and thus a great family is
a kingdom, and a little kingdom a family. Let us return
again to the state of nature, and consider men as if but
even now sprung out of the earth, and suddenly, like
mushrooms, come to full maturity, without all kind of
engagement to each other. There are but three ways only,

whereby one can have a dominion over the person of another; whereof the first is, if by mutual contract made
between themselves, for peace and self-defence's sake,
they have willingly given up themselves to the power and
authority of some man, or council of men; and of this we
have already spoken. The second is, if a man taken
prisoner in the wars, or overcome, or else distrusting his
own forces, to avoid death, promises the conqueror or the
stronger party his *service*, that is, to do all whatsoever he
shall command him. In which contract, the good which
the vanquished or inferior in strength doth receive, is the
grant of his life, which by the right of war in the natural
state of men he might have|been deprived of;|but the
good which he promises, is his service and obedience. By
virtue therefore of this promise, there is as absolute service and obedience due from the vanquished to the van-
quisher, as possibly can be, excepting what repugns the
divine laws; for he who is obliged to obey the commands
of any man before he knows what he will command him,
is simply and without any restriction tied to the performance of all commands whatsoever. Now he that is thus
tied, is called a *servant*; he to whom he is tied, a
lord. Thirdly, there is a right acquired over the person
of a man by generation; of which kind of acquisition
somewhat shall be spoken in the following chapter.

2. Every one that is taken in the war, and hath his life
spared him, is not supposed to have contracted with his
lord; for every one is not trusted with so much of his natural liberty, as to be able, if he desired it, either to fly
away, or quit his service, or contrive any mischief to his
lord. And these serve indeed, but within prisons or bound
within irons; and therefore they were called not by the
common name of *servant* only, but by the peculiar name
of *slave*; even as now at this day, *un serviteur*, and *un serf*,
or *un esclave* have diverse significations.

3. The obligation therefore of a *servant* to his *lord*,

ariseth not from a simple grant of his life; but from hence rather, that he keeps him not bound or imprisoned. For all obligation derives from contract; but where is no trust, there can be no contract, as appears by chap. II. art. 9; where a compact is defined to be the promise of him who is trusted. There is therefore a confidence and trust which accompanies the benefit of pardoned life, whereby the *lord* affords him his corporal liberty; so that if no obligation nor bonds of contract had happened, he might not only have made his escape, but also have killed his lord who was the preserver of his life.

4. Wherefore such kind of *servants* as are restrained by imprisonment or bonds, are not comprehended in that definition of *servants* given above; because those serve not for the contract's sake, but to the end they may not suffer. And therefore if they fly, or kill their *lord*, they offend not against the laws of nature. For to bind any man, is a plain sign that the binder supposes him that is bound, not to be sufficiently tied by any other obligation.

5. The lord therefore hath no less dominion over a servant that is not, than over one that is bound; for he hath a supreme power over both, and may say of his servant no less than of another thing, whether animate or inanimate, *this is mine*. Whence it follows, that whatsoever the servant had before his servitude, that afterwards becomes the lord's; and whatsoever he hath gotten, it was gotten for his lord. For he that can by right dispose of the *person* of a man, may surely dispose of all those things which that *person* could dispose of. There is therefore nothing which the servant may retain as his own against the will of his lord; yet hath he, by his lord's distribution, a propriety and dominion over his own goods: insomuch as one servant may keep and defend them against the invasion of his fellow-servant, in the same manner as hath been showed before, that a subject hath nothing properly *his own* against the will of the supreme authority, but

every subject hath a propriety against his fellow subject.

6. Since therefore both the servant himself, and all that belongs to him are his lord's, and by the right of nature every man may dispose of his own in what manner he pleases; the lord may either sell, lay to pledge, or by testament convey the dominion he hath over his servant, according to his own will and pleasure.

7. Furthermore, what hath before been demonstrated concerning subjects in an *institutive* government, namely, that he who hath the supreme power can do his subject no injury; is true also concerning *servants*, because they have subjected their will to the will of the lord. Wherefore, whatsoever he doth, it is done with their wills; but no injury can be done to him that willeth it.

8. But if it happen that the *lord*, either by captivity or voluntary subjection, doth become a *servant* or *subject* to another, that other shall not only be lord of him, but also of his *servants*; supreme lord over these, immediate lord over him. Now because not the servant only, but also all he hath, are his lord's; therefore his servants now belong to this man, neither can the mediate lord dispose otherwise of them than shall seem good to the supreme. And therefore, if sometime in civil governments the lord have an absolute power over his servants, that is supposed to be derived from the right of nature, and not constituted, but slightly passed over by the civil law.

9. A servant is by the same manner freed from his servitude, that a subject in an institutive government is freed from his subjection. First, if his lord enfranchise him; for the right which the servant transferred to his lord over himself, the same may the lord restore to the servant again. And this manner of bestowing of liberty is called *manumission*; which is just as if a city should permit a citizen to convey himself under the jurisdiction of some other city. Secondly, if the lord cast off his servant from him; which in a city is *banishment*; neither differs it from

manumission in effect, but in manner only. For there, liberty is granted as a favour, here, as a punishment: in both, the dominion is renounced. Thirdly, if the servant be taken prisoner, the old servitude is abolished by the new; for as all other things, so servants also are acquired by war, whom in equity the lord must protect, if he will have them to be his. Fourthly, the servant is freed for want of knowledge of a successor, the lord dying (suppose) without any testament or heir. For no man is understood to be obliged, unless he know to whom he is to perform the obligation. Lastly, the servant that is put in bonds, or by any other means deprived of his corporal liberty, is freed from that other obligation of contract. For there can be no contract where there is no trust, nor can that faith be broken which is not given. But the *lord* who himself serves another, cannot so free his *servants*, but that they must still continue under the power of the supreme; for, as hath been showed before, such servants are not his, but the supreme lord's.

10. We get a right over irrational creatures, in the same manner that we do over the persons of men; to wit, by force and natural strength. For if in the state of nature it is lawful for every one, by reason of that war which is of all against all, to subdue and also to kill men as oft as it shall seem to conduce unto their good; much more will the same be lawful against brutes; namely, at their own discretion to reduce those to servitude, which by art may be tamed and fitted for use, and to persecute and destroy the rest by a perpetual war as dangerous and noxious. Our dominion therefore over beasts, hath its original from the *right of nature*, not from *divine positive right*. For if such a right had not been before the publishing of the Sacred Scriptures, no man by right might have killed a beast for his food, but he to whom the divine pleasure was made manifest by holy writ; a most hard condition for men indeed, whom the beasts might devour without

injury, and yet they might not destroy them. Forasmuch therefore as it proceeds from the right of nature, that a beast may kill a man, it is also by the same right that a man may slay a beast.

IX

Of the Right of Parents over Their Children, and of Hereditary Government

1. Paternal dominion ariseth not from generation. 2. Dominion over infants belongs to him or her who first hath them in their power. 3. Dominion over infants is originally the mother's. 4. The exposed infant is his, from whom he receives his preservation. 5. The child that hath one parent a subject, and the other a sovereign, belongs to him or her in authority. 6. In such a conjunction of man and woman, as neither hath command over the other, the children are the mother's, unless by compact or civil law it be otherwise determined. 7. Children are no less subject to their parents, than servants to their lords and subjects to their princes. 8. Of the honour of parents and lords. 9. Wherein liberty consists, and the difference of subjects and servants. 10. There is the same right over subjects in an hereditary government, which there is in an institutive government. 11. The question concerning the right of succession belongs only to monarchy. 12. A monarch may by his will and testament dispose of his supreme authority: 13. Or give it, or sell it. 14. A monarch dying without testament, is ever supposed to will that a monarch should succeed him: 15. And some one of his children: 16. And a male rather than female: 17. And the eldest rather than the younger: 18. And his brother, if he want issue, before all others. 19. In the same manner that men succeed to the power, do they also succeed to the right of succession.

1. *Socrates is a man, and therefore a living creature,* is right reasoning; and that most evident, because there is nothing needful to the acknowledging of the truth of the consequence, but that the word *man* be understood; because *a living creature* is in the definition itself of *a man,*

and every one makes up the proposition which was desired, namely this, *man is a living creature*. And this, *Sophroniscus is Socrates' father, and therefore his lord*, is perhaps a true inference, but not evident; because the word *lord* is not in the definition of *a father*: wherefore it is necessary, to make it more evident, that the connexion of *father* and *lord* be somewhat unfolded. Those that have hitherto endeavoured to prove the dominion of a parent over his children, have brought no other argument than that of *generation*; as if it were of itself evident, that what is begotten by me is mine; just as if a man should think, that because there is a triangle, it appears presently, without any further discourse, that its angles are equal to two right. Besides, since dominion, that is, supreme power is indivisible, insomuch as no man can serve two masters; but two persons, male and female, must concur in the act of generation; it is impossible that dominion should at all be acquired by generation only. Wherefore we will, with the more diligence, in this place inquire into the original of *paternal government*.

2. We must therefore return to the state of nature, in which, by reason of the equality of nature, all men of riper years are to be accounted equal. There *by right of nature* the conqueror is lord of the conquered. By the right therefore of *nature*, the dominion over the infant first belongs to him who first hath him in his power. But it is manifest that he who is newly born is in the *mother's* power before any others; insomuch as she may rightly, and at her own will, either breed him up or adventure him to fortune.

3. If therefore she breed him, because the state of nature is the state of war, she is supposed to bring him up on this condition; that being grown to full age he become not her enemy; which is, that he obey her. For since by natural necessity we all desire that which appears good unto us, it cannot be understood that any man hath on

such terms afforded life to another, that he might both get strength by his years, and at once become an enemy. But each man is an enemy to that other, whom he neither obeys nor commands. And thus in the state of nature, every woman that bears children, becomes both a *mother* and a *lord*. But what some say, that in this case the *father*, by reason of the pre-eminence of sex, and not the *mother* becomes *lord*, signifies nothing. For both reason shows the contrary; because the inequality of their natural forces is not so great, that the man could get the dominion over the woman without war. And custom also contradicts not; for women, namely Amazons, have in former times waged war against their adversaries, and disposed of their children at their own wills. And at this day, in divers places women are invested with the principal authority; neither do their husbands dispose of their children, but themselves; which in truth they do *by the right of nature;* forasmuch as they who have the supreme power, are not tied at all (as hath been showed) to the civil laws. Add also, that in the state of nature it cannot be known who is the *father*, but by the testimony of the *mother;* the child therefore is his whose the mother will have it, and therefore her's. Wherefore original dominion over *children* belongs to the *mother:* and among men no less than other creatures, the birth follows the belly.

4. The dominion passes from the mother to others, divers ways. First, if she quit and forsake her right by *exposing* the child. He therefore that shall bring up the child thus exposed, shall have the same dominion over it which the mother had. For that life which the mother had given it (not by *getting* but *nourishing* it), she now by *exposing* takes from it. Wherefore the obligation also which arose from the benefit of life, is by this exposition made void. Now the preserved oweth all to the preserver, whether in regard of his education as to a *mother*, or of his service as to a *lord*. For although the mother in the

state of nature, where all men have a right to all things, may recover her son again, namely, by the same right that anybody else might do it; yet may not the son rightly transfer himself again unto his mother.

5. Secondly, if the mother be taken prisoner, her son is his that took her; because that he who hath dominion over the person, hath also dominion over all belonging to the person; wherefore over the son also, as hath been showed in the foregoing chapter, in the fifth article. Thirdly, if the mother be a subject under what government soever, he that hath the supreme authority in that government, will also have the dominion over him that is born of her; for he is lord also of the mother, who is bound to obey him in all things. Fourthly, if a woman for society's sake give herself to a man on this condition, that he shall bear the sway; he that receives his being from the contribution of both parties, is the *father's*, in regard of the command he hath over the *mother*. But if a woman bearing rule shall have children by a subject, the children are the *mother's*; for otherwise the woman can have no children without prejudice to her authority. And universally, if the society of the male and female be such an union, as the one have subjected himself to the other, the children belong to him or her that commands.

6. But in the state of nature, if a man and woman contract so, as neither is subject to the command of the other, the children are the mother's, for the reasons above given in the third article; unless by pacts it be otherwise provided. For the *mother* may by pact dispose of her right as she lists; as heretofore hath been done by the Amazons, who of those children which have been begotten by their neighbours, have by pact allowed them the *males*, and retained the *females* to themselves. But in a civil government, if there be a contract of marriage between a man and woman, the children are the *father's*; because in all cities, to wit, constituted of *fathers*, not *mothers* govern-

ing their families, the domestical command belongs to the man; and such a contract, if it be made according to the civil laws, is called matrimony. But if they agree only to lie together, the children are the *father's* or the *mother's* variously, according to the differing civil laws of divers cities.

7. Now because, by the third article, the *mother is originally lord of her children,* and from her the father, or somebody else by derived right; it is manifest that the children are no less subject to those by whom they are nourished and brought up, than servants to their lords, and subjects to him who bears the supreme rule; and that a parent cannot be injurious to his son, as long as he is under his power. A son also is freed from subjection in the same manner as a subject and servant are. For *emancipation* is the same thing with *manumission,* and *abdication* with *banishment.*

8. The *enfranchised son* or *released servant,* do now stand in less fear of their *lord* and *father,* being deprived of his natural and lordly power over them; and, if regard be had to true and inward honour, do honour him less than before. For *honour,* as hath been said in the section above, is nothing else but the estimation of another's power; and therefore he that hath least power, hath always least *honour.* But it is not to be imagined, that the *enfranchiser* ever intended so to match the *enfranchised* with himself, as that he should not so much as acknowledge a benefit, but should so carry himself in all things as if he were become wholly his equal. It must therefore be ever understood, that he who is freed from subjection, whether he be a *servant, son,* or some *colony,* doth promise all those external signs at least, whereby superiors used to be honoured by their inferiors. From whence it follows, that the precept of *honouring our parents,* belongs to the law of nature, not only under the title of *gratitude,* but also of *agreement.*

9. What then, will some one demand, is the difference
between a *son,* or between a *subject* and a *servant?*
Neither do I know that any writer hath fully declared
what *liberty* and what *slavery* is. Commonly, to do all
things according to our own fancies, and that without
punishment, is esteemed to be *liberty;* not to be able to
do this, is judged *bondage;* which in a civil government,
and with the peace of mankind, cannot possibly be done;
because there is no city without a command and a re-
straining right. *Liberty,* that we may define it, is nothing
else but *an absence of the lets and hindrances of motion;*
as water shut up in a vessel is therefore not at liberty,
because the vessel hinders it from running out; which, the
vessel being broken, is made *free.* And every man hath
more or less *liberty,* as he hath more or less space in
which he employs himself: as he hath more *liberty,* who
is in a large, than he that is kept in a close prison. And a
man may be free toward one part, and yet not toward
another; as the traveller is bounded on this and that side
with hedges or stone walls, lest he spoil the vines or corn
neighbouring on the highway. And these kinds of lets are
external and absolute. In which sense all *servants* and
subjects are *free,* who are not fettered and imprisoned.
There are others which are arbitrary, which do not absolutely hinder motion, but by accident, to wit, by our
own choice; as he that is in a ship, is not so hindered but
he may cast himself into the sea, if he will. And here also
the more ways a man may move himself, the more *liberty*
he hath. And herein consists civil *liberty;* for no man,
whether *subject, son,* or *servant,* is so hindered by the
punishments appointed by the *city,* the *father,* or the *lord,*
how cruel soever, but that he may do all things, and make
use of all means necessary to the preservation of his life
and health. For my part therefore I cannot find what reason a mere *servant* hath to make complaints, if they
relate only to want of *liberty;* unless he count it a misery

to be restrained from hurting himself, and to receive that life, which by war, or misfortune, or through his own idleness was forfeited, together with all manner of sustenance, and all things necessary to the conservation of health, on this condition only, that he will be ruled. For he that is kept in by punishments laid before him, so as he dares not let loose the reins to his will in all things, is not oppressed by servitude, but is governed and sustained. But this privilege free subjects and sons of a family have above servants in every government and family where servants are; that they may both undergo the more honourable offices of the city or family, and also enjoy a larger possession of things superfluous. And herein lies the difference between a *free subject* and a *servant*, that he is *free* indeed, who serves his city only; but a *servant* is he, who also serves his fellow subject. All other liberty is an exemption from the laws of the city, and proper only to those that bear rule.

10. A *father* with his *sons* and *servants*, grown into a civil person by virtue of his paternal jurisdiction, is called a *family*. This *family*, if through multiplying of *children* and acquisition of *servants* it becomes numerous, insomuch as without casting the uncertain die of war it cannot be subdued, will be termed an *hereditary kingdom*. Which though it differ from an *institutive monarchy*, being acquired by force, in the original and manner of its constitution; yet being constituted, it hath all the same properties, and the right of authority is everywhere the same; insomuch as it is not needful to speak anything of them apart.

11. It hath been spoken, by what right supreme authorities are constituted. We must now briefly tell you, by what right they may be continued. Now the right by which they are continued, is that which is called the right of *succession*. Now because in a *democracy* the supreme authority is with the *people*, as long as there be any subjects in

being, so long it rests with the same person; for the people hath no successor. In like manner in an *aristocracy,* one of the nobles dying, some other by the rest is substituted in his place; and therefore except they all die together, which I suppose will never happen, there is no succession. The query therefore of the right of succession takes place only in an *absolute monarchy.* For they who exercise the supreme power for a time only, are themselves no *monarchs,* but *ministers* of state.

12. But first, if a monarch shall by testament appoint one to succeed him, the person appointed shall succeed. For if he be appointed by the *people,* he shall have all the right over the city which the *people* had, as hath been showed in chap. VII. art. 11. But the people might choose him; by the same right therefore may he choose another. But in an *hereditary kingdom,* there are the same rights as in an *institutive.* Wherefore every monarch may by his will make a *successor.*

13. But what a man may transfer on another by testament, that by the same right may he, yet living, give or sell away. To whomsoever therefore he shall make over the supreme power, whether by gift or sale, it is rightly made.

14. But if living he have not declared his will concerning his successor by testament nor otherwise, it is supposed, first, that he would not have his government reduced to an anarchy or the state of war, that is, to the destruction of his subjects; as well because he could not do that without breach of the laws of nature, whereby he was obliged to the performance of all things necessarily conducing to the preservation of peace; as also because, if that had been his will, it had not been hard for him to have declared that openly. Next, because the right passeth according to the will of the father, we must judge of the *successor* according to the signs of his will. It is understood therefore, that he would have his subjects to be

under a *monarchical* government, rather than any other, because he himself in ruling hath before approved of that state by his example, and hath not afterward either by any word or deed condemned it.

15. Furthermore, because by natural necessity all men wish them better, from whom they receive glory and honour, than others; but every man after death receives honour and glory from his children, sooner than from the power of any other men: hence we gather, that a father intends better for his children than any other person's. It is to be understood therefore, that the will of the father, dying without testament, was that some of his children should succeed him. Yet this is to be understood with this proviso, that there be no more apparent tokens to the contrary: of which kind, after many successions, custom may be one. For he that makes no mention of his *succession*, is supposed to consent to the customs of his realm.

16. Among children the males carry the pre-eminence; in the beginning perhaps, because for the most part, although not always, they are fitter for the administration of greater matters, but specially of wars; but afterwards, when it was grown a custom, because that custom was not contradicted. And therefore the will of the father, unless some other custom or sign do clearly repugn it, is to be interpreted in favour of them.

17. Now because the sons are equal, and the power cannot be divided, the eldest shall succeed. For if there be any difference by reason of age, the eldest is supposed more worthy; for nature being judge, the most in years (because usually it is so) is the wisest; but other judge there cannot be had. But if the brothers must be equally valued, the succession shall be *by lot*. But *primogeniture* is a natural lot, and by this the eldest is already preferred; nor is there any that hath power to judge, whether by this or any other kind of lots the matter is to be decided.

Now the same reason which contends thus for the first-born son, doth no less for the first-born daughter.

18. But if he have no children, then the command shall pass to his brothers and sisters; for the same reason that the children should have succeeded, if he had had them. For those that are nearest to us in nature, are supposed to be nearest in benevolence. And to his brothers sooner than his sisters, and to the elder sooner than the younger; for the reason is the same for these, that it was for the children.

19. Furthermore, by the same reason that men succeed to the power, do they also succeed to the right of succession. For if the first-born die before the father, it will be judged that he transferred his right of succession unto his children; unless the father have otherwise decreed it. And therefore the nephews will have a fairer pretence to the succession than the uncles. I say all these things will be thus, if the custom of the place (which the father by not contradicting will be judged to have consented to) do not hinder them.

X

Comparison between Three Kinds of Government According to Their Several Inconveniences

1. A comparison of the natural state with the civil. 2. The conveniences and inconveniences of the ruler and his subjects are alike. 3. The praise of monarchy. 4. The government under one, cannot be said to be unreasonable in this respect, namely, because one hath more power than all the rest. 5. A rejection of their opinion, who say, that a lord with his servants cannot make a city. 6. Exactions are more grievous under a popular state, than a monarchy. 7. Innocent subjects are less exposed to penalties under a monarch, than under the people. 8. The liberty of single subjects is not less under a monarch, than under a people. 9. It is no disadvantage to the subjects, that they are not all admitted to public deliberations. 10. Civil deliberations are unadvisedly committed to great assemblies, by reason of the unskilfulness of the most part of men: 11. In regard of eloquence: 12. In regard of faction: 13. In regard of the unstableness of the laws: 14. In regard of the want of secrecy. 15. That these inconveniences adhere to democracy, forasmuch as men are naturally delighted with the esteem of wit. 16. The inconveniences of a city arising from a king that is a child. 17. The power of generals is an evident sign of the excellence of monarchy. 18. The best state of a city is that, where the subjects are the ruler's inheritance. 19. The nearer aristocracy draws to monarchy, the better it is; the further it keeps from it, the worse.

1. What *democracy*, *aristocracy*, and *monarchy* are, hath already been spoken; but which of them tends most to the preservation of the subjects' peace and procuring

their advantages, we must see by comparing them together. But first let us set forth the advantages and disadvantages of a city in general; lest some perhaps should
think it better, that every man be left to live at his own
will, than to constitute any civil society at all. Every
man indeed out of the state of civil government hath a
most entire, but unfruitful liberty; because that he who
by reason of his own liberty acts all at his own will, must
also by reason of the same liberty in others suffer all at
another's will. But in a constituted city, every subject
retains to himself as much freedom as suffices him to live
well and quietly; and there is so much taken away from
others, as may make them not to be feared. Out of this
state, every man hath such a right to all, as yet he can
enjoy nothing; in it, each one securely enjoys his limited
right. Out of it, any man may rightly spoil or kill another;
in it, none but one. Out of it, we are protected by our
own forces; in it, by the power of all. Out of it, no man
is sure of the fruit of his labours; in it, all men are. Lastly,
out of it, there is a dominion of passions, war, fear, poverty, slovenliness, solitude, barbarism, ignorance, cruelty;
in it, the dominion of reason, peace, security, riches, de-
cency, society, elegancy, sciences, and benevolence.

2. Aristotle, in his seventh book and fourteenth chapter
of his *Politics*, saith, that there are two sorts of governments; whereof the one relates to the benefit of the *ruler*,
the other to that of the *subjects*. As if where *subjects* are
severely dealt with, there were one, and where more
mildly, there were another form of government. Which
opinion may by no means be subscribed to; for all the
profits and disprofits arising from government are the
same, and common both to the *ruler* and the *subject*. The
damages which befall some particular subjects through
misfortune, folly, negligence, sloth, or his own luxury,
may very well be severed from those which concern the
ruler. But those relate not to the government itself, being

such as may happen in any form of government whatsoever. If these same happen from the first institution of the city, they will then be truly called the inconveniences of government; but they will be common to the ruler with his subjects, as their benefits are common. But the first and greatest benefit, peace and defence,|is to|both; for both he that commands, and he who is commanded, to the end that he may defend his life makes use at once of all the forces of his fellow subjects. And in the greatest inconvenience that can befall a city, namely, the slaughter of subjects arising from anarchy, both the commander and the parties commanded are equally concerned. Next, if the ruler levy such a sum of vast monies from his subjects, as they are not able to maintain themselves and their families, nor conserve their bodily strength and vigor, the disadvantage is as much his as theirs, who, with never so great a stock or measure of riches, is not able to keep his authority or his riches without the bodies of his subjects. But if he raise no more than is sufficient for the due administration of his power, that is a benefit|equal|to himself and his subjects, tending to a common peace and defence. Nor is it imaginable which way *public* treasures can be a grievance to *private* subjects, if they be not so exhausted as to be wholly deprived from all possibility to acquire, even by their industry, necessaries to sustain the strength of their bodies and minds. For even thus the grievance would concern the ruler; nor would it arise from the ill-institution or ordination of the government, because in all manner of governments subjects may be oppressed; but from the ill-administration of a well-established government.

3. Now that *monarchy*, of the foresaid forms of *democracy, aristocracy*, and *monarchy*, hath the pre-eminence, will best appear by comparing the conveniences and inconveniences arising in each one of them. Those arguments therefore, that the *whole* universe is governed by

one God; that the ancients preferred the monarchical state before all others, ascribing the rule of the gods to one Jupiter; that in the beginning of affairs and of nations, the decrees of princes were held for laws; that paternal government, instituted by God himself in the creation, was monarchical; that other governments were compacted by the artifice of men* out of the ashes of monarchy, after it had been ruined with seditions; and that the people of God were under the jurisdiction of kings: although, I say, these do hold forth *monarchy* as the more eminent to us, yet because they do it by examples and testimonies, and not by solid reason, we will pass them over.

4. Some there are, who are discontented with the government under *one*, for no other reason but because it is under *one*; as if it were an unreasonable thing, that *one* man among so many should so far excel in power, as to be able at his own pleasure to dispose of all the rest. These men, sure, if they could, would withdraw themselves from under the dominion of *one* God. But this exception against *one* is suggested by envy, while they see one man in possession of what all desire. For the same cause, they would judge it to be as unreasonable if a *few* commanded, unless they themselves either were, or hoped to be of the number. For if it be an unreasonable thing that all men

---

* *Compacted by the artifice of men*, &c. It seems the ancients who made that same fable of Prometheus, pointed at this. They say that Prometheus, having stolen fire from the sun, formed a man out of clay, and that for this deed he was tortured by Jupiter with a perpetual gnawing in his liver. Which is, that by human invention, which is signified by Prometheus, laws and justice were by imitation taken from monarchy; by virtue whereof, as by fire removed from its natural orb, the multitude, as the dirt and dregs of men, was as it were quickened and formed into a civil person; which is termed aristocracy or democracy. But the author and abettors being found, who might securely and quietly have lived under the natural jurisdiction of kings, do thus smart for it; that being exposed still to alteration, they are tormented with perpetual cares, suspicions, and dissensions.

have not an equal right, surely an aristocracy must be unreasonable also. But because we have showed that the state of equality is the state of war, and that therefore inequality was introduced by a general consent; this inequality, whereby he whom we have voluntarily given more to, enjoys more, is no longer to be accounted an unreasonable thing. The inconveniences therefore which attend the dominion of *one* man, attend his *person*, not his *unity*. Let us therefore see whether brings with it the greater grievances to the subject, the command of *one* man, or of *many*.

5. But first we must remove their opinion, who deny that to be any city at all, which is compacted of never so great a number of servants under a common lord. In the ninth article of the fifth chapter, a city is defined to be *one person* made out of *many men*, whose will by their own contracts is to be esteemed as the wills of them all; insomuch as he may use the strength and faculties of each single person for the public peace and safety. And by the same article of the same chapter, *one person* is that, when the wills of many are contained in the will of one. But the will of each servant is contained in the will of his lord; as hath been declared in the fifth article of the eighth chapter; so as he may employ all their forces and faculties according to his own will and pleasure. It follows therefore that that must needs be a city, which is constituted by *a lord and many servants*. Neither can any reason be brought to contradict this, which doth not equally combat against a city constituted by *a father and his sons*. For to a lord who hath no children, *servants* are in the nature of *sons*; for they are both his honour and safeguard; neither are *servants* more subject to their *lords*, than *children* to their *parents*, as hath been manifested above in the fifth article of the eighth chapter.

6. Among other grievances of supreme authority one is, that the ruler, beside those monies necessary for pub-

lic charges, as the maintaining of public ministers, building, and defending of castles, waging wars, honourably sustaining his own household, may also, if he will, exact others through his lust, whereby to enrich his sons, kindred, favourites, and flatterers too. I confess this is a grievance, but of the number of those which accompany all kinds of government, but are more tolerable in a *monarchy* than in a *democracy*. For though the monarch would enrich them, they cannot be many, because belonging but to one. But in a *democracy*, look how many demagogues, that is, how many powerful orators there are with the people (which ever are many, and daily new ones growing), so many children, kinsmen, friends, and flatterers are to be rewarded. For every of them desire not only to make their families as potent, as illustrious in wealth, as may be, but also to oblige others to them by benefits, for the better strengthening of themselves. A *monarch* may in great part satisfy his officers and friends, because they are not many, without any cost to his subjects; I mean without robbing them of any of those treasures given in for the maintenance of war and peace. In a *democracy*, where many are to be satisfied, and always new ones, this cannot be done without the subject's oppression. Though a *monarch* may promote unworthy persons, yet oft times he will not do it; but in a *democracy*, all the popular men are therefore supposed to do it, because it is necessary; for else the power of them who did it, would so increase, as it would not only become dreadful to those others, but even to the whole city also.

7. Another grievance is, that same perpetual fear of death, which every man must necessarily be in while he considers with himself, that the ruler hath power not only to appoint what punishments he lists on any transgressions, but that he may also in his wrath and sensuality slaughter his innocent subjects, and those who never offended against the laws. And truly this is a very great

grievance in any form of government, wheresoever it happens; for it is therefore a grievance, because it is, not because it may be done. But it is the fault of the ruler, not of the government. For all the acts of Nero are not essential to monarchy; yet subjects are less often undeservedly condemned under *one ruler*, than under the *people*. For kings are only severe against those who either trouble them with impertinent counsels, or oppose them with reproachful words, or control their wills; but they are the cause that that excess of power which one subject might have above another, becomes harmless. Wherefore some Nero or Caligula reigning, no men can undeservedly suffer but such as are known to him, namely, courtiers, and such as are remarkable for some eminent charge; and not all neither, but they only who are possessed of what he desires to enjoy. For they that are offensive and contumelious, are deservedly punished. Whosoever therefore in a *monarchy* will lead a retired life, let him be what he will that reigns, he is out of danger. For the ambitious only suffer; the rest are protected from the injuries of the more potent. But in a popular dominion, there may be as many Neros as there are orators who soothe the *people*. For each one of them can do as much as the *people*, and they mutually give way to each other's appetite, as it were by this secret pact, *spare me to-day and I'll spare thee to-morrow*, while they exempt those from punishment, who to satisfy their lust and private hatred have undeservedly slain their fellow subjects. Furthermore, there is a certain limit in private power, which if it exceed, it may prove pernicious to the realm; and by reason whereof it is necessary sometimes for *monarchs* to have a care, that the commonweal do thence receive no prejudice. When therefore this power consisted in the multitude of riches, they lessened it by diminishing their heaps; but if it were in popular applause, the powerful party, without any other crime laid to his charge, was taken from among them. The same was usually practised in *democracies*. For the Athenians inflicted a punishment of ten years' banishment on those that were powerful, merely because of their powers, without the guilt of any other crime. And those who by liberal gifts did seek the favour of the common people, were put to death at Rome, as men ambitious of a kingdom. In this *democracy* and *monarchy* were even; yet differed they much in fame. Because fame derives from the people; and what is done by many, is commended by many. And therefore what the *monarch* does, is said to be done out of envy to their virtues; which if it were done by the *people*, would be accounted|policy.|

8. There are some, who therefore imagine *monarchy* to be more grievous than *democracy*, because there is less liberty in that, than in this. If by liberty they mean an exemption from that subjection which is due to the laws, that is, the commands of the *people*; neither in *democracy*, nor in any other state of government whatsoever, is there any such kind of liberty. If they suppose liberty to consist in this, that there be few laws, few prohibitions, and those too such, that except they were forbidden, there could be no peace; then I deny that there is more liberty in *democracy* than *monarchy*; for the one as truly consisteth with such a liberty as the other. For although the word *liberty* may in large and ample letters be written over the gates of any city whatsoever, yet is it not meant the *subject's*, but the *city's* liberty; neither can that word with better right be inscribed on a city which is governed by the *people*, than that which is ruled by a *monarch*. But when private men or subjects demand liberty, under the name of liberty they ask not for liberty, but *dominion*; which yet for want of understanding they little consider. For if every man would grant the same liberty to another, which he desires for himself, as is commanded by the law of nature; that same natural state would return again, in

which all men may by right do all things; which if they knew, they would abhor, as being worse than all kinds of civil subjection whatsoever. But if any man desire to have his single freedom, the rest being bound, what does he else demand but to have the *dominion?* For whoso is freed from all bonds, is lord over all those that still continue bound. Subjects therefore have no greater liberty in a *popular,* than in a *monarchical* state. That which deceives them is the equal participation of command and public places. For where the authority is in the people, single subjects do so far forth share in it, as they are parts of the people ruling; and they equally partake in public offices, so far forth as they have equal voices in choosing magistrates and public ministers. And this is that which Aristotle aimed at, himself also through the custom of that time miscalling dominion liberty (*Polit.* lib. vi. cap. 2). *In a popular state there is liberty by supposition; which is a speech of the vulgar, as if no man were free out of this state.* From whence, by the way, we may collect, that those subjects who in a *monarchy* deplore their lost liberty, do only stomach this, that they are not received to the steerage of the commonweal.

9. But perhaps for this very reason, some will say that a *popular* state is much to be preferred before a *monarchical;* because that where all men have a hand in public businesses, there all have an opportunity to show their wisdom, knowledge, and eloquence, in deliberating matters of the greatest difficulty and moment; which by reason of that desire of praise which is bred in human nature, is to them who excel in such-like faculties, and seem to themselves to exceed others, the most delightful of all things. But in a monarchy, this same way to obtain praise and honour is shut up to the greatest part of subjects; and what is a grievance if this be none? I will tell you: to see his opinion, whom we scorn, preferred before ours; to have our wisdom undervalued before our own faces;

by an uncertain trial of a little vain glory, to undergo
most certain enmities (for this cannot be avoided,
whether we have the better or the worse); to hate and to
be hated, by reason of the disagreement of opinions; to
lay open our secret councils and advices to all, to no purpose and without any benefit; to neglect the affairs of
our own family: these, I say, are grievances. But to be
absent from a trial of wits, although those trials are pleasant to the eloquent, is not therefore a grievance to them;
unless we will say, that it is a grievance to valiant men to
be restrained from fighting, because they delight in it.

10. Besides, there are many reasons why deliberations
are less successful in great assemblies than in lesser councils. Whereof one is, that to advise rightly of all things
conducing to the preservation of a commonweal, we must
not only understand matters at home, but foreign affairs
too. At home, by what goods the country is nourished
and defended, and whence they are fetched; what places
are fit to make garrisons of; by what means soldiers are
best to be raised and maintained; what manner of affections the subjects bear towards their prince or governors
of their country; and many the like. Abroad, what the
power of each neighbouring country is, and wherein it
consists; what advantage or disadvantage we may receive
from them; what their dispositions are both to usward,
and how affected to each other among themselves; and
what counsel daily passeth among them. Now, because
very few in a great assembly of men understand these
things, being for the most part unskilful, that I say not
incapable of them, what can that same number of advisers
with their impertinent opinions contribute to good counsels, other than mere lets and impediments?

11. Another reason why a great assembly is not so fit
for consultation is, because every one who delivers his
opinion holds it necessary to make a long-continued
speech; and to gain the more esteem from his auditors,

he polishes and adorns it with the best and smoothest language. Now the nature of eloquence is to make *good* and *evil, profitable* and *unprofitable, honest* and *dishonest,* appear to be more or less than indeed they are; and to make that seem *just* which is *unjust,* according as it shall best suit with his end that speaketh: for this is to persuade. And though they reason, yet take they not their rise from true principles, but from vulgar received opinions, which for the most part are erroneous. Neither endeavour they so much to fit their speech to the nature of the things they speak of, as to the passions of their minds to whom they speak; whence it happens, that opinions are delivered not by right reason, but by a certain violence of mind. Nor is this fault in the *man,* but in the nature itself of *eloquence,* whose end, as all the masters of rhetoric teach us, is not truth (except by chance), but victory; and whose property is not to inform, but to allure.

12. The third reason why men advise less successfully in a great convent is, because that thence arise *factions* in a commonweal; and out of *factions,* seditions and civil war. For when equal orators do combat with contrary opinions and speeches, the conquered hates the conqueror and all those that were of his side, as holding his council and wisdom in scorn, and studies all means to make the advice of his adversaries prejudicial to the state: for thus he hopes to see the glory taken from him, and restored unto himself. Furthermore, where the votes are not so unequal, but that the conquered have hopes, by the accession of some few of their own opinion, at another sitting to make the stronger party, the chief heads do call the rest together; they advise a part how they may abrogate the former judgment given; they appoint to be the first and earliest at the next convent; they determine what, and in what order each man shall speak, that the same business may again be brought to agitation; that so what was confirmed before by the number of their then

present adversaries, the same may now in some measure
become of no effect to them, being negligently absent.
And this same kind of industry and diligence which they
use to *make* a people, is commonly called a *faction*. But
when a *faction* is inferior in votes, and superior, or not
much inferior in power, then what they cannot obtain
by craft and language, they attempt by force of arms; and
so it comes to a civil war. But some will say, these things
do not necessarily, nor often happen. He may as well say,
that the chief parties are not necessarily desirous of vain
glory, and that the greatest of them seldom disagree in
great matters.

13. It follows hence, that when the legislative power
resides in such convents as these, the laws must needs be
inconstant; and change, not according to the alteration
of the state of affairs, nor according to the changeable-
ness of men's minds, but as the major part, now of this,
then of that *faction*, do convene. Insomuch as the laws
do float here and there, as it were upon the waters.

14. In the fourth place, the counsels of great assemblies
have this inconvenience; that whereas it is oft of great
consequence that they should be kept secret, they are for
the most part discovered to the enemy before they
can be brought to any effect; and their power and will is
as soon known abroad, as to the *people* itself commanding at home.

15. These inconveniences, which are found in the deliberations of great assemblies, do so far forth evince *monarchy* to be better than *democracy*, as in *democracy*
affairs of great consequence are oftener trusted to be discussed by such like committees, than in a *monarchy*. Neither can it easily be done otherwise. For there is no reason why every man should not naturally mind his *own
private*, than the *public* business, but that here he sees a
means to declare his eloquence, whereby he may gain the
reputation of being ingenious and wise, and returning

home to his friends, to his parents, to his wife and children, rejoice and triumph in the applause of his dexterous behaviour. As of old, all the delight Marcus Coriolanus had in his warlike actions, was to see his praises so well pleasing to his mother. But if the *people* in a democracy would bestow the power of deliberating in matters of war and peace, either on one, or some very few, being content with the nomination of magistrates and public ministers, that is to say, with the authority without the ministration; then it must be confessed, that in this particular *democracy* and *monarchy* would be equal.

16. Neither do the conveniences or inconveniences which are found to be more in one kind of government than another, arise from hence, namely, because the government itself, or the administration of its affairs, are better committed to one than many; or on the other side, to many than to some few. For government is the *power*, the administration of it is the *act*. Now the *power* in all kinds of government is equal; the *acts* only differ, that is to say, the *actions* and *motions* of a commonweal, as they flow from the deliberations of many or few, of skilful or impertinent men. Whence we understand, that the conveniences or inconveniences of any government depend not on him in whom the authority resides, but on his officers; and therefore nothing hinders but that the commonweal may be well governed, although the *monarch* be a woman, or youth, or infant, provided that they be fit for affairs who are endued with the public offices and charges. And that which is said, *woe to the land whose king is a child,* doth not signify the condition of a monarchy to be inferior to a popular state; but contrariwise, that by accident it is the grievance of a kingdom, that the *king being a child,* it often happens, that many by ambition and power intruding themselves into public councils, the government comes to be administered in a

democratical manner; and that thence arise those infelici-
ties, which for the most part accompany the *dominion of
the people.*

17. But it is a manifest sign that the most absolute *monarchy* is the best state of government, that not only kings,
but even those cities which are subject to the *people* or
to *nobles*, give the whole command of war to one only;
and that so absolute, as nothing can be more. Wherein,
by the way, this must be noted also; that no king can give
a general greater authority over his army, than he himself
by right may exercise over all his subjects. *Monarchy*
therefore is the best of all governments in the camps. But
what else are many commonwealths, than so many camps
strengthened with arms and men against each other;
whose state, because not restrained by any common
power, howsoever an uncertain peace, like a short truce,
may pass between them, is to be accounted for the state
of nature; which is the state of war.

18. Lastly, since it was necessary for the preservation
of ourselves to be subject to some *man* or *council*, we cannot on better condition be subject to any, than one whose
interest depends upon our safety and welfare; and this
then comes to pass, when we are the inheritance of the
ruler. For every man of his own accord endeavours the
preservation of his inheritance. But the 'lands and monies
of the subjects are not only the prince's treasure, but their
bodies and wily minds. Which will be easily granted by
those, who consider at how great rates the dominion of
lesser countries is valued; and how much easier it is for
men to procure money, than money men. Nor do we
readily meet with any example that shows us when any
subject, without any default of his own, hath by his
prince been despoiled of his life or goods, through the
sole licentiousness of his authority.

19. Hitherto we have compared a *monarchical* with a
popular state; we have said nothing of *aristocracy*. We

may conclude of this, by what hath been said of those, that that which is hereditary, and content with the election of magistrates; which transmits its deliberations to some few, and those most able; which simply imitates the government of *monarchs* most, and the *people* least of all; is for the subjects both better and more lasting than the rest.

XI

Places and Examples of Scripture of the Rights of Government, Agreeable to What Hath Been Said Before

1. The beginning of institutive government from the consent of the people. 2. Judicature and wars depend on the will of supreme commanders. 3. That they who have the chief authority, are by right unpunishable. 4. That without a supreme power there is no government, but anarchy. 5. That from servants and sons there is a simple obedience due to their lords and parents. 6. Absolute authority proved by most evident places, as well of the New as the Old Testament.

1. We have, in the sixth chapter and the second article, so derived the original of institutive or political government from the consent of the multitude, that it appears they must either all consent, or be esteemed as enemies. Such was the beginning of God's government over the Jews instituted by Moses (Exod. xix. 5–8): *If ye will obey my voice indeed, &c. Ye shall be unto me a kingdom of priests, &c. And Moses came and called the elders of the people, &c. And all the people answered, and said: All that the Lord hath spoken we will do.* Such also was the beginning of Moses's power under God, or his vicegerency (Exod. xx. 18–19): *And all the people saw the thunderings and lightenings, and the noise of the trumpet, &c. And they said unto Moses, speak thou unto us, and we will hear.* The like beginning also had Saul's kingdom (1 Sam. xii. 12, 13): *When ye saw that Nahash king of the children of Ammon came out against you, ye said unto me, nay, but a king shall reign over us, when*

*the Lord your God was your king. Now therefore behold
the king whom ye have chosen, and whom ye have desired.* But the major part only consenting, and not all;
for there were certain *sons of Belial,* who said (1 Sam. x.
27), *How shall this man save us? And they despised him;*
those who did not consent, were put to death as enemies.
And the people said unto Samuel (1 Sam. xi. 12): *Who
is he that said, shall Saul reign over us? Bring the men,
that we may put them to death.*

2. In the same sixth chapter, the sixth and seventh
articles, I have showed that all *judgment* and *wars* depend upon the will and pleasure of him who bears the
supreme authority; that is to say, in a *monarchy,* on a
monarch or king; and this is confirmed by the people's
own judgment. 1 Sam. viii. 20; *We also will be like all the
nations, and our king shall judge us, and go out before
us, and fight our battles.* And what pertains to *judgments,*
and all other matters whereof there is any controversy,
whether they be *good* or *evil,* is confirmed by the testimony of King Solomon (1 Kings iii. 9): *Give therefore
thy servant an understanding heart to judge thy people,
that I may discern between good and evil.* And that of
Absolom (2 Sam. xv. 3): *There is no man deputed of
the king to hear thee.*

3. That kings may not be punished by their subjects,
as hath been showed above in the sixth chapter and the
twelfth article, King David also confirms; who, though
Saul sought to slay him, did notwithstanding refrain his
hand from killing him, and forbade Abishai, saying (1
Sam. xxvi. 9): *Destroy him not; for who can stretch forth
his hand against the Lord's anointed, and be innocent?*
And when he had cut off the skirt of his garment (1 Sam.
xxiv. 6): *The Lord forbid,* saith he, *that I should do this
thing unto my master the Lord's anointed, to stretch
forth mine hand against him.* And (2 Sam. i. 15) com-

manded the Amalekite, who for his sake had slain Saul, to be put to death.

4. That which is said in the seventeenth chapter of *Judges*, at the sixth verse: *In those days there was no king in Israel, but every man did that which was right in his own eyes:* as though where there were not a *monarchy*, there were an *anarchy* or confusion of all things: may be brought as a testimony to prove the excellency of monarchy above all other forms of government; unless that by the word *king* may perhaps be understood not *one man* only, but also a *court*; provided that in it there reside a supreme power. Which if it be taken in this sense, yet hence it may follow, that without a supreme and absolute power (which we have endeavoured to prove in the sixth chapter) there will be a liberty for every man to do what he hath a mind, or whatsoever shall seem right to himself; which cannot stand with the preservation of mankind. And therefore in all government whatsoever, there is ever a supreme power understood to be somewhere existent.

5. We have, in chap. VIII. art. 7 and 8, said that *servants* must yield a simple obedience to their *lords*, and in chap. IX. art. 7, that *sons* owe the same obedience to their *parents*. Saint Paul says the same thing concerning servants (Coloss. iii. 22): *Servants obey in all things your masters according to the flesh, not with eye-service, as men-pleasers, but in singleness of heart, fearing God.* Concerning sons (Coloss. iii. 20): *Children obey your parents in all things, for this is well-pleasing unto the Lord.* Now as we by simple obedience understand all things which are not contrary to the laws of God; so in those cited places of St. Paul, after the word *all things*, we must suppose, *excepting those which are contrary to the laws of God.*

6. But that I may not thus by piecemeal prove the right of princes, I will now instance those testimonies which

altogether establish the whole power; namely, that there
is an absolute and simple obedience due to them from
their subjects. And first out of the New Testament:
Matth. xxiii. 2, 3: *The Scribes and Pharisees sit in Moses'
seat; all therefore, whatsoever they bid you observe, that
observe and do.* Whatsoever they bid you (says he) *observe,* that is to say, *obey simply.* Why? Because they *sit
in Moses' seat;* namely, the *civil magistrate's,* not Aaron,
the priest's. Rom. xiii. 1, 2: *Let every soul be subject to
the higher powers; for there is no power but of God; the
powers that be are ordained of God; whosoever therefore
resisteth the power, resisteth the ordinance of God; and
they that resist, shall receive to themselves damnation.*
Now because the powers that were in St. Paul's time, were
ordained of God, and all kings did at that time require an
absolute entire obedience from their subjects, it follows
that such a power was ordained of God. 1 Peter ii. 13–15:
*Submit yourselves unto every ordinance of man for the
Lord's sake, whether it be to the king as supreme, or unto
governors as unto them that are sent by him for the punishment of wicked doers, and for the praise of them that
do well; for so is the will of God.* Again St. Paul to Titus
(chap. iii. 1): *Put them in mind to be subject to principalities and powers, to obey magistrates,* &c. What principalities? Was it not to the principalities of those times,
which required an absolute obedience? Furthermore, that
we may come to the example of Christ himself, to whom
the kingdom of the Jews belonged by hereditary right
derived from David himself; he, when he lived in the manner of a subject, both paid tribute unto Cæsar, and pronounced it to be due to him, Matth. xxii. 21: *Give unto
Cæsar* (saith he) *the things which are Cæsar's, and unto
God the things which are God's.* When it pleased him
to show himself a king, he required entire obedience,
Matth. xxi. 2, 3: *Go* (said he) *into the village over against
you, and straight-way ye shall find an ass tied, and a colt*

with her; loose them, and bring them unto me; and if any man say aught unto you, ye shall say the Lord hath need of them. This he did therefore by the right of being lord, or a king of the Jews. But to take away a subject's goods on this pretence only, because *the Lord hath need of them,* is an absolute power. The most evident places in the Old Testament are these: Deut. v. 27: *Go thou near, and hear all that the Lord our God shall say; and speak thou unto us all that the Lord our God shall speak unto thee, and we will hear it, and do it.* But under the word *all,* is contained absolute obedience. Again to Joshua (Joshua i. 16–18): *And they answered Joshua, saying, all that thou commandest us, we will do; and whithersoever thou sendest us, we will go; according as we hearkened unto Moses in all things, so will we hearken unto thee; only the Lord thy God be with thee, as he was with Moses; whosoever he be that doth rebel against thy commandment, and will not hearken unto thy words in all that thou commandest him, he shall be put to death.* And the parable of the bramble (Judges ix. 14, 15): *Then said all the trees unto the bramble, Come thou and reign over us. And the bramble said unto the trees, If in truth ye anoint me king over you, then come and put your trust in my shadow; and if not, let fire come out of the bramble, and devour the cedars of Lebanon.* The sense of which words is, that we must acquiesce to their sayings, whom we have truly constituted to be kings over us, unless we would choose rather to be consumed by the fire of a civil war. But the regal authority is more particularly described by God himself, in 1 Sam. viii. 9, &c.: *Show them the right of the king that shall reign over them, &c. This shall be the right of the king that shall reign over you; he will take your sons, and appoint them for himself, for his chariots, and to be his horsemen, and some shall run before his chariots, &c. And he will take your daughters to be confectionaries, &c. And he will take your vineyards,*

and give them to his servants, &c. Is not this power absolute? And yet it is by God himself styled the *king's
right.* Neither was any man among the Jews, no not the
high-priest himself, exempted from this obedience. For
when the king, namely, Solomon, said to Abiathar the
priest (1 Kings ii. 26, 27): *Get thee to Anathoth unto
thine own fields; for thou art worthy of death; but I will
not at this time put thee to death, because thou barest
the ark of the Lord God before David my father, and because thou hast been afflicted in all wherein my father
was afflicted. So Solomon thrust out Abiathar from being
priest unto the Lord;* it cannot by any argument be
proved, that this act of his displeased the Lord; neither
read we, that either Solomon was reproved, or that his
person at that time was any whit less acceptable to God.

XII

Of the Internal Causes Tending to the Dissolution of Any Government

1. That *the judging of good and evil belongs to private persons* is a seditious opinion. 2. That *subjects do sin by obeying their princes* is a seditious opinion. 3. That *tyrannicide is lawful* is a seditious opinion. 4. That *those who have the supreme power are subject to the civil laws* is a seditious opinion. 5. That *the supreme power may be divided* is a seditious opinion. 6. That *faith and sanctity are not acquired by study and reason, but always supernaturally infused and inspired,* is a seditious opinion. 7. That *each subject hath a propriety or absolute dominion of his own goods* is a seditious opinion. 8. Not to understand the difference between the people and the multitude, prepares toward sedition. 9. Too great a tax of monies, though never so just and necessary, prepares toward sedition. 10. Ambition disposeth us to sedition. 11. So doth the hope of success. 12. Eloquence alone without wisdom, is the only faculty needful to raise seditions. 13. How the folly of the common people, and the elocution of ambitious men, concur to the destruction of a commonweal.

1. Hitherto hath been spoken, by what causes and pacts commonweals are constituted, and what the rights of princes are over their subjects. Now we will briefly say somewhat concerning the causes which dissolve them, or the reasons of seditions. Now as in the motion of natural bodies three things are to be considered, namely, *internal disposition,* that they be susceptible of the motion to be produced; the *external agent,* whereby a certain and determined motion may in act be produced; and the *action*

itself: so also in a commonweal where the subjects begin
to raise tumults, three things present themselves to our
regard; first, the *doctrines* and the *passions* contrary to
peace, wherewith the minds of men are fitted and disposed; next, their quality and condition who solicit, assemble, and direct them, already thus disposed, to take
up arms and quit their allegiance; lastly, the manner how
this is done, or the *faction* itself. But one and the first
which disposeth them to sedition, is this, *that the knowledge of good and evil belongs to each single man.* In the
state of nature indeed, where every man lives by equal
right, and has not by any mutual pacts submitted to the
command of others, we have granted this to be true; nay,
[proved it] in chap. I. art. 9. [But in the civil state it is
false. For it was shown (chap. VI. art. 9)] that the civil
laws were the rules of *good* and *evil*, *just* and *unjust*, *honest* and *dishonest*; that therefore what the legislator commands, must be held for *good*, and what he forbids for
evil. And the legislator is ever that person who hath the
supreme power in the commonweal, that is to say, the
monarch in a monarchy. We have confirmed the same
truth in chap. XI. art. 2, out of the words of Solomon. For
if private men may pursue that as good and shun that as
evil, which appears to them to be so, to what end serve
those words of his: *Give therefore unto thy servant an
understanding heart, to judge thy people, that I may discern between good and evil?* Since therefore it belongs to
kings to discern between *good* and *evil*, wicked are those,
though usual, sayings, *that he only is a king who does
righteously*, and *that kings must not be obeyed unless
they command us just things*; and many other such like.
Before there was any government, *just* and *unjust* had
no being, their nature only being relative to some command: and every action in its own nature is indifferent;
that it becomes *just* or *unjust*, proceeds from the right
of the magistrate. Legitimate kings therefore make the

things they command just, by commanding them, and those which they forbid, unjust, by forbidding them. But private men, while they assume to themselves the knowledge of *good* and *evil*, desire to be even as kings; which cannot be with the safety of the commonweal. The most ancient of all God's commands is (Gen. ii. 17): *Thou shalt not eat of the tree of knowledge of good and evil:* and the most ancient of all diabolical temptations (Gen. iii. 5): *Ye shall be as gods, knowing good and evil;* and God's first expostulation with man (verse 11): *Who told thee that thou wert naked? Hast thou eaten of the tree, whereof I commanded thee that thou shouldst not eat?* As if he had said, how comest thou to judge that nakedness, wherein it seemed good to me to create thee, to be shameful, except thou have arrogated to thyself the knowledge of *good and evil.*

2. Whatsoever any man doth against his conscience, is a sin; for he who doth so, contemns the law. But we must distinguish. That is my sin indeed, which committing I do believe to be my sin; but what I believe to be another man's sin, I may sometimes do that without any sin of mine. For if I be commanded to do that which is a sin in him who commands me, if I do it, and he that commands me be by right lord over me, I sin not. For if I wage war at the commandment of my prince, conceiving the war to be unjustly undertaken, I do not therefore do unjustly; but rather if I refuse to do it, arrogating to myself the knowledge of what is just and unjust, which pertains only to my prince. They who observe not this distinction, will fall into a necessity of sinning, as oft as anything is commanded them which either is, or seems to be unlawful to them: for if they obey, they sin against their conscience; and if they obey not, against right. If they sin against their conscience, they declare that they fear not the pains of the world to come; if they sin against right, they do, as much as in them lies, abolish human society and the civil

life of the present world. Their opinion therefore who teach, *that subjects sin when they obey their prince's commands which to them seem unjust,* is both erroneous, and to be reckoned among those which are contrary to civil obedience; and it depends upon that original error which we have observed above, in the foregoing article. For by our taking upon us to judge of *good* and *evil,* we are the occasion that as well our obedience, as disobedience, becomes sin unto us.

3. The third seditious doctrine springs from the same root, that *tyrannicide is lawful*; nay, at this day it is by many divines, and of old it was by all the philosophers, Plato, Aristotle, Cicero, Seneca, Plutarch, and the rest of the maintainers of the Greek and Roman anarchies, held not only lawful, but even worthy of the greatest praise. And under the title of *tyrants,* they mean not only monarchs, but all those who bear the chief rule in any government whatsoever; for not Pisistratus only at Athens, but those Thirty also who succeeded him, and ruled together, were all called *tyrants.* But he whom men require to be put to death as being *a tyrant,* commands either by right or without right. If without right, he is an enemy, and by right to be put to death; but then this must not be called the *killing a tyrant,* but an *enemy.* If by right, then the divine interrogation takes place: *Who hath told thee that he was a tyrant? Hast thou eaten of the tree, whereof I commanded thee that thou shouldst not eat?* For why dost thou call him a *tyrant,* whom God hath made a *king,* except that thou, being a private person, usurpest to thyself the knowledge of *good* and *evil?* But how pernicious this opinion is to all governments, but especially to that which is *monarchical,* we may hence discern; namely, that by it every *king,* whether good or ill, stands exposed to be condemned by the judgment, and slain by the hand of every murderous villain.

4. The fourth|opinion adversary|to civil society, is their's

who hold, *that they who bear rule are subject also to the civil laws.* Which hath been sufficiently proved before not to be true, in chap. vi. art. 14, from this argument: that a city can neither be bound to itself, nor to any subject; not to itself, because no man can be obliged except it be to another; not to any subject, because the single wills of the subjects are contained in the will of the city; insomuch that if the city will be free from all such obligation, the subjects will so too; and by consequence she is so. But that which holds true in a city, that must be supposed to be true in a man, or an assembly of men who have the supreme authority; for they make a city, which hath no being but by their supreme power. Now that this opinion cannot consist with the very being of government, is evident from hence; that by it the knowledge of what is *good* and *evil*, that is to say, the definition of what is, and what is not against the laws, would return to each single person. Obedience therefore will cease, as oft as anything seems to be commanded contrary to the civil laws, and together with it all coercive jurisdiction; which cannot possibly be without the destruction of the very essence of government. Yet this error hath great props, Aristotle and others; who, by reason of human infirmity, suppose the supreme power to be committed with most security to the laws only. But they seem to have looked very shallowly into the nature of government, who thought that the constraining power, the interpretation of laws, and the making of laws, all which are powers necessarily belonging to government, should be left wholly to the laws themselves. Now although particular subjects may sometimes contend in judgment, and go to law with the supreme magistrate; yet this is only then, when the question is not what the magistrate may, but what by a certain rule he hath declared he would do. As, when by any law the judges sit upon the life of a subject, the question is not whether the magistrate could by his absolute right

deprive him of his life; but whether by that law his will
was that he should be deprived of it. But his will was, he
should, if he brake the law; else his will was, he should
not. This therefore, that a subject may have an action of
law against his supreme magistrate, is not strength of argument sufficient to prove that he is tied to his own laws.
On the contrary, it is evident that he is not tied to his
own laws; because no man is bound to himself. Laws
therefore are set for Titius and Caius, not for the ruler.
However, by the ambition of lawyers it is so ordered, that
the laws to unskilful men seem not to depend on the authority of the magistrate, but their prudence.

5. In the fifth place, *that the supreme authority may
be divided*, is a most fatal opinion to all commonweals.
But diverse men divide it diverse ways. For some divide
it, so as to grant a supremacy to the civil power in matters pertaining to peace and the benefits of this life; but
in things concerning the salvation of the soul they transfer it on others. Now, because justice is of all things most
necessary to salvation, it happens that subjects measuring
justice, not as they ought, by the civil laws, but by the
precepts and doctrines of them who, in regard of the
magistrate, are either private men or strangers, through
a superstitious fear dare not perform the obedience due
to their princes; through fear falling into that which they
most feared. Now what can be more pernicious to any
state, than that men should, by the apprehension of everlasting torments, be deterred from obeying their princes,
that is to say, the laws; or from being just? There are also
some, who divide the supreme authority so as to allow
the power of war and peace unto one whom they call a
monarch; but the right of raising money they give to some
others, and not to him. But because monies are the
sinews of war and peace, they who thus divide the authority, do either really not divide it at all, but place it wholly
in them in whose power the money is, but give the name

of it to another: or if they do really divide it, they dissolve the government. For neither upon necessity can war be waged, nor can the public peace be preserved without money.

6. It is a common doctrine, *that faith and holiness are not acquired by study and natural reason, but are always supernaturally infused and inspired into men*. Which, if it were true, I understand not why we should be commanded to give an account of our faith; or why any man, who is truly a Christian, should not be a prophet; or lastly, why every man should not judge what is fit for him to do, what to avoid, rather out of his own inspiration, than by the precepts of his superiors or right reason. A return therefore must be made to the private knowledge of *good* and *evil*; which cannot be granted without the ruin of all governments. This opinion hath spread itself so largely through the whole Christian world, that the number of apostates from natural reason is almost become infinite. And it sprang from sick-brained men, who having gotten good store of holy words by frequent reading of the Scriptures, made such a connexion of them usually in their preaching, that their sermons, signifying just nothing, yet to unlearned men seemed most divine. For he whose nonsense appears to be a divine speech, must necessarily seem to be inspired from above.

7. The seventh doctrine opposite to government, is this; *that each subject hath an absolute dominion over the goods he is in possession of*: that is to say, such a *propriety* as excludes not only the right of all the rest of his fellow subjects to the same goods, but also of the magistrate himself. Which is not true; for they who have a *lord* over them, have themselves no *lordship*, as hath been proved chap. VIII. art. 5. Now the magistrate is lord of all his subjects, by the constitution of government. Before the yoke of civil society was undertaken, no man had any *proper right*; all things were *common* to all men. Tell me

therefore, how gottest thou this *propriety* but from the magistrate? How got the magistrate it, but that every man transferred his right on him? And thou therefore hast also given up thy right to him. Thy *dominion* therefore, and *propriety*, is just so much as he will, and shall last so long as he pleases; even as in a family, each son hath such *proper* goods, and so long lasting, as seems good to the father. But the greatest part of men who profess civil prudence, reason otherwise. We are equal, say they, by nature; there is no reason why any man should by better right take my goods from me, than I his from him. We know that money sometimes is needful for the defence and maintenance of the public; but let them who require it, show us the present necessity, and they shall willingly receive it. They who talk thus know not, that what they would have, is already done from the beginning, in the very constitution of government; and therefore speaking as in a dissolute multitude and yet not fashioned government, they destroy the frame.

8. In the last place, it is a great hindrance to civil government, especially monarchical, that men distinguish not enough between a *people* and a *multitude*. The *people* is somewhat that is *one*, having *one will*, and to whom *one action* may be attributed; none of these can properly be said of a multitude. The *people* rules in all governments. For even in *monarchies* the *people* commands; for the *people* wills by the will of *one man*; but the multitude are citizens, that is to say, subjects. In a *democracy* and *aristocracy*, the citizens are the *multitude*, but the *court* is the *people*. And in a *monarchy*, the subjects are the *multitude*, and (however it seem a paradox) the king is the *people*. The common sort of men, and others who little consider these truths, do always speak of a *great number* of men as of the *people*, that is to say, the *city*. They say, that the *city* hath rebelled against the *king* (which is impossible), and that the *people* will and nill

what murmuring and discontented subjects would have or would not have; under pretence of the *people* stirring up the *citizens* against the *city*, that is to say, the *multitude* against the *people*. And these are almost all the opinions, wherewith subjects being tainted do easily tumult. And forasmuch as in all manner of government majesty is to be preserved by him or them, who have the supreme authority; the *crimen læsæ majestatis* naturally cleaves to these opinions.

9. There is nothing more afflicts the mind of man than *poverty*, or the want of those things which are necessary for the preservation of life and honour. And though there be no man but knows that riches are gotten with industry, and kept by frugality, yet all the poor commonly lay the blame on the evil government, excusing their own sloth and luxury; as if their private goods forsooth were wasted by public exactions. But men must consider, that they who have no patrimony, must not only labour that they may live, but fight too that they may labour. Every one of the Jews, who in Esdras' time built the walls of Jerusalem, did the work with one hand, and held the sword in the other. In all government, we must conceive that the hand which holds the sword is the *king* or *supreme council*, which is no less to be sustained and nourished by the subjects' care and industry, than that wherewith each man procures himself a private fortune; and that *customs* and *tributes* are nothing else but their reward who watch in arms for us, that the labours and endeavours of single men may not be molested by the incursion of enemies; and that their complaint, who impute their poverty to public persons, is not more just, than if they should say that they are become in want by paying of their debts. But the most part of men consider nothing of these things. For they suffer the same thing with them who have a disease they call an *incubus*; which springing from gluttony, it makes men believe they are invaded, op-

pressed, and stifled with a great weight. Now it is a thing manifest of itself, that they who seem to themselves to be burthened with the whole load of the commonweal, are prone to be seditious; and that they are affected with change, who are distasted at the present state of things.

10. Another noxious disease of the mind is theirs, who having little employment, want honour and dignity. All men naturally strive for honour and preferment; but chiefly they, who are least troubled with caring for necessary things. For these men are invited by their vacancy, sometimes to disputation among themselves concerning the commonweal, sometimes to an easy reading of histories, politics, orations, poems, and other pleasant books; and it happens that hence they think themselves sufficiently furnished both with wit and learning, to administer matters of the greatest consequence. Now because all men are not what they appear to themselves; and if they were, yet all (by reason of the multitude) could not be received to public offices; it is necessary that many must be passed by. These therefore conceiving themselves affronted, can desire nothing more, partly out of envy to those who were preferred before them, partly out of hope to overwhelm them, than ill-success to the public consultations. And therefore it is no marvel, if with greedy appetites they seek for occasions of innovations.

11. *The hope of overcoming* is also to be numbered among other seditious inclinations. For let there be as many men as you will, infected with opinions repugnant to peace and civil government; let there be as many as there can, never so much wounded and torn with affronts and calumnies by them who are in authority; yet if there be no *hope of having the better of them*, or it appear not sufficient, there will no sedition follow; every man will dissemble his thoughts, and rather content himself with the present burthen than hazard a heavier weight. There are four things necessarily requisite to this *hope*. Num-

bers, instruments, mutual trust, and commanders. To resist public magistrates without a great number, is not sedition, but desperation. By instruments of war, I mean
all manner of arms, munition, and other necessary provision: without which number can do nothing. Nor arms
neither, without mutual trust. Nor all these, without
union under some commander, whom of their own accord they are content to obey; not as being engaged by
their submission to his command (for we have already in
this very chapter, supposed these kind of men not to understand being obliged beyond that which seems right
and good in their own eyes); but for some opinion they
have of his virtue, or military skill, or resemblance of hu-
mours. If these four be near at hand to men grieved with
the present state, and measuring the justice of their actions by their own judgments; there will be nothing wanting to sedition and confusion of the realm, but one to
stir up and *quicken them*.

12. Sallust's character of Cataline, than whom there
never was a greater artist in raising seditions, is this: *that
he had great eloquence, and little wisdom*. He separates
wisdom from *eloquence*; attributing this as necessary to a
man born for commotions; adjudging that as an instruc-
tress of peace and quietness. Now eloquence is twofold.
The one is an elegant and clear expression of the conceptions of the mind; and riseth partly from the contemplation of the things themselves, partly from an understanding of words taken in their own proper and
definite signification. The other is a commotion of the
passions of the mind, such as are *hope, fear, anger, pity*;
and derives from a metaphorical use of words fitted to
the passions. That forms a speech from true principles;
this from opinions already received, what nature soever
they are of. The art of that is logic, of this rhetoric; the
end of that is truth, of this victory. Each hath its use; that
in deliberations, this in exhortations; for that is never

disjoined from *wisdom*, but this almost ever. But that
this kind of powerful *eloquence*, separated from the true
knowledge of things, that is to say, from wisdom, is the
true character of them who solicit and stir up the people
to innovations, may easily be gathered out of the work
itself which they have to do. For they could not poison
the people with those absurd opinions contrary to peace
and civil society, unless they held them themselves; which
sure is an ignorance greater than can well befall any wise
man. For he that knows not whence the laws derive their
power, which are the rules of *just* and *unjust*, *honest* and
dishonest, *good* and *evil*; what makes and preserves peace
among men, what destroys it; what is *his*, and what *another's*; lastly, what he would have done to himself, that
he may do the like to others: is surely to be accounted
but meanly wise. But that they can turn their auditors
out of fools into madmen; that they can make things to
them who are ill-affected, seem worse, to them who are
well-affected, seem evil; that they can enlarge their
hopes, lessen their dangers beyond reason: this they have
from that sort of eloquence, not which explains things
as they are, but from that other, which by moving their
minds, makes all things to appear to be such as they in
their minds, prepared before, had already conceived them.

13. Many men, who are themselves very well affected
to civil society, do through want of knowledge co-operate
to the disposing of subjects' minds to *sedition*, whilst
they teach young men a doctrine conformable to the said
opinions in their schools, and all the people in their pulpits. Now they who desire to bring this disposition into
act, place their whole endeavour in this: first, that they
may join the ill-affected together into *faction* and *con-
spiracy*; next, that themselves may have the greatest
stroke in the *faction*. They gather them into *faction*,
while they make themselves the relators and interpreters
of the counsels and actions of single men, and nominate

the persons and places to assemble and deliberate of such things whereby the present government may be reformed, according as it shall seem best to their interests. Now to the end that they themselves may have the chief rule in the *faction*, the *faction* must be kept in a *faction*; that is to say, they must have their secret meetings apart with a few, where they may order what shall afterward be propounded in a general meeting, and by whom, and on what subject, and in what order each of them shall speak, and how they may draw the powerfullest and most popular men of the *faction* to their side. And thus when they have gotten a faction big enough, in which they may rule by their eloquence, they move it to take upon it the managing of affairs. And thus they sometimes oppress the commonwealth, namely, where there is no other faction to oppose them; but for the most part they rend it, and introduce a civil war. For *folly* and *eloquence* concur in the subversion of government, in the same manner (as the fable hath it) as heretofore the daughters of Pelias, king of Thessaly, conspired with Medea against their father. They going to restore the decrepit old man to his youth again, by the counsel of Medea they cut him into pieces, and set him in the fire to boil; in vain expecting when he would live again. So the common people, through their folly, like the daughters of Pelias, desiring to renew the ancient government, being drawn away by the *eloquence* of ambitious men, as it were by the witchcraft of Medea; divided into *faction* they consume it rather by those flames, than they reform it.

XIII

Concerning the Duties of Them Who Bear Rule

1. The right of supreme authority is distinguished from its exercise. 2. The safety of the people is the supreme law. 3. It behoves princes to regard the common benefit of many, |not the peculiar interest of|this or that man. 4. That by safety is understood all manner of conveniences. 5. A query, whether it be the duty of kings to provide for the salvation of their subjects' souls, as they shall judge best according to their own consciences. 6. Wherein the safety of the people consists. 7. That discoverers are necessary for the defence of the people. 8. That to have soldiers, arms, garrisons, and monies in readiness, in time of peace, is also necessary for the defence of the people. 9. A right instruction of subjects in civil doctrines, is necessary for the preserving of peace. 10. Equal distributions of public offices conduces much to the preservation of peace. 11. It is natural equity, that monies be taxed according to what every man spends, not what he possesses. 12. It conduceth to the preservation of peace, to keep down ambitious men. 13. And to break factions. 14. Laws whereby thriving arts are cherished and great costs restrained, conduce to the enriching of the subject. 15. That more ought not to be defined by the laws, than the benefit of the prince and his subjects requires. 16. That greater punishments must not be inflicted, than are prescribed by the laws. 17. Subjects must have right done them against corrupt judges.

1. By what hath hitherto been said, the *duties* of citizens and subjects in any kind of government whatsoever, and the *power* of the supreme ruler over them are apparent. But we have as yet said nothing of the *duties* of rulers, and how they ought to behave themselves towards their subjects. We must then distinguish between the

right and the *exercise* of supreme authority; for they can be divided. As for example, when he who hath the *right*, either cannot or will not be present in judging trespasses, or deliberating of affairs. For kings sometimes by reason of their age cannot order their affairs; sometimes also, though they can do it themselves, yet they judge it fitter, being satisfied in the choice of their officers and counsellors, to exercise their power by them. Now where the *right* and *exercise* are severed, there the government of the commonweal is like the ordinary government of the world; in which God, the mover of all things, produceth natural effects by the means of secondary causes. But where he to whom the right of ruling doth belong, is himself present in all judicatures, consultations, and public actions, there the administration is such, as if God, beyond the ordinary course of nature, should immediately apply himself unto all matters. We will therefore in this chapter summarily and briefly speak somewhat concerning their *duties*, who exercise authority, whether by their own or other's right. Nor is it my purpose to descend into those things, which being diverse from others, some princes may do, for this is to be left to the political practices of each commonweal.

2. Now all the duties of rulers are contained in this one sentence, *the safety of the people is the supreme law*. For although they who among men obtain the chiefest dominion, cannot be subject to laws properly so called, that is to say, to the will of men, because to be chief and subject are contradictories; yet is it their *duty* in all things, as much as possibly they can, to yield obedience unto right reason, which is the natural, moral, and divine law. But because dominions were constituted for peace's sake, and peace was sought after for safety's sake; he, who being placed in authority, shall use his power otherwise than to the safety of the people, will act against the reasons of peace, that is to say, against the laws of nature. Now as

the safety of the people dictates a law by which princes know their *duty*, so doth it also teach them an art how to procure themselves a benefit; for the power of the citizens is the power of the city, that is to say, his that bears the chief rule in any state.

3. By the people in this place we understand, not one civil person, namely, the city itself which governs, but the multitude of subjects which are governed. For the city was not instituted for its own, but for the subjects' sake: and yet a particular care is not required of *this* or *that* man. For the ruler (as such) provides no otherwise for the safety of his people, than by his laws, which are universal; and therefore he hath fully *discharged* himself, if he have thoroughly endeavoured by wholesome constitutions to establish the welfare of the most part, and made it as lasting as may be; and that no man suffer ill, but by his own default, or by some chance which could not be prevented. But it sometimes conduces to the safety of the most part, that wicked men do suffer.

4. But by *safety* must be understood, not the sole preservation of life in what condition soever, but in order to its happiness. For to this end did men freely assemble themselves and *institute* a government, that they might, as much as their human condition would afford, live delightfully. They therefore who had undertaken the administration of power in such a kind of government, would sin against the law of nature (because against their trust, who had committed that power unto them), if they should not study, as much as by good laws could be effected, to furnish their subjects abundantly, not only with the good things belonging to life, but also with those which advance to delectation. They who have acquired dominion by arms, do all desire that their subjects may be strong in body and mind, that they may serve them the better. Wherefore if they should not endeavour to provide them, not only with such things whereby they

may live, but also with such whereby they may grow strong
and lusty, they would act against their own scope and
end.

5. And first of all, princes do believe that it mainly concerns *eternal salvation*, what opinions are held of the
Deity, and what manner of worship he is to be adored
with. Which being supposed, it may be demanded
whether chief rulers, and whosoever they be, whether
one or more, who exercise supreme authority, sin not
against the law of nature, if they cause not such a doctrine and worship to be taught and practised, or permit
a contrary to be taught and practised, as they believe necessarily conduceth to the *eternal salvation* of their subjects. It is manifest that they act against their conscience;
and that they will, as much as in them lies, the eternal
perdition of their subjects. For if they willed it not, I see
no reason why they should suffer (when being supreme
they cannot be compelled) such things to be taught and
done, for which they believe them to be in a damnable
state. But we will leave this difficulty in suspense.

6. The benefits of subjects, respecting this life only,
may be distributed into four kinds. 1. That they be defended against foreign enemies. 2. That peace be preserved at home. 3. That they be enriched, as much as may
consist with public security. 4. That they enjoy a harmless
liberty. For supreme commanders can confer no more to
their civil happiness, than that being preserved from foreign and civil wars, they may quietly enjoy that wealth
which they have purchased by their own industry.

7. There are two things necessary for the people's defence; *to be warned and to be forearmed.* For the state
of commonwealths considered in themselves, is natural,
that is to say, hostile. Neither if they cease from fighting,
is it therefore to be called peace; but rather a breathing
time, in which one enemy observing the motion and
countenance of the other, values his security not accord-

ing to the pacts, but the forces and counsels of his adversary. And this by natural right, as hath been showed in chap. II. art. 11, from this, that contracts are invalid in the state of nature, as oft as any just fear doth intervene. It is therefore necessary to the defence of the city, first, that there be some who may, as near as may be, *search into* and *discover* the counsels and motions of all those who may prejudice it. For *discoverers* to ministers of state, are like the beams of the sun to the human soul. And we may more truly say in vision political, than natural, that the sensible and intelligible species of outward things, not well considered by others, are by the air transported to the soul; that is to say, to them who have the supreme authority: and therefore are they no less necessary to the preservation of the state, than the rays of the light are to the conservation of man. Or if they be compared to spiders' webs, which, extended on all sides by the finest threads, do warn them, keeping in their small|holes,|of all outward motions; they who bear rule, can no more know what is necessary to be commanded for the defence of their subjects without *spies,* than those spiders can, when they shall go forth, and whither they shall repair, without the motion of those threads.

8. Furthermore, it is necessarily requisite to the people's defence, that they be *forearmed.* Now to be forearmed is to be furnished with soldiers, arms, ships, forts, and monies, before the danger be instant; for the listing of soldiers and taking up of arms after a blow is given, is too late at least, if not impossible. In like manner, not to raise forts and appoint garrisons in convenient places before the frontiers are invaded, is to be like those country swains (as Demosthenes said), who ignorant of the art of fencing, with their bucklers guarded those parts of the body where they first felt the smart of the strokes. But they who think it then seasonable enough to raise monies for the maintenance of soldiers and other charges of war,

when the danger begins to show itself, they consider not, surely, how difficult a matter it is to wring suddenly out of close-fisted men so vast a proportion of monies. For almost all men, what they once reckon in the number of their goods, do judge themselves to have such a right and propriety in it, as they conceive themselves to be injured whensoever they are forced to employ but the least part of it for the public good. Now a sufficient stock of monies to defend the country with arms, will not soon be raised out of the treasure of imposts and customs. We must therefore, for fear of war, in time of peace hoard up good sums, if we intend the safety of the commonweal. Since therefore it necessarily belongs to rulers, for the subjects' safety to discover the enemy's counsel, to keep garrisons, and to have money in continual readiness; and that princes are, by the law of nature, bound to use their whole endeavour in procuring the welfare of their subjects: it follows, that it is not only lawful for them to send out spies, to maintain soldiers, to build forts, and to require monies for these purposes; but also not to do thus is unlawful. To which also may be added, whatsoever shall seem to conduce to the lessening of the power of foreigners whom they suspect, whether by slight or force. For rulers are bound according to their power to prevent the evils they suspect; lest peradventure they may happen through their negligence.

9. But many things are required to the conservation of inward peace; because many things concur (as hath been showed in the foregoing chapter) to its perturbation. We have there showed, that some things there are, which dispose the minds of men to sedition, others which move and quicken them so disposed. Among those which dispose them, we have reckoned in the first place certain perverse doctrines. It is therefore the duty of those who have the chief authority, to root those out of the minds of men, not by commanding, but by teaching; not by the terror of

penalties, but by the perspicuity of reasons. The laws whereby this evil may be withstood, are not to be made against the persons erring, but against the errors themselves. Those errors which, in the foregoing chapter, we affirmed were inconsistent with the quiet of the commonweal, have crept into the minds of ignorant men, partly from the pulpit, partly from the daily discourses of men, who, by reason of little employment otherwise, do find leisure enough to study; and they got into these men's minds by the teachers of their youth in public schools. Wherefore also, on the other side, if any man would introduce sound doctrine, he must begin from the *academies*. There the true and truly demonstrated foundations of civil doctrine are to be laid; wherewith young men, being once endued, they may afterward, both in private and public, instruct the vulgar. And this they will do so much the more cheerfully and powerfully, by how much themselves shall be more certainly convinced of the truth of those things they profess and teach. For seeing at this day men receive propositions, though false, and no more intelligible than if a man should join together a company of terms drawn by chance out of an urn, by reason of the frequent use of hearing them; how much more would they for the same reason entertain true doctrines, suitable to their own understandings and the nature of things? I therefore conceive it to be the duty of supreme officers, to cause the true elements of civil doctrine to be written, and to command them to be taught in all the colleges of their several dominions.

10. In the next place we showed that grief of mind arising from *want* did dispose the subjects to sedition; which want, although derived from their own luxury and sloth, yet they impute it to those who govern the realm, as though they were drained and oppressed by public pensions. Notwithstanding, it may sometimes happen that this complaint may be just; namely, when the burthens of

the realm are unequally imposed on the subjects; for that
which to all together is but a light weight, if many withdraw themselves it will be very heavy, nay, even intolerable
to the rest: neither are men wont so much to grieve at the
burthen itself, as at the inequality. With much earnestness
therefore men strive to be freed from taxes; and in this
conflict the less happy, as being overcome, do envy the
more fortunate. To remove therefore all just complaint, it
is the interest of the public quiet, and by consequence it
concerns the duty of the magistrate, to see that the public
burthens be equally borne. Furthermore, since what is
brought by the subjects to public use, is nothing else but
the price of their bought peace, it is good reason that they
who equally share in the peace, should also pay an equal
part, either by contributing their monies or their labours
to the commonweal. Now it is the law of nature (by art.
15, chap. III), that every man in distributing right to
others, do carry himself equal to all. Wherefore rulers are,
by the natural law, obliged to lay the burthens of the commonweal equally on their subjects.

11. Now in this place we understand an equality, not of
money, but of burthen; that is to say, an equality of reason between the burthens and the benefits. For although
all equally enjoy peace, yet the benefits springing from
thence are not equal to all; for some get greater possessions, others less; and again, some consume less, others
more. It may therefore be demanded, whether subjects
ought to contribute to the public according to the rate of
what they gain, or of what they spend: that is to say,
whether the persons must be taxed, so as to pay contribution according to their wealth; or the goods themselves,
that every man contribute according to what he spends.
But if we consider, where monies are raised according to
wealth, there they who have made equal gain, have not
equal possessions, because that one preserves what he hath
got by frugality, another wastes it by luxury, and therefore

equally rejoicing in the benefit of peace, they do not equally sustain the burthens of the commonweal: and on the other side, where the goods themselves are taxed, there every man, while he spends his private goods, in the very act of consuming them he undiscernably pays part due to the commonweal, according to, not what he hath, but what by the benefit of the realm he hath had: it is no more to be doubted, but that the former way of commanding monies is against equity, and therefore against the duty of rulers; the latter is agreeable to reason, and the exercise of their authority.

12. In the third place we said, that that trouble of mind which riseth from *ambition,* was offensive to public peace. For there are some, who seeming to themselves to be wiser than others, and more sufficient for the managing of affairs than they who at present do govern, when they can no otherwise declare how profitable their virtue would prove to the commonweal, they show it by harming it. But because ambition and greediness of honours cannot be rooted out of the minds of men, it is not the duty of rulers to endeavour it; but by constant application of rewards and punishments they may so order it, that men may know that the way to honour is not by contempt of the present government, nor by factions and the popular air, but by the contraries. They are good men who observe the decrees, the laws, and rights of their fathers. If with a constant order we saw these adorned with honours, but the factious punished and had in contempt by those who bear command, there would be more ambition to obey than withstand. Notwithstanding, it so happens sometimes, that as we must stroke a horse by reason of his too much fierceness, so a stiff-necked subject must be flattered for fear of his power; but as that happens when the rider, so this when the commander is in danger of falling. But we speak here of those whose authority and power is entire. Their duty, I say, it is to cherish obedient subjects,

and to depress the factious all they can; nor can the public power be otherwise preserved, nor the subjects' quiet without it.

13. But if it be the duty of princes to restrain the factious, much more does it concern them to dissolve and dissipate the factions themselves. Now I call a *faction*, a multitude of subjects gathered together either by mutual *contracts* among themselves, or by the power of some one, without his or their authority who bear the supreme rule. A *faction*, therefore, is as it were a city in a city: for as by an union of men in the state of nature a city receives its being, so by a new union of subjects there ariseth a *faction*. According to this definition, a multitude of subjects who have bound themselves simply to obey any foreign prince or subject, or have made any pacts or leagues of mutual defence between themselves against all men, not excepting those who have the supreme power in the city, is a *faction*. Also favour with the vulgar, if it be so great that by it an army may be raised, except public caution be given either by hostages or some other pledges, contains *faction* in it. The same may be said of private wealth, if it exceed; because all things obey money. Forasmuch therefore as it is true, that the state of cities among themselves is natural and hostile, those princes who permit factions, do as much as if they received an enemy within their walls: which is contrary to the subjects' safety, and therefore also against the law of nature.

14. There are two things necessary to the enriching of the subjects, *labour* and *thrift*; there is also a third which helps, to wit, the *natural increase of the earth and water*; and there is a fourth too, namely, *the militia*, which sometimes augments, but more frequently lessens the subjects' stock. The two first|only are|necessary. For a city constituted in an island of the sea, no greater than will serve for dwelling, may grow rich without sowing or fishing, by merchandize and handicrafts only; but there is no doubt, if

they have a territory, but they may be richer with the same number, or equally rich being a greater number. But the fourth, namely, *the militia,* was of old reckoned in the number of the gaining arts, under the notion of *booting* or *taking prey*; and it was by mankind, dispersed by families before the constitution of civil societies, accounted just and honourable. For preying is nothing else but a war waged with small forces. And great commonweals, namely, that of Rome and Athens, by the spoils of war, foreign tribute, and the territories they have purchased by their arms, have sometimes so improved the commonwealth, that they have not only not required any public monies from the poorer sort of subjects, but have also divided to each of them both monies and lands. But this kind of increase of riches is not to be brought into rule and fashion. For the militia, in order to profit, is like a die; wherewith many lose their estates, but few improve them. Since therefore there are three things only, *the fruits of the earth and water, labour,* and *thrift,* which are expedient for the enriching of subjects, the duty of commanders in chief shall be conversant only about those three. For the first those laws will be useful, which countenance the arts that improve the increase of the earth and water; such as are *husbandry* and *fishing*. For the second all laws against idleness, and such as quicken industry, are profitable; the *art of navigation,* by help whereof the commodities of the whole world, bought almost by labour only, are brought into one city; and the *mechanics,* under which I comprehend all the arts of the most excellent workmen; and the *mathematical sciences,* the fountains of navigatory and mechanic employments, are held in due esteem and honour. For the third those laws are useful, whereby all inordinate expense, as well in meats as in clothes, and universally in all things which are consumed with usage, is forbidden. Now because such laws are beneficial to the

ends above specified, it belongs also to the office of supreme magistrates to establish them.

15. The liberty of subjects consists not in being exempt
from the laws of the city, or that they who have the supreme power cannot make what laws they have a mind
to. But because all the motions and actions of subjects are
never circumscribed by laws, nor can be, by reason of their
variety; it is necessary that there be infinite cases which
are neither commanded nor prohibited, but every man
may either do or not do them as he lists himself. In these,
each man is said to enjoy his liberty; and in this sense liberty is to be understood in this place, namely, for that part
of natural right which is granted and left to subjects by
the civil laws. As water inclosed on all hands with banks,
stands still and corrupts; having no bounds, it spreads too
largely, and the more passages it finds the more freely it
takes its current; so subjects, if they might do nothing
without the commands of the law, would grow dull and
unwieldy; if all, they would be dispersed; and the more is
left undetermined by the laws, the more liberty they enjoy. Both extremes are faulty; for laws were not invented
to take away, but to direct men's actions; even as nature
ordained the banks, not to stay, but to guide the course of
the stream. The measure of this liberty is to be taken from
the subjects' and the city's good. Wherefore, in the first
place, it is against the charge of those who command and
have the authority of making laws, that there should be
more laws than necessarily serve for good of the magistrate
and his subjects. For since men are wont commonly to debate what to do or not to do, by natural reason rather
than any knowledge of the laws, where there are more
laws than can easily be remembered, and whereby such
things are forbidden as reason of itself prohibits not of
necessity, they must through ignorance, without the least
evil intention, fall within the compass of laws, as gins laid
to entrap their harmless liberty; which supreme com-

manders are bound to preserve for their subjects by the laws of nature.

16. It is a great part of that *liberty*, which is harmless to civil government and necessary for each subject to live happily, that there be no penalties dreaded but what they may both foresee and look for; and this is done, where there are either no punishments at all defined by the laws, or greater not required than are defined. Where there are none defined, there he that hath first broken the law, expects an indefinite or arbitrary punishment; and his fear is supposed boundless, because it relates to an unbounded evil. Now the law of nature commands them who are not subject to any civil laws, by what we have said in chap. iii. art. 11, and therefore supreme commanders, that in taking revenge and punishing they must not so much regard the past evil as the future good; and they sin, if they entertain any other measure in arbitrary punishment than the public benefit. But where the punishment is defined; either by a law prescribed, as when it is set down in plain words that *he that shall do thus or thus, shall suffer so and so;* or by practice, as when the penalty, not by any law prescribed, but arbitrary from the beginning, is afterward determined by the punishment of the first delinquent (for natural equity commands that equal transgressors be equally punished); there to impose a greater penalty than is defined by the law, is against the law of nature. For the end of punishment is not to compel the will of man, but to fashion it, and to make it such as he would have it who hath set the penalty. And deliberation is nothing else but a weighing, as it were in scales, the conveniences and inconveniences of the fact we are attempting; where that which is more weighty, doth necessarily according to its inclination prevail with us. If therefore the legislator doth set a less penalty on a crime, than will make our fear more considerable with us than our lust, that excess of lust above the fear of punishment, whereby sin is committed,

is to be attributed to the legislator, that is to say, to the supreme; and therefore if he inflict a greater punishment than himself hath determined in his laws, he punisheth that in another in which he sinned himself.

17. It pertains therefore to the harmless and necessary *liberty* of subjects, that every man may without fear enjoy the rights which are allowed him by the laws. For it is in vain to have *our own* distinguished by the laws from *another's*, if by wrong judgment, robbery, or theft, they may be again confounded. But it falls out so, that these do happen where judges are corrupted. For the fear whereby men are deterred from doing evil, ariseth not from hence, namely, because penalties are set, but because they are executed. For we esteem the future by what is past, seldom expecting what seldom happens. If therefore judges corrupted either by gifts, favour, or even by pity itself, do often forbear the execution of the penalties due by the law, and by that means put wicked men in hope to pass unpunished: honest subjects encompassed with murderers, thieves, and knaves, will not have the liberty to converse freely with each other, nor scarce to stir abroad without hazard; nay, the *city* itself is dissolved, and every man's right of protecting himself at his own will returns to him. The law of nature therefore gives this precept to supreme commanders, that they not only do righteousness themselves, but that they also by penalties cause the judges, by them appointed, to do the same; that is to say, that they hearken to the complaints of their subjects; and as oft as need requires, make choice of some extraordinary judges, who may hear the matter debated concerning the ordinary ones.

XIV

Of Laws and Trespasses

1. How law differs from counsel. 2. How from covenant.
3. How from right. 4. Division of laws into divine and
human: the divine into natural and positive; and the natural into the laws of single men and of nations. 5. The
division of human, that is to say, of civil laws into sacred
and secular. 6. Into distributive and vindicative. 7. That
distributive and vindicative are not species, but parts of
the laws. 8. All law is supposed to have a penalty annexed
to it. 9. The precepts of the decalogue of honouring parents, of murder, adultery, theft, false witness, are civil
laws. 10. It is impossible to command aught by the civil
law contrary to the law of nature. 11. It is essential to a
law, both that itself and also the lawgiver be known. 12.
Whence the lawgiver comes to be known. 13. Publishing
and interpretation are necessary to the knowledge of a law.
14. The division of the civil law into written and unwritten. 15. The natural laws are not written laws; neither are
the wise sentences of lawyers nor custom laws of themselves,
but by the consent of the supreme power. 16. What the
word sin, most largely taken, signifies. 17. The definition of sin. 18. The difference between a sin of infirmity and malice. 19. Under what kind of sin atheism is
contained. 20. What treason is. 21. That by treason not
the civil, but the natural laws are broken. 22. And that
therefore it is to be punished not by the right of dominion,
but by the right of war. 23. That obedience is not rightly
distinguished into active and passive.

1. They who less seriously consider the force of words,
do sometimes confound *law* with *counsel*, sometimes with
covenant, sometimes with *right*. They confound *law* with
counsel, who think that it is the duty of monarchs not

only to give ear to their *counsellors*, but also to obey
them; as though it were in vain to take *counsel*, unless it
were also followed. We must fetch the distinction between *counsel* and *law*, from the difference between
counsel and *command*. Now *counsel* is a *precept*, in which
the reason of my obeying it is taken from *the thing itself
which is advised*; but *command* is a *precept*, in which
the cause of my obedience depends on *the will of the commander*. For it is not properly said, *thus I will and thus I
command*, except the will stand for a reason. Now when
obedience is yielded to the laws, not for the thing itself,
but by reason of the adviser's will, the law is not a
counsel, but a *command*, and is defined thus: *law is the
command of that person, whether man or court, whose
precept contains in it the reason of obedience*: as the
precepts of God in regard of men, of magistrates in respect of their subjects, and universally of all the powerful
in respect of them who cannot resist, may be termed
their laws. *Law* and *counsel* therefore differ many ways.
Law belongs to him who hath power over them whom he
adviseth; *counsel* to them who have no power. To follow
what is prescribed by *law*, is *duty*; what by *counsel*, is
free-will. *Counsel* is directed to his end, that receives it;
law, to his that gives it. *Counsel* is given to none but the
willing; *law* even to the unwilling. To conclude, the right
of the *counsellor* is made void by the will of him to whom
he gives counsel; the right of the *lawgiver* is not abrogated
at the pleasure of him who hath a *law* imposed.

2. They confound *law* and *covenant*, who conceive the
laws to be nothing else but certain ὁμολογήματα, or
forms of living determined by the common consent of
men. Among whom is Aristotle, who defines *law* on this
manner; Νόμος ἐστὶ λόγος ὡρισμένος καθ᾽ ὁμολογίαν
κοινὴν πόλεως, μηνύων πῶς δεῖ πράττειν ἕκαστα: that
is to say, *law is a speech, limited according to the common
consent of the city, declaring every thing that we ought to*

do. Which definition is not simply of *law*, but of the *civil law*. For it is manifest that the *divine laws* sprang not from the consent of men, nor yet the *laws of nature*. For if they had their original from the consent of men, they might also by the same consent be abrogated; but they are unchangeable. But indeed, that is no right definition of a *civil law*. For in that place, a city is taken either for one civil person, having one will; or for a multitude of men, who have each of them the liberty of their private wills. If for one person, those words *common consent* are ill-placed here; for *one* person hath no *common consent*. Neither ought he to have said, *declaring* what was needful to be done, but *commanding*; for what the city declares, it commands its subjects. He therefore by a city understood a multitude of men, declaring by common consent (imagine it a writing confirmed by votes) some certain forms of living. But these are nothing else but some mutual contracts, which oblige not any man (and therefore are no laws) before that a supreme power being constituted, which can compel, have sufficient remedy against the rest, who otherwise are not likely to keep them. Laws therefore, according to this definition of Aristotle, are nothing else but naked and weak contracts; which then at length, when there is one who by right doth exercise the supreme power, shall either become *laws* or *no laws* at his will and pleasure. Wherefore he confounds *contracts* with *laws*, which he ought not to have done; for contract is *a promise*, law a *command*. In contracts we say, *I will do this*; in laws, *do this*. Contracts oblige us;* laws tie us fast,

---

* *Contracts oblige us.* To be obliged, and to be tied being obliged, seems to some men to be one and the same thing; and that therefore here seems to be some distinction in words, but none indeed. More clearly therefore, I say thus: that a man is obliged by his contracts, that is, that he ought to perform for his promise sake; but that the law ties him being obliged, that is to say, it compels him to make good his promise for fear of the punishment appointed by the law.

being obliged. A *contract* obligeth of *itself;* the *law* holds
the party obliged by virtue of the universal *contract* of
yielding obedience. Therefore in *contract*, it is first determined what is to be done, before we are obliged to do it;
but in *law*, we are first obliged to perform, and what is to
be done is determined afterwards. Aristotle therefore
ought to have defined a *civil law* thus: *a civil law is a speech
limited by the will of the city, commanding everything
behoveful to be done.* Which is the same with that we have
given above, in chap. VI. art. 9: to wit, *that the civil laws
are the command of him, whether man or court of men,
who is endued with supreme power in the city, concerning the future actions of his subjects.*

3. They confound *laws* with *right*, who continue still to
do what is permitted by *divine right*, notwithstanding it
be forbidden by *the civil law.* That which is prohibited by
the *divine law*, cannot be permitted by the *civil;* neither
can that which is commanded by the *divine law*, be prohibited *by the civil.* Notwithstanding, that which is permitted by the *divine right*, that is to say, that which may
be done by *divine right*, doth no whit hinder why the
same may not be forbidden by the *civil laws;* for *inferior
laws* may restrain the liberty allowed by the *superior*, although they cannot enlarge them. Now *natural liberty* is
a right not constituted, but allowed by the laws. For the
laws being removed, our *liberty* is absolute. This is first
restrained by the *natural* and *divine laws;* the residue is
bounded by the *civil law;* and what remains, may again be
restrained by the *constitutions* of particular towns and
societies. There is great difference therefore between *law*
and *right*. For law is *a fetter*, right is *freedom;* and they
differ like contraries.

4. All *law* may be divided, first according to the diversity
of its authors into *divine* and *human*. The *divine*, according to the two ways whereby God hath made known his
will unto men, is twofold; *natural* or *moral*, and *positive*.

Natural is that which God hath declared to all men by his *eternal word* born with them, to wit, their *natural reason;* and this is that law, which in this whole book I have endeavoured to unfold. *Positive* is that which God hath revealed to us by *the word of prophecy,* wherein he hath spoken unto men as a man. Such are the laws which he gave to the Jews concerning their government and divine worship; and they may be termed the *divine civil laws,* because they were peculiar to the civil government of the Jews, his peculiar people. Again, *the natural law* may be divided into that of *men,* which alone hath obtained the title of the *law of nature;* and *that of cities,* which may be called *that of nations,* but vulgarly it is termed the *right of nations.* The precepts of both are alike. But because cities once instituted do put on the personal proprieties of men, that *law,* which speaking of the duty of single men we call *natural,* being applied to whole cities and nations, is called the *right of nations.* And the same elements of *natural law and right,* which have hitherto been spoken of, being transferred to *whole cities* and *nations,* may be taken for the elements of the *laws* and *right of nations.*

5. All *human law* is civil. For the state of men considered out of civil society, is hostile; in which, because one is not subject to another, there are no other laws beside the dictates of natural reason, which is the divine law. But in civil government the city only, that is to say, that man or court to whom the supreme power of the city is committed, is the legislator; and the laws of the city are civil. *The civil laws* may be divided, according to the diversity of their subject matter, into *sacred* or *secular. Sacred* are those which pertain to religion, that is to say, to the ceremonies and worship of God: to wit, what persons, things, places, are to be consecrated, and in what fashion; what opinions concerning the Deity are to be taught publicly; and with what words and in what order supplications

are to be made; and the like; and are not determined by any divine positive law. For the *civil sacred laws* are the *human laws* (which are also called *ecclesiastical*) concerning *things sacred;* but *the secular,* under a general notion, are usually called the *civil* laws.

6. Again, the *civil law* (according to the two offices of the legislator, whereof one is to judge, the other to constrain men to acquiesce to his judgments) hath two parts; the one *distributive,* the other *vindicative* or *penal. By the distributive* it is, that every man hath his proper right; that is to say, it sets forth rules for all things, whereby we may know what is properly our's, what another man's; so as others may not hinder us from the free use and enjoyment of our own, and we may not interrupt others in the quiet possession of their's; and what is lawful for every man to do or omit, and what is not lawful. *Vindicative* is that, whereby it is defined what punishment shall be inflicted on them who break the law.

7. Now *distributive* and *vindicative* are not two several *species* of the laws, but two *parts* of the same law. For if the law should say no more, but (for example) *whatsoever you take with your net in the sea, be it yours,* it is in vain. For although another should take that away from you which you have caught, it hinders not but that it still remains yours. For in the state of nature where all things are common to all, *yours* and *others* are all one; insomuch as what the law defines to be *yours,* was *yours* even before the law, and after the law ceases not to be *yours,* although in another man's possession. Wherefore the law doth nothing, unless it be understood to be so *yours,* as all other men be forbidden to interrupt your free use and secure enjoyment of it at all times, according to your own will and pleasure. For this is that which is required to a propriety of goods; not that a man may be able to use them, but to use them alone; which is done by prohibiting others to be an hinderance to him. But in vain do they

also prohibit any men, who do not withal strike a fear of punishment into them. In vain therefore is the law, unless it contain both parts, that which *forbids* injuries to be done, and that which *punisheth* the doers of them. The first of them, which is called *distributive*, is *prohibitory*, and speaks to all; the second, which is styled *vindicative* or *penary*, is *mandatory*, and only speaks to public ministers.

8. From hence also we may understand, *that every civil law hath a penalty annexed to it*, either explicitly or implicitly. For where the penalty is not defined, neither by any writing, nor by example of any who hath suffered the punishment of the transgressed law, there the penalty is understood to be arbitrary; namely, to depend on the will of the legislator, that is to say, of the supreme commander. For in vain is that law, which may be broken without punishment.

9. Now because it comes from the civil laws, both that every man have *his proper right* and distinguished from *another's*, and also that he is forbidden to invade another's rights; it follows that these precepts: *Thou shalt not refuse to give the honour defined by the laws, unto thy parents: Thou shalt not kill the man, whom the laws forbid thee to kill: Thou shalt avoid all copulation forbidden by the laws: Thou shalt not take away another's goods, against the lord's will: Thou shalt not frustrate the laws and judgments by false testimony*: are civil laws. The natural laws command the same things, but implicitly. For the law of nature (as hath been said in chap. III. art. 2) commands us to *keep contracts*; and therefore also to perform obedience, when we have convenanted obedience, and to abstain from another's goods, when it is determined by the civil law what belongs to another. But all subjects (by chap. VI. art. 13) do *covenant* to obey his commands who hath the supreme power, that is to say, the civil laws, in the very constitution of government, even before it is pos-

sible to break them. For the law of nature did oblige in
the state of nature; where first, because nature hath given
all things to all men, nothing did properly belong to another, and therefore it was not possible to invade another's right; next, where all things were common, and
therefore all carnal copulations lawful; thirdly, where was
the state of war, and therefore lawful to kill; fourthly,
where all things were determined by every man's own
judgment, and therefore paternal respects also; lastly,
where there were no public judgments, and therefore no
use of bearing witness, either true or false.

10. Seeing therefore our obligation to observe those
laws is more ancient than the promulgation of the laws
themselves, as being contained in the very constitution of
the city; by the virtue of the natural law which forbids
breach of covenant, the law of nature commands us to
keep all the civil laws. For where we are tied to obedience before we know what will be commanded us, there
we are universally tied to obey in all things. Whence it
follows, that no civil law whatsoever, which tends not to
a reproach of the Deity (in respect of whom cities themselves have no right of their own, and cannot be said to
make laws), can possibly be against the law of nature.
For though the law of nature forbid theft, adultery, &c.;
yet if the civil law command us to invade anything, that
invasion is not theft, adultery, &c. For when the
Lacedæmonians of old permitted their youths, by a certain law, to take away other men's goods, they commanded that these goods should not be accounted other
men's, but their own who took them; and therefore such
surreptions were no thefts. In like manner, copulations of
heathen sexes, according to their laws, were lawful marriages.

11. It is necessary to the essence of a law, that the
subjects be acquainted with two things: first, what man
or court hath the supreme power, that is to say, the right

of making laws; secondly, what the law itself says. For he that neither knew either to whom or what he is tied to, cannot obey; and by consequence is in such a condition as if he were not tied at all. I say not that it is necessary to the essence of a law, that either one or the other be perpetually known, but only that it be once known. And if the subject afterward forget either the right he hath who made the law, or the law itself, that makes him no less tied to obey; since he might have remembered it, had he had a will to obey.

12. *The knowledge of the legislator* depends on the subject himself; for the right of making laws could not be conferred on any man without his own consent and covenant, either expressed or supposed; expressed, when from the beginning the citizens do themselves constitute a form of governing the city, or when by promise they submit themselves to the dominion of any one; or supposed at least, as when they make use of the benefit of the realm and laws for their protection and conservation against others. For to whose dominion we require our fellow subjects to yield obedience for our good, his dominion we acknowledge to be legitimate by that very request. And therefore ignorance of the power of making laws, can never be a sufficient excuse; for every man knows what he hath done himself.

13. *The knowledge of the laws* depends on the legislator; who must publish them; for otherwise they are not laws. For law is the command of the law-maker, and his command is the declaration of his will; it is not therefore a law, except the will of the law-maker be declared, which is done by *promulgation*. Now in *promulgation* two things must be manifest; whereof one is, that he or they who publish a law, either have a right themselves to make laws, or that they do it by authority derived from him or them who have it; the other is the sense of the law itself. Now, that the first, namely, published laws, proceed from

him who hath the supreme command, cannot be manifest
(speaking exactly and philosophically) to any, but them
who have received them from the mouth of the commander. The rest believe; but the reasons of their belief
are so many, that it is scarce possible they should not believe. And truly in a *democratical* city, where every one
may be present at the making of laws if he will, he that
shall be absent, must believe those that were present. But
in *monarchies* and *aristocracies*, because it is granted but
to few to be present, and openly to hear the commands
of the *monarch* or the *nobles*, it was necessary to bestow
a power on those few of publishing them to the rest. And
thus we believe those to be the *edicts* and *decrees* of
princes, which are propounded to us for such, either by
the writings or voices of them whose office it is to publish
them. But yet, when we have these causes of belief; that
we have seen the prince or supreme counsel constantly
use such *counsellors, secretaries, publishers,* and *seals,* and
the like arguments for the declaring of his will; that he
never took any authority from them; that they have been
punished, who not giving credit to such like promulga-
tions have transgressed the law; not only he who thus believing shall obey the *edicts* and *decrees* set forth by them,
is everywhere excused, but he that not believing shall not
yield obedience, is punished. For the constant permission
of these things is a manifest sign enough and evident declaration of the commander's will; provided there be nothing contained in the *law, edict,* or *decree,* derogatory
from his supreme power. For it is not to be imagined that
he would have aught taken from his power by any of his
officers, as long as he retains a will to govern. Now the
sense of the *law,* when there is any doubt made of it, is
to be taken from them to whom the supreme authority
hath committed the *knowledge of causes* or *judgments;*
for to *judge,* is nothing else than by *interpretation* to
apply the *laws* to particular cases. Now we may know who

they are that have this office granted them, in the same manner as we know who they be that have authority given them to publish laws.

14. Again the *civil law*, according to its twofold manner of publishing, is of two sorts, *written* and *unwritten*. By *written*, I understand that which wants a voice, or some other sign of the will of the legislator, that it may become a law. For all kind of laws are of the same age with mankind, both in nature and time; and therefore of more antiquity than the invention of letters, and the art of writing. Wherefore not a *writing*, but a *voice* is necessary for a *written law*; this alone is requisite to the *being*, that to the *remembrance* of a law. For we read, that before letters were found out for the help of memory, that *laws*, contracted into metre, were wont to be sung. The *unwritten*, is that which wants no other publishing than the voice of nature or natural reason; such are the *laws of nature*. For the natural law, although it be distinguished from the civil, forasmuch as it commands the will; yet so far forth as it relates to our actions, it is civil. For example, this same, *thou shalt not covet*, which only appertains to the mind, is a natural law only; but this, *thou shalt not invade*, is both natural and civil. For seeing it is impossible to prescribe such universal rules, whereby all future contentions, which perhaps are infinite, may be determined; it is to be understood that in all cases not mentioned by the *written laws*, the *law of natural equity* is to be followed, which commands us to distribute equally to equals; and this by the virtue of the *civil law*, which also punisheth those who knowingly and willingly do actually transgress the *laws of nature*.

15. These things being understood, it appears, first, that the *laws of nature*, although they were described in the books of some philosophers, are not for that reason to be termed *written laws*: and that the writings of the interpreters of the laws, were no laws, for want of the supreme

authority; nor yet those *orations of the wise*, that is to say, *judges*, but so far forth as by the consent of the supreme power they part into custom; and that then they are to be received among the *written laws*, not for the custom's sake (which by its own force doth not constitute a law), but for the will of the supreme commander; which appears in this, that he hath suffered his *sentence*, whether equal or unequal, to pass into custom.

16. *Sin*, in its largest signification, comprehends every *deed*, *word*, and *thought* against right reason. For every man, by reasoning, seeks out the means to the end which he propounds to himself. If therefore he reason right; that is to say, beginning from most evident principles he makes a discourse out of consequences continually necessary, he will proceed in a most direct way. Otherwise he will go astray, that is to say, he will either *do, say*, or *endeavour* somewhat against his proper end; which when he hath done, he will indeed in reasoning be said to have *erred*, but in action and will to have *sinned*. For *sin* follows *error*, just as the *will* doth the *understanding*. And this is the most general acception of the word; under which is contained every *imprudent* action, whether against the law, as to overthrow another man's house, or not against the law, as to build his own upon the sand.

17. But when we speak of *the· laws*, the word *sin* is taken in a more strict sense, and signifies not every thing done against right reason, but that only which is *blameable*; and therefore it is called *malum culpæ*, the evil of fault. But yet if anything be culpable, it is not presently to be termed *a sin* or *fault*; but only if it be blameable with reason. We must therefore enquire what it is to be *blameable with reason*, what *against reason*. Such is the nature of man, that every one calls that *good* which he desires, and *evil* which he eschews. And therefore through the diversity of our affections it happens, that one counts that *good*, which another counts

evil; and the same man what now he esteemed for *good,* he immediately after looks on as *evil:* and the same thing which he calls *good* in himself, he terms *evil* in another. For we all measure *good* and *evil* by the pleasure or pain we either feel at present, or expect hereafter. Now seeing the prosperous actions of enemies, because they increase their honours, goods, and power; and of equals, by reason of that strife of honours which is among them; both seem and are *irksome,* and therefore *evil* to all; and men use to repute those *evil,* that is to say, to *lay some fault* to their charge, from whom they receive *evil;* it is impossible to be determined by the consent of single men, whom the same things do not please and displease, what actions are, and what not to be blamed. They may agree indeed in some certain general things, as that *theft, adultery,* and the like are *sins;* as if they should say that all men account those things *evil,* to which they have given names which are usually taken in an *evil* sense. But we demand not whether theft be a sin, but what is to be termed theft; and so concerning others, in like manner. Forasmuch therefore as in so great a diversity of censurers, what is by reason blameable is not to be measured by the reason of one man more than another, because of the equality of human nature; and there are no other reasons in being, but only those of *particular men,* and that of the *city:* it follows, that the *city* is to determine what *with reason is culpable.* So as a *fault,* that is to say, a *sin,* is that which a man does, omits, says, or wills, against the reason of *the city,* that is, contrary to the laws.

18. But a man may do somewhat against the laws through human infirmity, although he desire to fulfil them; and yet his action, as being against the laws, is rightly blamed, and called a *sin.* But there are some who *neglect* the laws; and as oft as any hope of gain and impunity doth appear to them, no conscience of contracts and betrothed faith can withhold them from their

violation. Not only the deeds, but even the minds of these men are against the laws. They who sin only through infirmity, are *good men* even when they sin; but these, even when they do not sin, are wicked. For though both the action and the mind be repugnant to the laws, yet those repugnances are distinguished by different appellations. For the irregularity of the action is called ἀδίκημα, *unjust deed*; that of the mind ἀδικία and κακία, *injustice* and *malice*; that is the infirmity of a disturbed soul, this the *pravity* of a sober mind.

19. But seeing there is no sin which is not against some law, and that there is no law which is not the command of him who hath the supreme power, and that no man hath a supreme power which is not bestowed on him by our own consent; in what manner will he be said to sin, who either denies that there is a God, or that he governs the world, or casts any other reproach upon him? For he will say: *that he never submitted his will to God's will, not conceiving him so much as to have any being: and granting that his opinion were erroneous, and therefore also a sin, yet were it to be numbered among those of imprudence or ignorance, which by right cannot be punished.* This speech seems so far forth to be admitted, that though this kind of sin be the greatest and most hurtful, yet is it to be referred to sins of imprudence;† but that

† *Yet is it to be referred to sins of imprudence.* Many find fault that I have referred atheism to imprudence, and not to injustice; yea by some it is taken so, as if I had not declared myself an enemy bitter enough against atheists. They object further, that since I had elsewhere said that it might be known *there is a God* by natural reason, I ought to have acknowledged that they sin at least against the law of nature, and therefore are not only guilty of imprudence, but injustice too. But I am so much an enemy to atheists, that I have both diligently sought for, and vehemently desired to find some law whereby I might condemn them of injustice. But when I found none, I inquired next what name God himself did give to men so detested by him. Now God speaks thus of the atheist: *The fool hath said in his heart, there is no God.* Wherefore I placed their sin in that rank which God himself refers to. Next I show them to be

it should be excused by imprudence or ignorance, is absurd. For the atheist is punished either immediately by God himself, or by kings constituted under God; not as a subject is punished by a king, because he keeps not the laws; but as one enemy by another, because he would not accept of the laws; that is to say, by the right of war, as the giants warring against God. For whosoever are not subject either to some common lord, or one to another, are enemies among themselves.

20. Seeing that from the virtue of the covenant, whereby each subject is tied to the other to perform absolute and universal obedience (such as is defined above, chap. vi. art. 13) to the city, that is to say, to the sovereign power, whether that be one man or council, there is an obligation derived to observe each one of the civil laws; so that that covenant contains in itself all the laws at once; it is manifest that the subject who shall renounce the general covenant of obedience, doth at once renounce all the laws. Which trespass is so much worse than any other one sin, by how much to sin *always*, is worse than to sin *once*. And this is that sin which is called *treason*; and it is a word or deed whereby the citizen or subject declares, that he will no longer obey that man or court to whom the supreme power of the city is en-

---

enemies of God. But I conceive the name of an enemy to be sometimes somewhat sharper, than that of an unjust man. Lastly, I affirm that they may under that notion be justly punished both by God, and supreme magistrates; and therefore by no means excuse or extenuate this sin. Now that I have said, that it might be known by natural reason *that there is a God*, is so to be understood, not as if I had meant that all men might know this; except they think, that because Archimedes by natural reason found out what proportion the circle hath to the square, it follows thence, that every one of the vulgar could have found out as much. I say therefore, that although it may be known to some by the light of reason that there is a God; yet men that are continually engaged in pleasures or seeking of riches and honour; also men that are not wont to reason aright, or cannot do it, or care not to do it; lastly, fools, in which number are atheists, cannot know this.

trusted. And the subject declares this same will of his by deed, when he either doth or endeavours to do violence to the sovereign's person, or to them who execute his commands. Of which sort are traitors, regicides, and such as take up arms against the city, or during a war fly to the enemy's side. And they show the same will in word, who flatly deny that themselves or other subjects are tied to any such kind of obedience, either in the whole, as he who should say that we must not obey him (keeping the obedience which we owe to God entire) simply, absolutely, and universally; or in part, as he who should say, that he had no right to wage war at his own will, to make peace, list soldiers, levy monies, electing magistrates and public ministers, enacting laws, deciding controversies, setting penalties, or doing aught else without which the state cannot stand. And these and the like words and deeds are treason by the natural, not the civil law. But it may so happen, that some action, which before the civil law was made, was not treason, yet will become such if it be done afterwards. As if it be declared by the law, that it shall be accounted for a sign of renouncing public obedience, that is to say, for treason, if any man shall coin monies, or forge the privy-seal; he that after that declaration shall do this, will be no less guilty of treason than the other. Yet he sins less, because he breaks not all the laws at once, but one law only. For the law by calling that treason which by nature is not so, doth indeed by right set a more odious name, and perhaps a more grievous punishment on the guilty persons; but it makes not the sin itself more grievous.

21. But that sin, which by the law of nature is treason, is a transgression of the natural, not the civil law. For since our obligation to civil obedience, by virtue whereof the civil laws are valid, is before all civil law, and the sin of treason is naturally nothing else but the breach of that obligation; it follows, that by the sin of treason that law

is broken which preceded the civil law, to wit, the natural, which forbids us to violate covenants and betrothed faith. But if some sovereign prince should set forth a law on this manner, *thou shalt not rebel*, he would effect just nothing. For except subjects were before obliged to obedience, that is to say, not to rebel, all law is of no force. Now the obligation which obligeth to what we were before obliged to, is superfluous.

22. Hence it follows, that *rebels, traitors,* and all others *convicted of treason,* are punished not by *civil,* but *natural* right; that is to say, not as *civil subjects,* but as *enemies to the government;* not by the *right of sovereignty* and *dominion,* but by the *right of war.*

23. There are some who think that those acts which are done against the law, when the punishment is determined by the law itself, are expiated, if the punished willingly undergo the punishment; and that they are not guilty before God of breaking the natural law (although by breaking the civil laws, we break the natural too, which command us to keep the civil), who have suffered the punishment which the law required; as if by the law the fact were not prohibited, but a punishment were set instead of a price, whereby a license might be bought of doing what the law forbids. By the same reason they might infer too, that no transgression of the law were a sin; but that every man might enjoy the liberty which he hath bought by his own peril. But we must know, that the words of the law may be understood in a twofold sense. The one as containing two parts (as hath been declared above in art. 7), namely, that of absolutely prohibiting, as, *thou shalt not do this;* and revenging, as, *he that doth this, shall be punished.* The other, as containing a condition, for example, *thou shalt not do this thing, unless thou wilt suffer punishment;* and thus the law forbids not simply, but conditionally. If it be understood in the first sense, he that doth it sins, because he doth what

the law forbids to be done; if in the second, he sins not, because he cannot be said to do what is forbidden him, that performs the condition. For in the first sense, all men are forbidden to do it; in the second, they only who keep themselves from the punishment. In the first sense, the vindicative part of the law obligeth not the guilty, but the magistrate to require punishment; in the second, he himself that owes the punishment, is obliged to exact it; to the payment whereof, if it be capital or otherwise grievous, he cannot be obliged. But in what sense the law is to be taken, depends on the will of him who hath the sovereignty. When therefore there is any doubt of the meaning of the law, since we are sure they sin not who do it not, it will be sin if we do it, howsoever the law may afterward be explained. For to do that which a man doubts whether it be a sin or not, when he hath freedom to forbear it, is a contempt of the laws; and therefore by chap. III. art. 28, a sin against the law of nature. Vain therefore is that same distinction of *obedience* into *active* and *passive*; as if that could be expiated by penalties constituted by human decrees, which is a sin against the law of nature, which is the law of God; or as though they sinned not, who sin at their own peril.

RELIGION

XV

Of the Kingdom of God by Nature

1. The proposition of the following contents. 2. Over whom God is said to rule by nature. 3. The word of God threefold; reason, revelation, prophecy. 4. The kingdom of God twofold; natural, and prophetic. 5. The right whereby God reigns, is seated in his omnipotence. 6. The same proved from Scripture. 7. The obligation of yielding obedience to God, proceeds from human infirmity. 8. The laws of God in his natural kingdom, are those which are recited above in chapters II and III. 9. What honour and worship is. 10. Worship consists either in attributes or in actions. 11. And there is one sort natural, another arbitrary. 12. One commanded, another voluntary. 13. What the end or scope of worship is. 14. What the natural laws are concerning God's attributes. 15. What the actions are whereby naturally we do give worship. 16. In God's natural kingdom, the city may appoint what worship of God it pleaseth. 17. God ruling by nature only, the city, that is to say, that man or court who under God hath the sovereign authority of the city, is the interpreter of all the laws. 18. Certain doubts removed. 19. What sin is in the natural kingdom of God; and what treason against the Divine Majesty.

1. We have already in the foregoing chapters, proved both by reason and testimonies of holy writ, that the

estate of nature, that is to say, of absolute liberty, such
as is theirs who neither govern nor are governed, is an
anarchy or hostile state; that the precepts whereby to
avoid this state, are *the laws of nature;* that there can be
no civil government without a sovereign; and that they
who have gotten this sovereign command, must be
obeyed simply, that is to say, in all things which repugn
not the commandments of God. There is this one thing
only wanting to the complete understanding of all civil
duty, and that is, to know which are the laws and commandments of God. For else we cannot tell whether that
which the civil power commands us, be against the laws
of God, or not; whence it must necessarily happen, that
either by too much obedience to the civil authority we
become stubborn against the divine Majesty; or for fear of
sinning against God we run into disobedience against the
civil power. To avoid both these rocks, it is necessary to
know the divine laws. Now because the knowledge of the
laws depends on the knowledge of the kingdom, we must
in what follows speak somewhat concerning the *kingdom
of God.*

2. *The Lord is king, the earth may be glad thereof;*
saith the psalmist (Psalm xcvii. 1). And again the same
psalmist (Psalm xcix. 1): *The Lord is king, be the people never so impatient; he sitteth between the cherubims,
be the earth never so unquiet;* to wit, whether men will
or not, God is the king over all the earth; nor is he moved
from his throne, if there be any who deny either his *existence* or his *providence.* Now although God govern all
men so by his power, that none can do anything which
he would not have done: yet this, to speak properly and
accurately, is not to reign. For he is said to reign, who
rules not by *acting,* but *speaking,* that is to say, by *precepts* and *threatenings.* And therefore we count not inanimate nor irrational bodies for subjects in the kingdom of
God, although they be subordinate to the divine power;

because they *understand not the commands and threats* of God: nor yet the atheists, because they believe not that there is a God; nor yet those who believing there is a God, do not yet believe that he rules these inferior things: for even these, although they be governed by the power of God, yet do they not acknowledge any of his *commands*, nor stand in awe of his *threats*. Those only therefore are supposed to belong to God's kingdom, who acknowledge him to be the governor of all things, and that he hath given *his commands* to men, and appointed *punishments* for the transgressors. The rest we must not call subjects, but enemies of God.

3. But none are said to govern by *commands*, but they who openly declare them to those who are governed by them. For the *commands* of the rulers, are the *laws* of the ruled; but *laws* they are not, if not perspicuously published, insomuch as all excuse of ignorance may be taken away. Men indeed publish their laws by *word* or *voice*; neither can they make their will universally known any other way. But God's *laws* are declared after a threefold manner: first, *by the tacit dictates of right reason;* next, by *immediate revelation,* which is supposed to be done either by a supernatural voice, or by a vision or dream, or divine inspiration; thirdly, by the *voice of one man,* whom God recommends to the rest, as worthy of belief, by the working of true miracles. Now he whose voice God thus makes use of to signify his will unto others, is called a *prophet.* These three manners may be termed the *threefold word of God,* to wit, the *rational word,* the *sensible word,* and *the word of prophecy.* To which answer the three manners whereby we are said to hear God; *right reasoning, sense,* and *faith.* God's *sensible word* hath come but to few; neither hath God spoken to men by revelation, except particularly to some, and to diverse diversely; neither have any laws of his kingdom been published on this manner unto any people.

4. And according to the difference which is between the *rational word* and the *word of prophecy*, we attribute a twofold kingdom unto God: *natural*, in which he reigns by the dictates of right reason; and which is universal over all who acknowledge the divine power, by reason of that rational nature which is common to all: and *prophetical*, in which he rules also by the *word of prophecy*; which is peculiar, because he hath not given positive laws to all men, but to his peculiar people and some certain men elected by him.

5. God in his *natural kingdom* hath a right to rule, and to punish those who break his laws, from his sole *irresistible power*. For all right over others is either from *nature*, or from *contract*. How the right of governing springs from *contract*, we have already showed in chap. vi. And the same right is derived from *nature*, in this very thing, that it is not by nature taken away. For when by nature all men had a right over all things, every man had a right of ruling over all as ancient as nature itself. But the reason why this was abolished among men, was no other but mutual fear, as hath been declared above in chap. ii. art. 3; reason, namely, dictating that they must forego that right for the preservation of mankind; because the equality of men among themselves, according to their strength and natural powers, was necessarily accompanied with war; and with war joins the destruction of mankind. Now if any man had so far exceeded the rest in power, that all of them with joined forces could not have resisted him, there had been no cause why he should part with that right, which nature had given him. The right therefore of dominion over all the rest would have remained with him, by reason of that excess of power whereby he could have preserved both himself and them. They therefore whose power cannot be resisted, and by consequence God *Almighty* derives his right of sovereignty from the *power* itself. And as oft as God punisheth or slays a

sinner, although he therefore punish him because he sinned, yet may we not say that he could not justly have punished or killed him although he had not sinned. Neither, if the will of God in punishing may perhaps have regard to some sin antecedent, doth it therefore follow, that the right of afflicting and killing depends not on *divine power*, but on *men's sins*.

6. That question made famous by the disputations of the ancients: *why evil things befall the good, and good things the evil*: is the same with this of ours; *by what right God dispenseth good and evil things unto men*; and with its difficulty it not only staggers the faith of the vulgar concerning the divine Providence, but also of philosophers, and which is more, even of holy men. Psalm lxxiii. 1, 2, 3: *Truly God is good to Israel, even to such as are of a clean heart; but as for me, my feet were almost gone, my steps had well nigh slipped. And why? I was grieved at the wicked; I do also see the ungodly in such prosperity*. And how bitterly did Job expostulate with God, that being *just* he should yet be afflicted with so many calamities! God himself with open voice resolved this difficulty in the case of Job, and hath confirmed his right by arguments drawn not from Job's sin, but from his own power. For Job and his friends had argued so among themselves; that they would needs make him guilty, because he was punished; and he would reprove their accusation by arguments fetched from his own innocence. But God, when he had heard both him and them, refutes his expostulation, not by condemning him of injustice or any sin, but by declaring his own power (Job xxxviii. 4): *Where wast thou* (says he) *when I laid the foundation of the earth*, &c. And for his friends, God pronounces himself angry against them (Job xlii. 7): *Because they had not spoken of him the thing that is right, like his servant Job*. Agreeable to this is that speech of our Saviour's in the man's case who was born blind: when his disciples

asking him whether he or his parents had sinned, that he was born blind, he answered (John ix. 3): *Neither hath this man sinned, nor his parents; but that the works of God should be manifest in him.* For though it be said (Rom. v. 12), *that death entered into the world by sin:* it follows not but that God by his right might have made men subject to diseases and death, although they had never sinned; even as he hath made the other animals mortal and sickly, although they cannot sin.

7. Now if God have the right of sovereignty from his power, it is manifest that the *obligation* of yielding him obedience lies on men by reason of their weakness.* For that *obligation* which rises from contract, of which we have spoken in chap. II. can have no place here; where the right of ruling, no covenant passing between, rises only from nature. But there are two species of *natural obligation.* One, when liberty is taken away by corporal impediments, according to which we say that heaven and earth, and all creatures, do obey the common laws of their creation. The other, when it is taken away by hope or fear, according to which the weaker, despairing of his own power to resist, cannot but yield to the stronger. From this last kind of obligation, that is to say, from fear or conscience of our own weakness in respect of the divine power, it comes to pass that we are obliged to obey God in his natural kingdom; reason dictating to all, acknowledging the divine power and providence, *that there is no kicking against the pricks.*

* *By reason of their weakness.* If this shall seem hard to any man, I desire him with a silent thought to consider, if there were two Omnipotents, whether were bound to obey. I believe he will confess that neither is bound. If this be true, then it is also true what I have set down; that men are subject unto God, because they are not omnipotent. And truly our Saviour admonishing Paul, who at that time was an enemy to the Church, that he should not kick against the pricks; seems to require obedience from him for this cause, because he had not power enough to resist.

8. Because the *word of God*, ruling by nature only, is supposed to be nothing else but right reason, and the laws of kings can be known by their *word* only; it is manifest that the laws of God, ruling by nature alone, are only the *natural laws*; namely, those which we have set down in chaps. II. and III. and deduced from the dictates of reason, *humility, equity, justice, mercy*; and other *moral virtues* befriending *peace*, which pertain to the discharge of the duties of men one toward the other; and those which right reason shall dictate besides, concerning the honour and worship of the Divine Majesty. We need not repeat what those *natural laws* or *moral virtues* are; but we must see what honours and what divine worship, that is to say, what *sacred laws* the same *natural reason* doth dictate.

9. Honour to speak properly, is nothing else but an opinion of another's *power* joined with *goodness*; and to *honour* a man, is the same with highly esteeming him: and so honour is not in the party *honoured*, but in the *honourer*. Now three passions do necessarily follow *honour* thus placed in opinion; *love*, which refers to *goodness*; *hope* and *fear*, which regard *power*. And from these arise all outward actions, wherewith the powerful are appeased and become propitious; and which are the effects, and therefore also the natural signs of honour itself. But the word *honour* is transferred also to those outward effects of *honour*; in which sense, we are said to *honour* him, of whose power we testify ourselves, either in word or deed, to have a very great respect; insomuch as *honour* is the same with *worship*. Now *worship* is an outward act, the sign of inward honour; and whom we endeavour by our homage to appease if they be angry, or howsoever to make them favourable to us, we are said to *worship*.

10. All signs of the mind are either *words* or *deeds*; and therefore all *worship* consists either in *words* or *deeds*.

Now both the one and the other are referred to three kinds; whereof the first is *praise*, or *public declaration of goodness*; the second a *public declaration of present power*, which is to *magnify*, μεγάλυνειν; the third is a *public declaration of happiness*, or of *power secure also for the future*, which is called μακαρισμός. I say that all kinds of honour may be discerned, not in *words* only, but in *deeds* too. But we then praise and celebrate in *words*, when we do it by way of proposition, or *dogmatically*, that is to say, by *attributes* or *titles*; which may be termed praising and celebrating *categorically* and *plainly*; as when we declare him whom we honour to be *liberal, strong, wise*. And then in *deeds*, when it is done by *consequence* or by *hypothesis* or supposition; as by *thanksgiving*, which supposeth *goodness*; or by *obedience*, which supposeth *power*; or by *congratulation*, which supposeth *happiness*.

11. Now whether we desire to praise a man in *words* or *deeds*, we shall find some things which signify honour with all men: such as among *attributes*, are the general words of *virtues* and *powers*, which cannot be taken in ill sense; as *good, fair, strong, just*, and the like: and among *actions, obedience, thanksgiving, prayers*, and others of that kind, by which an acknowledgment of virtue and power is ever understood. Others, which signify honour but with some, and scorn with others, or else neither; such as in *attributes*, are those words, which, according to the diversity of opinions, are diversely referred to virtues or vices, to honest or dishonest things. As that a man slew his enemy, that he fled, that he is a philosopher, or an orator, and the like; which with some are had in honour, with others in contempt. In *deeds*, such as depend on the custom of the place, or prescriptions of civil laws; as in saluting to be bareheaded, to put off the shoes, to bend the body, to petition for anything standing, prostrate, kneeling, forms of ceremony, and the like. Now that *worship* which is always and by all men ac-

counted honourable, may be called *natural*; the other, which follows places and customs, *arbitrary*.

12. Furthermore, *worship* may be enjoined, to wit, by the *command* of him that is worshipped, and it may be *voluntary*, namely, such as seems good to the worshipper. If it be *enjoined*, the actions expressing it do not signify honour, as they signify actions, but as they are *enjoined*: for they signify *obedience* immediately, obedience *power*; insomuch as *worship enjoined* consists in obedience. *Voluntary* is honourable only in the nature of the actions; which if they do signify honour to the beholders, it is *worship*, if not, it is *reproach*. Again, *worship* may be either *public* or *private*. But *public*, respecting each single worshipper, may not be *voluntary*; respecting the city, it may. For seeing that which is done voluntarily, depends on the will of the doer, there would not one worship be given, but as many worships as worshippers; except the will of all men were united by the command of one. But *private* worship may be *voluntary*, if it be done secretly; for what is done openly, is restrained either by laws or through modesty; which is contrary to the nature of a *voluntary* action.

13. Now that we may know what the *scope* and *end* of *worshipping* others is, we must consider the cause why men delight in worship. And we must grant what we have showed elsewhere; that *joy* consists in this, that a man contemplates virtue, strength, science, beauty, friends, or any *power* whatsoever, as being, or as though it were his own; and it is nothing else but a *glory* or triumph of the mind, conceiving itself honoured, that is to say, loved and feared, that is to say, having the services and assistances of men in readiness. Now because men believe him to be powerful, whom they see honoured, that is to say, esteemed powerful by others; it falls out that honour is increased by worship; and by the opinion of power true power is acquired. His *end* therefore, who either com-

mands or suffers himself to be worshipped, is, that by this means he may acquire as many as he can, either through love or fear, to be obedient unto him.

14. But that we may understand what manner of *worship* of God *natural reason* doth assign us, let us begin from his *attributes*. Where first, it is manifest that *existence* is to be allowed him; for there can be no will to honour him, who, we think, hath no being. Next, those philosophers who said, that God was the world or the world's soul, that is to say, a part of it, spake unworthily of God; for they attribute nothing to him, but wholly deny his being. For by the word God we understand the *world's cause*. But in saying that the *world is God*, they say *that it hath no cause*, that is as much as *there is no God*. In like manner, they who maintain the world not to be created, but eternal; because there can be no cause of an eternal thing, in denying *the world to have a cause*, they deny also that *there is a God*. They also have a wretched apprehension of God, who imputing idleness to him, do take from him the government of the world and of mankind. For say, they should acknowledge him omnipotent; yet if he mind not these inferior things, that same thread-bare sentence will take place with them: *quod supra nos, nihil ad nos;* what is above us, doth not concern us. And seeing there is nothing for which they should either love or fear him, truly he will be to them as though he were not at all. Moreover, in *attributes* which signify *greatness* or *power*, those which signify some finite or limited thing, are not signs at all of an honouring mind. For we honour not God worthily, if we ascribe less *power* or *greatness* to him than possibly we can. But every finite thing is less than we can; for most easily we may always assign and attribute more to a finite thing. No *shape* therefore must be assigned to God, for all *shape* is *finite;* nor must he be said to be conceived or comprehended by imagination, or any other faculty of

our soul; for whatsoever we conceive is *finite*. And although this word *infinite* signify a conception of the mind, yet it follows not that we have any conception of an *infinite thing*. For when we say that a thing is *infinite*, we signify nothing really, but the impotency in our own mind; as if we should say, we know not whether or where it is limited. Neither speak they honourably enough of God, who say we have an *idea* of him in our mind: for an idea is our conception; but conception we have none, except of a *finite* thing. Nor they, who say that he hath *parts*, or that he is some certain *entire* thing; which are also attributes of *finite* things. Nor that he is in any place; for nothing can be said to be in a *place*, but what hath *bounds* and *limits* of its greatness on all sides. Nor that he is *moved* or *is at rest*; for either of them suppose a *being in some place*. Nor that there are|more|Gods; because not|more|infinites. Furthermore, concerning *attributes of happiness*, those are unworthy of God which signify *sorrow* (unless they be taken not for any passion, but, by a metonomy, for the effect); such as *repentance, anger, pity*. Or *want*; as *appetite, hope, concupiscence*, and that *love* which is also called *lust*; for they are signs of *poverty*; since it cannot be understood that a man should *desire, hope*, and *wish* for aught, but what he wants and stands in need of. Or any *passive faculty*; for *suffering* belongs to a limited power, and which depends upon another. When we therefore attribute a *will* to God, it is not to be conceived like unto ours, which is called *a rational desire* (for if God *desires*, he *wants*, which for any man to say, is a contumely); but we must suppose some resemblance which we cannot conceive. In like manner when we attribute *sight* and other *acts of the senses* to him, or *knowledge*, or *understanding*, which in us are nothing else but a tumult of the mind, raised from outward objects pressing the organs; we must not think that any such thing befalls the Deity; for it is a sign

of power *depending* upon some other, which is not the
most blessed thing. He therefore who would not ascribe
any other titles to God than what reason commands, must
use such as are either *negative*, as *infinite, eternal, incomprehensible*, &c.; or *superlative*, as *most good, most great,
most powerful*, &c.; or *indefinite*, as *good, just, strong,
creator, king*, and the like; in such sense, as not desiring
to declare what he *is* (which were to circumscribe him
within the narrow limits of our phantasy); but to confess
his own admiration and obedience, which is the property
of humility and of a mind yielding all the honour it possibly can do. For reason dictates one name alone which
doth signify the *nature* of God, that is, *existent*, or simply,
that he is; and one in *order* to, and in *relation* to us,
namely *God*, under which is contained both *King*, and
Lord, and *Father*.

15. Concerning the *outward actions* wherewith God is
to be worshipped, as also concerning his *titles*; it is a most
general command of reason, that they be signs of a mind
yielding honour. Under which are contained in the first
place, *prayers*.

> "Qui fingit sacros auro vel marmore vultus,
> Non facit ille deos; qui rogat, ille facit."

For *prayers* are the signs of hope; and hope is an acknowledgment of the divine *power* or *goodness*.

In the second place, *thanksgiving*; which is a sign of
the same affection, but that *prayers go before* the benefit, and *thanks follow it*.

In the third, *gifts*, that is to say, *oblations* and *sacrifices*;
for these are *thanksgivings*.

In the fourth, *not to swear by any other*. For a man's
oath is an imprecation of his wrath against him if he deceive, who both knows whether he do or not, and can
punish him if he do, though he be never so powerful;
which only belongs to God. For if there were any man

from whom his subjects' *malice* could not lie hid, and whom no human power could resist, plighted faith would suffice without swearing; which broken, might be punished by that man. And for this very reason there would be no need of an oath.

In the fifth place, *to speak warily of God*; for that is a sign of *fear*, and *fear* is an acknowledgment of *power*. It follows from this precept, *that we may not take the name of God in vain, or use it rashly*; for either are inconsiderate. *That we must not swear, where there is no need*; for that is in vain. But need there is none, unless it be between cities, to avoid or take away contention by force, which necessarily must arise where there is no faith kept in promises: or in a city, for the better certainty of judicature. Also, *that we must not dispute of the divine nature*; for it is supposed *that all things in the natural kingdom of God are inquired into by reason only*, that is to say, out of the principles of natural science. But we are so far off by these to attain to the knowledge of the nature of God, that we cannot so much as reach to the full understanding of all the qualities of our own bodies, or of any other creatures. Wherefore there comes nothing from these disputes, but a rash imposition of names to the divine Majesty according to the small measure of our conceptions. It follows also (which belongs to the right of God's kingdom), that their speech is inconsiderate and rash, who say, *that this or that doth not stand with divine justice*. For even men count it an affront that their children should dispute their right, or measure their justice otherwise than by the rule of their commands.

In the sixth, *whatsoever is offered up in prayers, thanksgivings, and sacrifices, must in its kind be the best and most betokening honour*; namely, *prayers* must not be rash, or light, or vulgar, but beautiful, and well composed. For though it were absurd in the heathen to worship God in an image, yet was it not against reason to use poetry and music in their churches.

Also *oblations must be clean, and presents sumptuous;* and such as are significative either of submission or gratitude, or commemorative of benefits received. For all these proceed from a desire of honouring.

In the seventh, *that God must be worshipped not privately only, but openly and publicly in the sight of all men;* because that worship is so much more acceptable, by how much it begets honour and esteem in others; as hath been declared before in art. 13. Unless others therefore see it, that which is most pleasing in our worship vanisheth.

In the last place, *that we use our best endeavour to keep the laws of nature.* For the undervaluing of our master's command, exceeds all other affronts whatsoever; as on the other side, obedience is more acceptable than all other sacrifices.

And these are principally the natural laws concerning the worship of God; those, I mean, which reason dictates to every man. But to whole cities, every one whereof is one person, the same natural reason further commands an *uniformity of public worship.* For the actions done by particular persons, according to their private reasons, are not the city's actions; and therefore not the city's worship. But what is done by the city, is understood to be done by the command of him or them who have the sovereignty; wherefore also together with the consent of all the subjects, that is to say, *uniformly.*

16. The *natural laws* set down in the foregoing article concerning the divine worship, only command the giving of natural signs of honour. But we must consider that there are two kinds of signs; the one *natural;* the other done upon *agreement,* or by express or tacit composition. Now because in every language the use of *words* and *names* come by appointment, it may also by appointment

be altered; for that which depends on and derives its force from the will of men, can by the will of the same men agreeing be changed again or abolished. Such *names* therefore as are *attributed* to God by the appointment of men, can by the same appointment be taken away. Now what can be done by the appointment of men, that the city may do. The city therefore by right, that is to say, they who have the power of the whole city, shall judge what *names* or *appellations* are more, what less *honourable* for God; that is to say, what doctrines are to be held and professed concerning the nature of God and his operations. Now actions do signify not by men's appointment, but naturally; even as the effects are signs of their causes. Whereof some are always signs of scorn to them before whom they are committed; as those whereby the body's uncleanness is discovered, and whatsoever men are ashamed to do before those whom they respect. Others are always signs of honour, as to draw near and discourse decently and humbly, to give way or to yield in any matter of private benefit. In these actions the city can alter nothing. But there are infinite others, which, as much as belongs to honour or reproach, are indifferent. Now these, by the institution of the city, may both be made signs of honour, and being made so, do in very deed become so. From whence we may understand, that we must obey the city in whatsoever it shall command to be used for a sign of honouring God, that is to say, for *worship*; provided it can be instituted for a sign of honour; because that is a sign of honour, which by the city's command is used for such.

17. We have already declared which were the laws of God, as well sacred as secular, in his government by the way of nature only. Now because there is no man but may be deceived in reasoning, and that it so falls out that men are of different opinions concerning the most actions; it may be demanded further, whom God would have to be

the *interpreter of right reason*, that is to say, of his laws.
And as for the *secular* laws (I mean those which concern
justice and the carriage of men towards men), by what
hath been said before of the constitution of a city, we
have demonstratively showed it agreeable to reason, that
all *judicature* belongs to the city; and that *judicature* is
nothing else but an *interpretation of the laws*; and by
consequence, that every where cities, that is to say, those
who have the sovereign power, are the *interpreters of the
laws*. As for the *sacred* laws, we must consider what hath
been before demonstrated in chap. v. art. 13, that every
subject hath transferred as much right as he could on him
or them who had the supreme authority. But he could
have transferred his right of judging the manner how God
is to be honoured; and therefore also he hath done it.
That he could, it appears hence; that the manner of
honouring God before the constitution of a city, was to
be fetched from every man's *private reason*. But every
man can subject his *private* reason to the reason of *the
whole city*. Moreover, if each man should follow his own
reason in the *worshipping* of God, in so great a diversity
of worshippers one would be apt to judge another's worship uncomely, or impious; neither would the one seem
to the other to honour God. Even that therefore which
were most consonant to reason, would not be a *worship*;
because that the nature of *worship* consists in this, that
it be the *sign of inward honour*. But there is no sign, but
whereby somewhat becomes known to others; and therefore is there no sign of honour, but what seems so to
others. Again, that is a true sign, which by the consent of
men becomes a sign; therefore also that is honourable,
which by the consent of men, that is to say, by the command of the city, becomes a sign of honour. It is not
therefore against the will of God, declared by the way of
reason only, to give him such signs of honour as the city
shall command. Wherefore subjects can transfer their

right of judging the manner of God's worship, on him
or them who have the sovereign power. Nay, they must do
it; for else all manner of absurd opinions concerning the
nature of God, and all ridiculous ceremonies which have
been used by any nations, will be seen at once in the same
city. Whence it will fall out, that every man will believe
that all the rest do offer God an affront; so that it cannot
be truly said of any, that he worships God; for no man
worships God, that is to say, honours him outwardly, but
he who doth those things, whereby he appears to others
for to honour him. It may therefore be concluded, that
the *interpretation* of all laws, as well *sacred* as *secular*
(God ruling by the way of *nature* only), depends on the
authority of the city, that is to say, that man or counsel
to whom the sovereign power is committed; and that
whatsoever God commands, he commands by his voice.
And on the other side, that whatsoever is commanded
by them, both concerning the manner of honouring God,
and concerning secular affairs, is commanded by God
himself.

18. Against this, some man may demand, first, whether
it doth not follow that the city must be obeyed, if it
command us directly to affront God, or forbid us to worship him? I say, it does not follow, neither must we obey.
For to affront, or not to worship at all, cannot by any man
be understood for a manner of worshipping. Neither also
had any one, before the constitution of a city, of those
who acknowledge God to rule, a right to deny him the
honour which was then due unto him; nor could he
therefore transfer a right on the city of commanding any
such things. Next, if it be demanded whether the city
must be obeyed, if it command somewhat to be said or
done, which is not a disgrace to God directly, but from
whence by reasoning disgraceful consequences may be
derived; as for example, if it were commanded to worship God in an image, before those who account that

honourable: truly it is to be done.† For worship is instituted in sign of honour; but to worship him thus, is a sign
of honour, and increaseth God's honour among those
who do so account of it. Or if it be commanded to call
God by a name, which we know not what it signifies, or
how it can agree with this word *God*; that also must be
done. For what we do for honour's sake (and we know
no better), if it be taken for a sign of honour, it is a sign
of honour; and therefore if we refuse to do it, we refuse
the enlarging of God's honour. The same judgment must
be had of all the *attributes* and *actions* about the merely
rational worship of God, which may be controverted and
disputed. For though this kind of commands may be
sometimes contrary to right reason, and therefore sins
in them who command them; yet are they not against
right reason, nor sins in subjects; whose right reason, in
points of controversy, is that which submits itself to the
reason of the city. Lastly, if that man or counsel who hath
the supreme power, command himself to be worshipped
with the same *attributes* and *actions*, wherewith God is
to be worshipped; the question is, whether we must obey?
There are many things, which may be commonly attrib-

† *Truly it is to be done.* We said in art. 14 of this chapter, that
they who attributed limits to God, transgressed the natural law
concerning God's worship. Now they who worship him in an image,
assign him limits. Wherefore they do that which they ought not to
do. And this place seems to contradict the former. We must therefore know first, that they who are constrained by authority, do not
set God any bounds; but they who command them. For they who
worship unwillingly, do worship in very deed: but they either stand
or fall there, where they are commanded to stand or fall by a lawful
sovereign. Secondly, I say it must be done, not at all times and
everywhere, but on supposition that there is no other rule of worshipping God, beside the dictates of human reason; for then the will
of the city stands for reason. But in the kingdom of God by way of
covenant, whether old or new, where idolatry is expressly forbid,
though the city commands us to worship thus, yet must we not do
it. Which, if he shall consider, who conceived some repugnancy between this and art. 14, will surely cease to think so any longer.

uted both to God and men; for even men may be *praised* and *magnified*. And there are many actions, whereby God and men may be worshipped. But the significations of the *attributes* and *actions* are only to be regarded. Those *attributes* therefore, whereby we signify ourselves to be of an opinion, that there is any man endued with a sovereignty independent from God, or that he is immortal, or of infinite power, and the like; though commanded by princes, yet must they be abstained from. As also from those *actions* signifying the same; as prayer to the absent; to ask those things which God alone can give, as rain and fair weather; to offer him what God can only accept, as oblations, holocausts; or to give a worship, than which a greater cannot be given, as sacrifice. For these things seem to tend to this end, that God may not be thought to rule; contrary to what was supposed from the beginning. But genuflection, prostration, or any other act of the body whatsoever, may be lawfully used even in civil worship; for they may signify an acknowledgment of the civil power only. For divine worship is distinguished from civil, not by the motion, placing, habit, or gesture of the body, but by the declaration of our opinion of him whom we do worship. As if we cast down ourselves before any man, with intention of declaring by that sign that we esteem him as God, it is divine worship; if we do the same thing as a sign of our acknowledgment of the civil power, it is civil worship. Neither is the *divine worship* distinguished from *civil*, by any action usually understood by the words λατρεία and δουλεία; whereof the former marking out the *duty* of servants, the latter their *destiny*, they are words of the same action in degree.

19. From what hath been said may be gathered, that God reigning by the way of natural reason only, subjects do sin, first if they break the moral laws; which are unfolded in chapters II. and III. Secondly, if they break the laws or commands of the city, in those things which per-

tain to justice. Thirdly, if they worship not God κατὰ τὰ νόμικα. Fourthly, if they confess not before men, both in words and deeds, that there is one God most good, most great, most blessed, the Supreme King of the world and of all worldly kings; that is to say, if they do not worship God. This fourth sin in the natural kingdom of God, by what hath been said in the foregoing chapter in art. 2, is the *sin of treason against the Divine Majesty*. For it is a denying of the Divine Power, or *atheism*. For sins proceed here, just as if we should suppose some man to be the sovereign king, who being himself absent, should rule by his viceroy. Against whom sure they would transgress, who should not obey his viceroy in all things; except he usurped the kingdom to himself, or would give it to some other. But they who should so absolutely obey him, as not to admit of this exception, might be said to be guilty of treason.

XVI

Of the Kingdom of God under the Old Covenant

1. Superstition possessing foreign nations, God instituted the true religion by the means of Abraham. 2. By the covenant between God and Adam, all dispute is forbidden concerning the commands of superiors. 3. The manner of the covenant between God and Abraham. 4. In that covenant is contained an acknowledgment of God, not simply, but of him who appeared unto Abraham. 5. The laws unto which Abraham was tied, were no other beside those of nature, and the law of circumcision. 6. Abraham was the interpreter of the word of God, and of all laws among those that belonged to him. 7. Abraham's subjects could not sin by obeying him. 8. God's covenant with the Hebrews at Mount Sinai. 9. From thence God's government took the name of a kingdom. 10. What laws were by God given to the Jews. 11. What the word of God is, and how to be known. 12. What was held the written word of God among the Jews. 13. The power of interpreting the word of God, and the supreme civil power, were united in Moses while he lived. 14. They were also united in the high-priest, during the life of Joshua. 15. They were united too in the high-priest until king Saul's time. 16. They were also united in the kings until the captivity. 17. They were so in the high-priests after the captivity. 18. Denial of the Divine Providence, and idolatry, were the only treasons against the Divine Majesty among the Jews; in all things else they ought to obey their princes.

1. Mankind, from conscience of its own weakness and admiration of natural events, hath this; that most men believe God to be the invisible maker of all |invisible| things; whom they also fear, conceiving that they have

not a sufficient protection in themselves. But the imper-
fect use they had of their reason, the violence of their passions did so cloud them, that they could not rightly worship him. Now the fear of invisible things, when it is
severed from right reason, is superstition. It was therefore almost impossible for men, without the special assistance of God, to avoid both rocks of *atheism* and *superstition*. For this proceeds from fear without right reason;
that, from an opinion of right reason without fear.
Idolatry therefore did easily fasten upon the greatest part
of men; and almost all nations did worship God in images
and resemblances of finite things; and they worshipped
spirits or vain visions, perhaps out of fear calling them
devils. But it pleased the Divine Majesty, as we read it
written in the sacred history, out of all mankind to call
forth Abraham, by whose means he might bring men to
the true worship of him; and to reveal himself supernaturally to him, and to make that most famous covenant with
him and his seed, which is called the *old covenant* or *testament*. He therefore is the head of true religion; he was
the first that *after the deluge taught, that there was one
God, the Creator of the universe*. And from him the *kingdom of God by way of covenants*, takes its beginning.
Joseph. Antiq. Jews, lib. i. cap. 7.

2. In the beginning of the world God reigned indeed,
not only naturally, but also *by way of covenant*, over
Adam and Eve; so as it seems he would have no obedience
yielded to him, beside that which natural reason should
dictate, but *by the way of covenant*, that is to say, by the
consent of men themselves. Now because this *covenant*
was presently made void, nor ever after renewed, the
original of God's *kingdom* (which we treat of in this
place) is not to be taken thence. Yet this is to be noted by
the way; that by that precept of not eating of the tree of
the knowledge of good and evil (whether the judicature
of good and evil, or the eating of the fruit of some tree

were forbidden), God did require a most simple obedience to his commands, without dispute whether that were *good* or *evil* which was commanded. For the fruit of the tree, if the command be wanting, hath nothing in its own nature, whereby the eating of it could be morally *evil*, that is to say, *a sin*.

3. Now the covenant between God and Abraham was made in this manner (Gen. xvii. 7, 8): *I will establish my covenant between me and thee, and thy seed after thee in their generations, for an everlasting covenant, to be a God unto thee and to thy seed after thee. And I will give unto thee and to thy seed after thee, the land wherein thou art a stranger, all the land of Canaan, for an everlasting possession; and I will be their God.* Now it was necessary to institute some sign, whereby Abraham and his seed should retain the memory of this covenant; wherefore *circumcision* was added to the covenant, but yet as a sign only (verse 10, 11): *This is my covenant which ye shall keep between me and thee, and thy seed after thee; every man-child among you shall be circumcised, and ye shall circumcise the flesh of your foreskin; and it shall be a token of the covenant between me and you.* It is therefore covenanted, that Abraham shall acknowledge God to be his God and the God of his seed, that is to say, that he shall submit himself to be governed by him; and that God shall give unto Abraham the inheritance of that land wherein he then dwelt but as a pilgrim; and that Abraham, for a memorial sign of this covenant, should take care to see himself and his male seed *circumcised*.

4. But seeing that Abraham, even before the covenant, acknowledged God to be the Creator and King of the world (for he never doubted either of the *being* or the *providence* of God); how comes it not to be superfluous, that God would purchase to himself with a price and by *contract* an obedience which was due to him by nature;

namely, by promising Abraham the land of Canaan, upon
condition that he would receive him for his God; when
by the right of nature he was already so? By those words
therefore, *to be a God unto thee and to thy seed after
thee*, we understand not that Abraham satisfied this
covenant by a bare acknowledgment of the power and
dominion which God had naturally over men, that is to
say, by acknowledging God indefinitely, which belongs to
natural reason; but he must definitely acknowledge him,
who said unto him (Gen. xii. 1, 2): *Get thee out of thy
country*; &c. (Gen. xiii. 14): *Lift up thine eyes*, &c.:
who appeared unto him (Gen. xviii. 1, 2), in the shape
of three celestial men; and (Gen. xv. 1), in a *vision*; and
(verse 13), in a *dream*, which is *matter of faith*. In what
shape God appeared unto Abraham, by what kind of
sound he spake to him, is not expressed. Yet it is plain
that Abraham believed that voice to be the voice of God
and a true revelation, and would have all his to worship
him, who had so spoken unto him, for God the Creator of
the world; and that his faith was grounded on this, not
that he believed *God to have a being* or *that he was true*
in his promises, that which all men believe, but that he
doubted not him to be God, whose voice and promises
he had heard, and that the *God* of Abraham signified not
simply *God*, but *that God which appeared unto him*; even
as the worship, which Abraham owed unto God in that
notion, was not the worship of *reason*, but of *religion* and
faith, and that which not reason, but God had *supernaturally* revealed.

5. But we read of no laws given by God to Abraham, or
by Abraham to his family, either then or after, secular
or sacred; excepting the commandment of *circumcision*,
which is contained in the *covenant* itself. Whence it is
manifest, that there were no other laws or worship which
Abraham was obliged to, but the laws of nature, rational
worship, and circumcision.

6. Now Abraham was the *interpreter* of all *laws*, as well sacred as secular, among those that belonged to him; not merely naturally, as using the laws of nature only, but even by the form of the covenant itself; in which obedience is promised by Abraham, not for himself only, but for his seed also; which had been in vain, except his children had been tied to obey his commands. And how can that be understood, which God says (Gen. xviii. 18, 19): *All the nations of the earth shall be blessed in him; for I know him, that he will command his children and his household after him, and they shall keep the way of the Lord to do justice and judgment*: unless his children and his household were supposed to be obliged to yield obedience unto his commands?

7. Hence it follows, that Abraham's subjects could not sin in obeying him, provided that Abraham commanded them not to deny God's *existence* or *providence*, or to do somewhat expressly contrary to the honour of God. In all other things, *the word of God* was to be fetched from his lips only, as being the interpreter of all the *laws* and *words* of God. For Abraham alone could teach them who was the God of Abraham, and in what manner he was to be worshipped. And they who after Abraham's death were subject to the sovereignty of Isaac or Jacob, did by the same reason obey them in all things without sin, as long as they acknowledged and professed *the God of Abraham* to be their God. For they had submitted themselves *to God* simply, before they did it to Abraham, and to Abraham before they did it to the God of Abraham: again, to the God of Abraham, before they did it to Isaac. In Abraham's subjects therefore, to deny God was the only *treason against the divine Majesty*; but in their posterity, it was also treason *to deny the God of Abraham*, that is to say, to worship God otherwise than was instituted by Abraham, to wit, in images made with

hands,* as other nations did; which for that reason were called *idolaters*. And hitherto, subjects might easily enough discern what was to be observed, what avoided in the commands of their princes.

8. To go on now, following the guidance of the holy Scripture; the same *covenant* was renewed (Gen. xxvi. 3, 4) with Isaac; and (Gen. xxviii. 13, 14) with Jacob; where God styles himself not simply God, whom nature doth dictate him to be, but distinctly the *God of Abraham and Isaac*. Afterward being about to renew the same *covenant* by Moses with the whole people of Israel (Exod. iii. 6): *I am*, saith he, *the God of thy Father, the God of Abraham, the God of Isaac, and the God of Jacob*. Afterward, when that people, not only the freest, but also the greatest enemy to human subjection, by reason of the fresh memory of their Egyptian bondage, abode in the wilderness near Mount Sinai, that *ancient covenant* was propounded to them all to be renewed in this manner (Exod. xix. 5, 6): *Therefore if ye will obey my voice indeed, and keep my covenant* (to wit, that covenant which was made with Abraham, Isaac and Jacob); *then shall ye be a peculiar treasure unto me, above all people; for all the earth is mine, and ye shall be to me a kingdom of priests, and an holy nation. And· all the people answered together, and said* (verse 8), *All that the Lord hath spoken, will we do.*

9. In this covenant, among other things, we must consider well the appellation of *kingdom*, not used before. For although God, both by *nature* and by *covenant* made

---

* *In images made with hands*. In chap. xv. art. 14, there we have showed such a kind of worship to be irrational. But if it be done by the command of a city, to whom the written word of God is not known nor received, we have then showed this worship (in article 18) to be rational. But where God reigns by way of covenant, in which it is expressly warned not to worship thus, as in the covenant made with Abraham; there, whether it be with or without the command of the city, it is ill done.

with Abraham, was their king, yet owed they him an obedience and worship only natural, as being his subjects; and religious, such as Abraham instituted, as being the subjects of Abraham, Isaac, and Jacob, their natural princes. For they had received no *word of God* beside the natural word of right reason; neither had any *covenant* passed between God and them, otherwise than as their wills were included in the will of Abraham, as their *prince*. But now by the covenant made at Mount Sinai, the consent of each man being had, there becomes an *institutive kingdom of God* over them. That *kingdom of God*, so renowned in Scriptures and writings of divines, took its beginning from this time; and hither tends that which God said to Samuel, when the Israelites asked a king (1 Sam. viii. 7): *They have not rejected thee, but they have rejected me, that I should not reign over them;* and that which Samuel told the Israelites (1 Sam. xii. 12): *Ye said unto me, nay, but a king shall reign over us, when the Lord your God was your king;* and that which is said, Jer. xxxi. 31: *I will make a new covenant, &c. although I was an husband unto them;* and the doctrine also of Judas Galilæus, where mention is made in *Josephus' Antiq. of the Jews* (Book xviii. chap. 2), in these words: *But Judas Galilæus was the first author of this fourth way of those who followed the study of wisdom. These agree in all the rest with the Pharisees, excepting that they burn with a most constant desire of liberty; believing God alone to be held for their Lord and prince; and will sooner endure even the most exquisite kinds of torments, together with their kinsfolks and dearest friends, than call any mortal man their Lord.*

10. The right of the kingdom being thus constituted by way of *covenant*, let us see in the next place, what *laws* God propounded to them. Now those are known to all, to wit, the *decalogue*, and those other, as well *judicial* as *ceremonial laws*, which we find from the twentieth chap-

ter of Exodus to the end of Deuteronomy and the death
of Moses. Now of those *laws*, delivered in general by the
hand of Moses, some there are which oblige *naturally*,
being made by God, as the *God of nature*, and had their
force even before Abraham's time. Others there are which
oblige by virtue of the *covenant* made with Abraham, being made by God as the God of Abraham, which had
their force even before Moses's time, by reason of the
former *covenant*. But there are *others* which oblige by
virtue of that covenant only, which was made last with
the people themselves; being made by God, as being
the peculiar king of the Israelites. Of the first sort are all
the precepts of the decalogue which pertain unto manners; such as, *honour thy parents, thou shalt not kill, thou
shalt not commit adultery, thou shalt not steal, thou shalt
not bear false witness, thou shalt not covet;* for they
are the laws of nature. Also the precept of not taking
God's name in vain; for it is a part of natural worship, as
hath been declared in the foregoing chapter (art. 15). In
like manner the second commandment, of not worshipping by way of any image made by themselves; for this
also is a part of natural religion, as hath been showed in
the same article. Of the second sort is the first commandment of the decalogue, *of not having any other Gods;*
for in that consists the essence of the *covenant* made with
Abraham, by which God requires nothing else, but that
he should be his God, and the God of his seed. Also the
precept of *keeping holy the Sabbath;* for the sanctifica-
tion of the seventh day is instituted in memorial of the
six days' creation, as appears out of these words (Exod.
xxxi. 16–17): *It is a perpetual covenant* (meaning *the
Sabbath), and a sign between me and the children of Israel for ever; for in six days the Lord made heaven and
earth, and on the seventh day he rested, and was re-
freshed.* Of the third kind are the *politic, judicial,* and
ceremonial laws; which only belonged to the Jews. The

laws of the first and second sort written in *tables of stone,* to wit, the *decalogue,* was kept in the *ark* itself. The rest written in the *volume* of the whole law, were laid up in *the side of the ark* (Deut. xxxi. 26). For these, retaining the faith of Abraham, might be changed; those could not.

11. All God's *laws* are *God's word;* but all *God's word* is not his *law. I am the Lord thy God which brought thee out of the land of Egypt,* is the word of God; it is no law. Neither is all that, which for the better declaring of *God's word* is pronounced or written together with it, instantly to be taken for *God's word.* For, *Thus saith the Lord,* is not the voice of God, but of the preacher or prophet. All that, and only that, is the word of God, which a true prophet hath declared God to have spoken. Now the writings of the prophets, comprehending as well those things which God, as which the prophet himself speaks, are therefore called the word of God, because they contain the word of God. Now because all that, and that alone, is the *word of God,* which is recommended to us for such by a true prophet, it cannot be known what *God's word* is, before we know who is the true prophet; nor can we believe *God's word,* before we believe the prophet. Moses was believed by the people of Israel for two things; his *miracles* and his *faith.* For how great and most evident miracles soever he had wrought, yet would they not have trusted him, at least he was not to have been trusted, if he had called them out of Egypt to any other worship than the worship of the God of Abraham, Isaac, and Jacob their fathers. For it had been contrary to the *covenant* made by themselves with God. In like manner two things there are; to wit, *supernatural prediction of things to come,* which is a mighty miracle; and *faith in the God of Abraham, their deliverer out of Egypt;* which God proposed to all the Jews to be kept for marks of a true prophet. He that wants either of these, is no prophet; nor is it to be received for God's word, which

he obtrudes for such. If faith be wanting, he is rejected in these words (Deut. xiii. 1, 2, 3, 4, 5): *If there arise among you a prophet or a dreamer of dreams, and giveth thee a sign, or a wonder; and the sign or the wonder come to pass, whereof he spake unto thee, saying, Let us go after other gods, &c. that prophet, or that dreamer of dreams shall be put to death.* If prediction of events be wanting, he is condemned by these (Deut. xviii. 21, 22): *And if thou say in thine heart, how shall we know the word which the Lord hath not spoken? When a prophet speaketh in the name of the Lord, if the thing follow not nor come to pass, that is the thing which the Lord hath not spoken; but the prophet hath spoken it presumptuously.* Now, that that is the word of God which is published for such by a true prophet; and that he was held to be a true prophet among the Jews, whose faith was true, and to whose predictions the events answered; is without controversy. But what it is, to follow other gods, and whether the events which are affirmed to answer their predictions, do truly answer them or not, may admit many controversies; especially in predictions which obscurely and enigmatically foretell the event; such as the predictions of almost all the prophets are; as who saw not God apparently, like unto Moses, but *in dark speeches, and in figures* (Numb. xii. 8). But of these we cannot judge, otherwise than *by the way of natural reason;* because that judgment depends on the prophet's interpretation, and on its proportion with the event.

12. The Jews did hold the book of the whole law, which was called *Deuteronomy,* for *the written word of God;* and that only (forasmuch as can be collected out of sacred history) until the captivity. For this book was delivered by Moses himself to the priests, to be kept and laid up in the side of the ark of the covenant, and to be copied out by the kings; and the same a long time after, by the authority of king Josiah (2 Kings xxiii. 2), acknowl-

edged again for *the word of God*. But it is not manifest,
when the rest of the books of the Old Testament were
first received into canon. But what concerns the prophets,
Isaiah and the rest, since they foretold no other things
than what were to come to pass, either in or after the captivity, their writings could not at that time be held for
prophetic; by reason of the law cited above (Deut. xviii.
21, 22), whereby the Israelites were commanded not to
account any man for a true prophet, but him whose
prophecies were answered by the events. And hence peradventure it is, that the Jews esteemed the writings of
those whom they slew when they prophesied, for
prophetic afterward; that is to say, for the word of God.

13. It being known what laws there were under *the old
covenant*, and what *word of God* received from the beginning; we must furthermore consider, with whom the
authority of judging, whether the writings of the prophets
arising afterward were to be received for the *word of God*;
that is to say, whether the events did answer their predictions or not; and with whom also the authority of interpreting the laws already received, and the written word
of God, did reside: which thing is to be traced through
all the times and several changes of the commonwealth
of Israel. But it is manifest that this power, during the
life of Moses, was entirely in himself. For if he had not
been the *interpreter of the laws and word*, that office must
have belonged either to *every private person*, or to a *congregation* or *synagogue* of many, or to the *high-priest* or
to other *prophets*. First, that that office belonged not to
private men, or any congregation made of them, appears
hence; that they were not admitted, nay, they were prohibited with most heavy threats, *to hear God speak*, otherwise than by the means of Moses. For it is written (Exod.
xix. 24, 25): *Let not the priests and the people break
through, to come up unto the Lord, lest he break forth
upon them. So Moses went down unto the people, and*

spake unto them. It is further manifestly and expressly declared, upon occasion given by the rebellion of Corah, Dathan, and Abiram, and the two hundred and fifty princes of the assembly, that neither private men nor the congregation should pretend that God had spoken by them, and by consequence that they had the right of *interpreting God's word.* For they contending, that God spake no less by them than by Moses, argue thus (Numbers xvi. 3): *Ye take too much upon you, seeing all the congregation are holy, every one of them, and the Lord is among them. Wherefore then lift ye up yourselves above the congregation of the Lord?* But how God determined this controversy, is easily understood by verses 33 and 35 of the same chapter, where *Corah, Dathan, and Abiram went down alive into the pit,* &c. *And there came out fire from the Lord, and consumed the two hundred and fifty men that offered incense.* Secondly, that Aaron the high-priest had not this authority, is manifest by the like controversy between him (together with his sister Miriam) and Moses. For the question was, whether God spake by Moses only, or by them also; that is to say, whether Moses alone, or whether they also were *interpreters of the word of God.* For thus they said (Numb. xii. 2): *Hath the Lord indeed spoken only by Moses? Hath he not also spoken by us?* But God reproved them; and made a distinction between Moses and other prophets, saying (verse 6, 7, 8): *If there be a prophet among you, I the Lord will make myself known unto him in a vision, and will speak unto him in a dream: my servant Moses is not so,* &c. *For with him will I speak mouth to mouth, even apparently, and not in dark speeches, and the similitude of the Lord shall he behold. Wherefore then were ye not afraid to speak against my servant Moses?* Lastly, that *the interpretation of the word of God* as long as Moses lived, belonged not to any other prophets whatsoever, is collected out of that place which we now cited, concerning his eminency above all others; and out of natural reason, for as much as it belongs to the same prophet who brings the commands of God, to unfold them too; but there was then no other *word of God,* beside that which was declared by Moses. And out of this also, that there was no other prophet extant at that time, who prophesied to the people, excepting the seventy elders who prophesied by *the spirit* of Moses. And even that Joshua, who was then Moses' servant, his successor afterward, believed to be injuriously done, till he knew it was by Moses' consent; which thing is manifest by text of Scripture (Numb. xi. 25): *And the Lord came down in a cloud, &c. and took of the spirit that was upon Moses, and gave it unto the seventy elders.* Now after it was told that they prophesied, Joshua said unto Moses, *Forbid them, my lord.* But Moses answered: *Why enviest thou for my sake?* Seeing therefore Moses alone was the messenger of God's word, and that the authority of interpreting it pertained neither to *private men,* nor to *the synagogue,* nor to the *high-priest,* nor to other *prophets;* it remains that Moses alone was *the interpreter of God's word,* who also had the supreme power in civil matters; and that the conventions of Corah with the rest of his complices against Moses and Aaron, and of Aaron with his sister against Moses, were raised, not for the salvation of their souls, but by reason of their ambition and desire of dominion over the people.

14. In Joshua's time *the interpretation of the laws,* and *of the word of God,* belonged to Eleazar the high-priest; who was also, under God, their absolute king. Which is collected, first of all, out of the *covenant itself;* in which the commonwealth of Israel is called a *priestly kingdom,* or, as it is recited in 1 Peter ii. 9, a *royal priesthood.* Which could in no wise be said, unless by the institution and *covenant* of the people, the regal power were understood to belong to the *high-priest.* Neither doth this re-

pugn what hath been said before, where Moses, and not
Aaron, had the kingdom under God. Since it is necessary, that when one man institutes the form of a future
commonwealth, that one should govern the kingdom
which he institutes during his life (whether it be *monarchy, aristocracy,* or *democracy*); and have all that
power for the present, which he is bestowing on others
for the future. Now, that Eleazar the priest had not only
the priesthood, but also the *sovereignty,* is expressly set
down in Joshua's call to the administration. For thus it
is written (Numb. xxvii. 18, 19, 20, 21): *Take thee Joshua
the son of Nun, a man in whom is the Spirit, and lay
thine hand upon him, and set him before Eleazar the
priest, and before all the congregation, and give him a
charge in their sight; and thou shalt put some of thine
honour upon him, that all the congregation of the children of Israel may be obedient; and he shall stand before
Eleazar the priest, who shall ask counsel for him after
the judgment of Urim, before the Lord; at his word shall
they go out, and at his word shall they come in, and all
the children of Israel with him, even all the congregation.* Where *to ask counsel of God for whatsoever is to
be done,* that is, *to interpret God's word,* and in the name
of God to command in all matters, belongs to Eleazar;
and *to go out* and *to come in at his word,* that is to say, to
obey, belongs both to Joshua and *to all the people.* It is to
be observed also, that that speech, *part of thy glory,*
clearly denotes that Joshua had not a power equal with
that which Moses had. In the meantime it is manifest, that
even in Joshua's time the supreme power and authority
of interpreting the word of God, were both in one person.

15. After Joshua's death follow the times of the Judges
until king Saul; in which it is manifest that the right of
the *kingdom* instituted by God, remained with the *high-
priest.* For the *kingdom* was by covenant *priestly,* that
is to say, God's government by priests. And such ought

it to have been, until that form, with God's consent, were changed by the people themselves; which was not done before that requiring a king God consented unto them, and said unto Samuel (1 Sam. viii. 7): *Hearken unto the voice of the people in all that they say unto thee; for they have not rejected thee, but they have rejected me, that I should not reign over them.* The supreme civil power was therefore *rightly* due by God's own institution to the high-priest; but *actually* that power was in the prophets, to whom (being raised by God in an extraordinary manner) the Israelites, a people greedy of prophets, submitted themselves to be protected and judged, by reason of the great esteem they had of prophecies. The reason of this thing was, because that though penalties were set and judges appointed in the institution of God's priestly kingdom; yet, the right of inflicting punishment depended wholly on private judgment; and it belonged to a dissolute multitude and each single person to punish or not to punish, according as their private zeal should stir them up. And therefore Moses by his own command punished no man with death; but when any man was to be put to death, one or many stirred up the multitude against him or them, by divine authority, and saying, *Thus saith the Lord.* Now this was conformable to the nature of God's peculiar kingdom. For there God reigns indeed, where his laws are obeyed not for fear of men, but for fear of himself. And truly, if men were such as they should be, this were an excellent state of civil government; but as men are, there is a coercive power (in which I comprehend both right and might) necessary to rule them. And therefore also God, from the beginning, prescribed laws by Moses for the future kings (Deut. xvii. 14–20). And Moses foretold this in his last words to the people, saying (Deut. xxxi. 29): *I know that after my death ye will utterly corrupt yourselves, and turn aside from the way that I have commanded you,* &c. When therefore accord-

ing to this prediction there arose another generation
(Judges ii. 10–11) *who knew not the Lord, nor yet the
works which he had done for Israel, the children of Israel
did evil in the sight of the Lord, and served Balaam;* to
wit, they cast off God's government, that is to say, that
of the *priest*, by whom God ruled; and afterward, when
they were overcome by their enemies and oppressed with
bondage, they looked for God's will, not at the hands of
the *priest* any more, but of the prophets. These therefore
actually judged Israel; but their obedience was *rightly
due* to the high-priest. Although therefore the priestly
kingdom, after the death of Moses and Joshua, was without power; yet was it not without right. Now that the *interpretation of God's word* did belong to the same high-
priest, is manifest by this; that God, after the tabernacle
and the ark of the covenant was consecrated, spake no
more in Mount Sinai, but in the tabernacle of the covenant, from the propitiatory which was between the *cherubims*, whither it was not lawful for any to approach except the high-priest. If therefore regard be had to the
right of the kingdom, the supreme civil power and the
authority of interpreting God's word were joined in the
high-priest. If we consider the *fact*, they were united in
the prophets who judged Israel. For as *judges*, they had
the civil authority; as *prophets*, they interpreted God's
word. And thus every way hitherto these two powers continued inseparable.

16. Kings being once constituted, it is no doubt but
the *civil authority* belonged to them. For the kingdom of
God by the way of priesthood (God consenting to the
request of the Israelites) was ended; which Hierom also
marks, speaking of the books of Samuel. Samuel, says he,
Eli being dead and Saul slain, declares the old law abolished. Furthermore, the oaths of the new priesthood and
new sovereignty in Zadok and David, do testify that the
right, whereby the *kings* did rule, was founded in the very

concession of the people. |The priest could rightly do
only what God commanded him, whereas the king could
rightly do to every man whatsoever every man could
rightly do himself; for |the Israelites granted him *a right
to judge* of all things, and to *wage war* for all men;
in which two are contained all right whatsoever can be
conceived from man to man. *Our king* say they (1 Sam.
viii. 20) *shall judge us, and go out before us, and fight
our battles. Judicature* therefore belonged to the kings.
But to *judge* is nothing else, than by *interpreting* to ap-
ply the |*facts* to the *laws.* |To them therefore belonged the
interpretation *of laws* too. And because there was no
other written word of God acknowledged beside the *law
of* Moses, until the captivity; the authority *of interpreting God's word* did also belong to the kings. Nay, forasmuch as the word of God must be taken for a law, if there
had been another written word beside the Mosaical law,
seeing the interpretation of laws belonged to the kings,
the interpretation of it must also have belonged to them.
When the book of Deuteronomy, in which the whole Mosaical *law* was contained, being a long time lost was found
again; *the priests* indeed asked counsel of God concerning that book, but not by their own authority, but by the
commandment of Josiah; and not immediately neither,
but by the means of Holda the prophetess. Whence it
appears that the authority of admitting books for the
word of God, belonged not to the priest. Neither yet follows it, that that authority belonged to the prophetess;
because others did judge of the prophets, whether they
were to be held for true or not. For to what end did God
give signs and tokens to all the people, whereby the true
prophets might be discerned from the false; namely, the
event of predictions, and conformity with the religion
established by Moses; if they might not use those marks?
The authority therefore of admitting books for *the word
of God,* belonged to the king; and thus that book of the

law was approved, and received again by the authority of
king Josiah; as appears by the second book of the Kings,
chap. xxii. xxiii.: where it is reported that he gathered together all the several degrees of his kingdom, *the elders,
priests, prophets, and all the people; and he read in their
ears all the words of the covenant;* that is to say, he
caused that *covenant* to be acknowledged for the Mosaical *covenant;* that is to say, *for the word of God;* and
to be again received and confirmed by the Israelites. The
civil power therefore, and the power of discerning God's
word from the words of men, and of interpreting God's
word even in the days of the kings, was wholly belonging
to themselves. Prophets were sent not with authority, but
in the form and by the right of proclaimers and preachers,
of whom the hearers did judge. And if perhaps these were
punished who did not listen to them plainly, teaching
easy things; it doth not thence follow, that the kings were
obliged to follow all things which they, in God's name,
did declare were to be followed. For though Josiah, the
good king of Judah, were slain because he obeyed not
the word of the Lord from the mouth of Necho king of
Egypt; that is to say, because he rejected good counsel
though it seemed to come from an enemy; yet no man
I hope will say that Josiah was, by any bond either of divine or human laws, obliged to believe Pharaoh Necho
king of Egypt, because he said *that God had spoken to
him.* But what some man may object against kings, that
for want of learning they are seldom able enough to interpret those books of antiquity, in the which God's word
is contained; and that for this cause, it is not reasonable
that this office should depend on their authority; he may
object as much against the priests and all mortal men;
for they may err. And although priests were better
instructed in nature and arts than other men, yet kings
are able enough to appoint such interpreters under them;
and so, though kings did not themselves interpret the

word of God, yet the office of interpreting them might depend on their authority. And they who therefore refuse to yield up this authority to kings, because they cannot practice the office itself, do as much as if they should say, that the authority of teaching *geometry* must not depend upon kings, except they themselves were geometricians. We read that kings have prayed for the people; that they have blessed the people; that they have consecrated the temple; that they have commanded the priests; that they have removed priests from their office; that they have constituted others. Sacrifices indeed they have not offered; for that was hereditary to Aaron and his sons. But it is manifest, as in Moses' lifetime, so throughout all ages, from king Saul to the captivity of Babylon, that the priesthood was not a maistry, but a ministry.

17. After their return from Babylonian bondage, the *covenant* being renewed and signed, *the priestly kingdom* was restored to the same manner it was in from the death of Joshua to the beginning of the kings; excepting that it is not expressly set down, that the returned Jews did give up the right of sovereignty either to Esdras, by whose directions they ordered their state, or to any other beside God himself. That reformation seems rather to be nothing else, than the bare promises and vows of every man, to observe those things which were written in the book of the law. Notwithstanding (perhaps not by the people's intention), by virtue of the *covenant* which they then renewed (for the covenant was the same with that which was made at Mount Sinai), that same state was a *priestly kingdom*; that is to say, the supreme civil authority and the sacred were united in the priests. Now, howsoever through the ambition of those who strove for the priesthood, and by the interposition of foreign princes, it was so troubled till our Saviour Jesus Christ's time, that it cannot be understood out of the histories of those times, where that authority resided; yet it is plain, that in those

times the power *of interpreting God's word* was not severed from the supreme civil power.

18. Out of all this, we may easily know how the Jews, in all times from Abraham unto Christ, were to behave themselves in the commands of their *princes*. For as in kingdoms merely human, men must obey a subordinate magistrate in all things, excepting when his commands contain in them some treason; so in the kingdom of God, the Jews were bound to obey their *princes*, Abraham, Isaac, Jacob, Moses, the *priest*, the *king*, every one during their time in all things, except when their commands did contain some treason against *the Divine Majesty*. Now treason against the Divine Majesty was, first, *the denial of his divine providence*; for this was *to deny God to be a king by nature:* next, *idolatry*, or the worship not of other (for there is but one God), but of strange Gods; that is to say, a worship though of one God, yet under other *titles, attributes*, and *rites*, than what were established by Abraham and Moses; for this was to *deny the God of Abraham* to be their king *by covenant* made with Abraham and themselves. In all other things they were to obey. And if a king or priest, having the sovereign authority, had commanded somewhat else to be done which was against the laws, t1at had been his sin, and not his subject's; whose duty it is, not to dispute, but to obey the commands of his superiors.

XVII

Of the Kingdom of God by the New Covenant

1. The prophecies concerning Christ's dignity. 2. The prophecies concerning his humility and passion. 3. That Jesus was that Christ. 4. That the kingdom of God by the new covenant, was not the kingdom of Christ, as Christ, but as God. 5. That the kingdom by the new covenant is heavenly, and shall begin from the day of judgment. 6. That the government of Christ in this world was not a sovereignty, but counsel, or a government by the way of doctrine and persuasion. 7. What the promises of the new covenant are, on both parts. 8. That no laws are added by Christ, beside the institution of the sacraments. 9. Repent ye, be baptized, keep the commandments, and the like forms of speech, are not laws. 10. It pertains to the civil authority, to define what the sin of injustice is. 11. It pertains to the civil authority, to define what conduces to the peace and defence of the city. 12. It pertains to the civil authority, to judge (when need requires) what definitions and what inferences are true. 13. It belongs to the office of Christ, to teach | morally, not by the way of speculation, but as a law; to forgive sins, and to teach all things whereof there is no science, properly so called. 14. A distinction of things temporal from spiritual. 15. In how many several sorts the word of God may be taken. 16. That all which is contained in Holy Scripture, belongs not to the canon of Christian faith. 17. That the word of a lawful interpreter of Holy Scriptures, is the word of God. 18. That the authority of interpreting Scriptures, is the same with that of determining controversies of faith. 19. Divers significations of a Church. 20. What a Church is, to which we attribute rights, actions, and the like personal capacities. 21. A Christian city is the same with a Christian Church. 22. Many cities do not constitute one Church. 23. Who are ecclesiastical persons. 24. That the election

of ecclesiastical persons belongs to the Church, their consecration to pastors. 25. That the power of remitting the sins of the penitent, and retaining those of the impenitent, belongs to the pastors; but that of judging concerning repentance belongs to the Church. 26. What excommunication is, and on whom it cannot pass. 27. That the interpretation of Scripture depends on the authority of the city. 28. That a Christian city ought to interpret Scriptures by ecclesiastical pastors.

1. There are many clear prophecies extant in the Old Testament concerning our Saviour Jesus Christ, who was to restore the kingdom of *God* by a new covenant; partly foretelling his regal *dignity*, partly his *humility and passion*. Among others concerning his dignity, these. God, blessing Abraham, makes him a promise of his son Isaac; and adds (Gen. xvii. 16): *And kings of people shall be of him.* Jacob blessing his son Judah (Gen. xlix. 10): *The sceptre*, quoth he, *shall not depart from Judah.* God to Moses (Deut. xviii. 18): *A prophet,* saith he, *will I raise them up from among their brethren, like unto thee, and will put my words in his mouth, and he shall speak unto them all that I shall command him; and it shall come to pass, that whosoever will not hearken unto my words, which he shall speak in my name, I will require it of him.* Isaiah (Isai. vii. 14): *The Lord himself shall give thee a sign; Behold a virgin shall conceive and bear a son, and shall call his name Emmanuel.* The same prophet (Isaiah ix. 6): *Unto us a child is born, unto us a son is given, and the government shall be upon his shoulders; and his name shall be called wonderful, counsellor, the mighty God, the everlasting Father, the Prince of Peace.* And again (Isaiah xi. 1–5): *There shall come forth a rod out of the stem of Jesse, and a branch shall grow out of his roots; the spirit of the Lord shall rest upon him,* &c.; *He shall not judge after the sight of his eyes, neither reprove after the hearing of his ears; but with righteous-*

ness shall he judge the poor, &c.; *And he shall smite the earth with the rod of his mouth, and with the breath of his lips shall he slay the wicked.* Furthermore in the same Isaiah (chapters li. to lxii.), there is almost nothing else contained but a description of the coming and the works of Christ. Jeremiah (Jerem. xxxi. 31): *Behold the days come, saith the Lord, that I will make a new covenant with the house of Israel, and with the house of Judah.* And Baruch (Bar. iii. 35–37): *This is our God,* &c. *Afterward did he show himself upon earth, and conversed with men.* Ezekiel (Ezek. xxxiv. 23–25): *I will set up one shepherd over them, and he shall feed them; even my servant David. And I will make with them a covenant of peace,* &c. Daniel (Dan. vii. 13–14): *I saw in the night visions; and behold one like the Son of Man came with the clouds of heaven, and came to the ancient of days; and they brought him near before him; and there was given him dominion, and glory, and a kingdom, that all people, nations, and languages should serve him; his dominion is an everlasting dominion,* &c. Haggai (Haggai ii. 6–7): *Yet once it is a little while, and I will shake the heaven, and the earth, and the sea, and the dry land; and I will shake all nations; and the desire of all nations shall come.* Zachariah, under the type of Joshua the high-priest (Zach. iii. 8): *I will bring forth my servant the branch,* &c. And again (Zach. vi. 12): *Behold the man whose name is the Branch.* And again (Zach. ix. 9): *Rejoice greatly O daughter of Zion, shout O daughter of Jerusalem; behold thy king cometh to thee; he is just, having salvation.* The Jews moved by these and other prophecies, expected Christ their king to be sent from God; who should redeem them, and furthermore bear rule over all nations. Yea, this prophecy had spread over the whole Roman empire; which Vespasian too, though falsely, interpreted in favour of his own enterprises; *that out of Judea should come he that should have dominion.*

2. Now the prophecies of *Christ's humility and passion,*
amongst others are these: (Isaiah liii. 4): *He hath borne
our griefs, and carried our sorrows; yet we did esteem him
stricken, smitten of God, and afflicted;* and by and by
(verse 7): *He was oppressed, he was afflicted, yet he
opened not his mouth; he is brought as a lamb to the
slaughter, and as a sheep before her shearer is dumb, so
opened he not his mouth,* &c. And again (verse 8): *He
was cut out of the land of the living; for the transgression
of my people was he stricken,* &c. (Verse 12): *Therefore
will I divide him a portion with the great, and he shall
divide the spoil with the strong; because he hath poured
out his soul unto death, and he was numbered with the
transgressors, and he bare the sin of many, and made in-
tercession for the transgressors.* And that of Zachariah
(Zach. ix. 9): *He is lowly, riding upon an ass, and upon
a colt the foal of an ass.*

3. In the reign of Tiberius Cæsar, Jesus our Saviour, a
Galilean, began to preach; the son, as was supposed, of
Joseph; declaring to the people of the Jews, that the
kingdom of God expected by them was now come, and
that himself was a *king,* that is to say, the Christ; explaining the *law,* choosing *twelve apostles,* and *seventy
disciples,* after the number of the *princes* of the tribes,
and seventy elders (according to the pattern of Moses)
to the ministry; *teaching the way of salvation* by himself
and them; purging the temple, doing great signs, and fulfilling all those things which the prophets had foretold
of Christ to come. That this man, hated of the Pharisees,
whose false doctrine and hypocritical sanctity he had reproved; and by their means, of the people accused of unlawful seeking for the kingdom, and crucified; was the true
Christ and *king* promised by God, and sent from his
Father to renew the *new covenant* between them and
God; both the evangelists do show, describing his genealogy, nativity, life, doctrine, death, and resurrection; and

by comparing the things which he did with those which were foretold of him, all Christians do consent to.

4. Now from this, that *Christ* was sent from God his Father to make a *covenant* between him and the people, it is manifest, that though Christ were equal to his Father according to his nature, yet was he inferior according to the right of the kingdom. For this office, to speak properly, was not that of a king, but of a viceroy; such as Moses' government was; for the kingdom was not his, but his *Father's*. Which Christ himself signified when he was baptized as a subject, and openly professed when he taught his disciples to pray, *Our Father, thy kingdom come,* &c.: and when he said (Matth. xxvi. 29): *I will not drink of the blood of the grape, until that day when I shall drink it new with you in the kingdom of my Father.* And St. Paul (1 Cor. xv. 22–24): *As in Adam all die, so in Christ shall all be made alive; but every man in his own order; Christ the first fruits; afterward they that are Christ's, who believed in his coming; then cometh the end when he shall have delivered up the kingdom to God even his Father* &c. The same notwithstanding is also called the *kingdom of Christ*: for both the mother of the sons of Zebedee petitioned Christ, saying (Matth. xx. 21): *Grant that these my two sons may sit, the one on thy right hand, the other on thy left, in thy kingdom:* and the thief on the cross (Luke xxiii. 42): *Lord remember me when thou comest into thy kingdom:* and St. Paul (Ephes. v. 5): *For this know ye, that no whoremonger,* &c. *shall enter into the kingdom of God, and of Christ:* and elsewhere (2 Tim. iv. 1): *I charge thee before God, and the Lord Jesus Christ, who shall judge the quick and dead at his appearing, and his kingdom,* &c. (verse 18): *And the Lord shall deliver me from every evil work, and will preserve me unto his heavenly kingdom.* Nor is it to be marveled at, that the same kingdom is attributed to them both; since both the Father and the

Son are the same God; and the new covenant concerning God's kingdom, is not propounded in the name of the *Father*; but in the name of the *Father*, of the *Son*, and of the *Holy Ghost*, as of one God.

5. But the kingdom of God, for restitution whereof Christ was sent from God his Father, takes not its beginning before his second coming; to wit, from the day of judgment, when he shall come in majesty accompanied with his angels. For it is promised the apostles, that in the kingdom of God they shall judge the twelve tribes of Israel (Matth. xix. 28): *Ye which have followed me in the regeneration, when the Son of man shall sit in the throne of his glory, ye also shall sit upon twelve thrones judging the twelve tribes of Israel:* which is not to be done till the day of judgment. Christ therefore is not yet in the throne of his majesty; nor is that time, when Christ was conversant here in the world, called a kingdom, but a *regeneration;* that is to say, a renovation or restitution of the kingdom of God, and a calling of them who were hereafter to be received into his kingdom. And where it is said (Matth. xxv. 31–32): *When the Son of man shall come in his glory, and all the holy angels with him, then shall he sit upon the throne of his glory, and before him shall be gathered all nations; and he shall separate them one from another, as a shepherd divideth his sheep from the goats:* we may manifestly gather that there will be no local separation of God's subjects from his enemies, but that they shall live mixed together until Christ's second coming. Which is also confirmed by the comparison of the kingdom of heaven with wheat mingled with darnell, and with a net containing all sorts of fish. But a multitude of men, enemies and subjects, living promiscuously together, cannot properly be termed a kingdom. Besides, the apostles, when they asked our Saviour, whether he would at that time when he ascended into heaven, restore the kingdom unto Israel; did openly tes-

tify, that they then, when Christ ascended, thought the kingdom of God not to be yet come. Furthermore, the words of Christ, *My kingdom is not of this world:* and, *I will not drink,* &c. *till the kingdom of God come:* and, *God hath not sent his Son into the world, to judge the world, but that the world through him might be saved:* and, *If any man|hear my words, and keep them not,|I judge him not; for I came not to judge the world, but to save the world:* and, *Man, who made me a judge or divider between you?* and the very appellation of *the kingdom of heaven* testifies as much. The same thing is gathered out of the words of the prophet Jeremiah, speaking of the kingdom of God by the new covenant (Jer. xxxi. 34): *They shall teach no more every man his neighbour; saying, Know the Lord. For they shall all know me, from the least of them to the greatest of them, saith the Lord:* which cannot be understood of a kingdom in this world. The kingdom of God therefore, for the restoring whereof Christ came into the world; of which the prophets did prophesy, and of which praying we say, *Thy kingdom come;* if it must have subjects locally separated from enemies, if judicature, if majesty, according as hath been foretold; shall begin from that time, wherein God shall separate the sheep from the goats; wherein the apostles shall judge the twelve tribes of Israel; wherein Christ shall come in majesty and glory; wherein lastly, all men shall so know God, that they shall not need to be taught; that is to say, at Christ's second coming, or the day of judgment. But if the kingdom of God were now already restored, no reason could be rendered why Christ, having completed the work for which he was sent, should come again; or why we should pray, *Thy kingdom come.*

6. Now, although the kingdom *of God* by Christ to be established with a *new covenant,* were heavenly; we must not therefore think, that they, who believing in Christ would make that covenant, were not so to be governed

here on the earth too, as that they should persevere in their faith and obedience promised by that covenant. For in vain had the kingdom of heaven been promised, if we were not to have been led into it; but none can be led, but those who are directed in the way. Moses, when he had instituted the *priestly kingdom*, himself though he were no priest, yet ruled and conducted the people all the time of their peregrination, until their entrance into the promised land. In the same manner is it our Saviour's office (whom God in this thing would have like unto Moses), as he was sent from his Father, so to govern the future subjects of his heavenly kingdom in this life, that they might attain to and enter into that; although the kingdom were not properly his, but his Father's. But the government whereby Christ rules the faithful ones in this life, is not properly a *kingdom* or *dominion*, but a *pastoral charge*, or *the right of teaching*; that is to say, God the Father gave him not a power to judge of *meum* and *tuum*, as he doth to the kings of the earth; nor a *coercive power*, nor *legislative*; but of showing to the world, and teaching them *the way and knowledge of salvation*; that is to say, of preaching and declaring what they were to do, who would enter into the kingdom of heaven. That Christ had received no power from his Father to judge in questions of *meum* and *tuum*, that is to say, in all questions of right among those who believed not, those words above cited do sufficiently declare: *Man, who made me a judge or divider between you?* And it is confirmed by reason. For seeing Christ was sent to make *a covenant* between God and men; and no man is obliged to perform obedience before the contract be made; if he should have judged of questions of *right*, no man had been tied to obey his sentence. But that the discerning of right was not committed to Christ in this world, neither among the faithful nor among infidels, is apparent in this; that that right without all controversy belongs to princes, as long as it is not by God himself derogated from their authority. But it is not derogated before the day of judgment; as appears by the words of St. Paul, speaking of the day of judgment (1 Cor. xv. 24): *Then cometh the end, when he shall have delivered up the kingdom to God even the Father, when he shall have put down all rule, and all authority, and power.* Secondly, the words of our Saviour reproving James and John, when they had said (Luke ix. 54): *Wilt thou that we call for fire from heaven, that it may consume them?* (namely the Samaritans, who had denied to receive him going up to Jerusalem): and replying (verse 56), *The Son of man is not come to destroy souls, but to save them;* and those words: *Behold I send you as sheep among wolves; Shake off the dust of your feet;* and the like; and those words, *God sent not his Son into the world, to judge the world, but that the world through him might be saved;* and those: *If any man hear my words, and keep them not, I judge him not; for I came not to judge the world,* &c.: do all show, that he had no power given him to condemn or punish any man. We read indeed, that *the Father judgeth no man, but hath committed all judgment to the Son;* but since that both may, and must be understood of the day of future judgment, it doth not at all repugn what hath been said before. Lastly, that he was not sent to make new laws, and that therefore by his office and mission he was no legislator properly so called, nor Moses neither, but a bringer and publisher of his Father's laws (for God only, and neither Moses nor Christ, was a king by covenant), is collected hence; that he said, *I came not to destroy* (to wit, the laws before given from God by Moses, which he presently interprets), *but to fulfil;* and, *He that shall break one of the least of these commandments, and shall teach men so, he shall be called least in the kingdom of heaven.* Christ therefore had not a royal or sovereign power committed to him from his Father in this world, but councillary and doctrinal only; which himself signifies, as well then when he calls his apostles not hunters, but fishers of men; as when he compares the kingdom of God to a grain of mustard-seed, and to a little leaven hid in meal.

7. God promised unto Abraham, first, a numerous seed, the possession of the land of Canaan, and a blessing upon all nations in his seed, on this condition; that he and his seed should serve him: next, unto the seed of Abraham according to the flesh, *a priestly* kingdom, a government most free, in which they were to be subject to no human power, on this condition; that they should serve the God of Abraham in that fashion which Moses should teach: lastly, both to them and to all nations, a heavenly and *eternal* kingdom, on condition that they should serve the God of Abraham in that manner which Christ should teach. For by *the new,* that is to say, *the Christian covenant,* it is covenanted on men's part, to serve the God of Abraham *on that manner which Jesus should teach:* on God's part, *to pardon their sins, and bring them into his celestial kingdom.* We have already spoken of the quality of the *heavenly* kingdom, above in art. 5; but it is usually called, sometimes the *kingdom of heaven,* sometimes the *kingdom of glory,* sometimes the *life eternal.* What is required on men's part, namely, to serve God as Christ should teach, contains two things; *obedience to be performed to God* (for this is to serve God); and *faith in Jesus,* to wit, that we believe *Jesus to be that Christ who was promised by God;* for that only is the cause why his doctrine is to be followed, rather than any other's. Now in holy Scriptures, *repentance* is often put instead of *obedience;* because Christ teacheth every where, that with God the will is taken for the deed; but *repentance* is an infallible sign of an obedient mind. These things being understood, it will most evidently appear out of many places of sacred Scripture, that those

are the conditions of *the Christian covenant* which we have named; to wit, giving remission of sins and eternal life on God's part; and repenting and believing in Jesus Christ, on men's part. First, the words (Mark i. 15): *The kingdom of God is at hand; Repent ye and believe the gospel,* contain the whole covenant. In like manner those (Luke xxiv. 46–47): *Thus it is written, and thus it behoved Christ to suffer, and to rise from the dead the third day; and that repentance and remission of sins should be preached in his name among all nations, beginning at Jerusalem.* And those (Acts iii. 19): *Repent and be converted, that your sins may be blotted out when the times of refreshing shall come,* &c. And sometimes one part is expressly propounded, and the other understood, as here (John iii. 36): *He that believeth in the Son, hath everlasting life; He that believeth not the Son, shall not see life, but the wrath of God abideth on him:* where *faith* is expressed, *repentance* not mentioned; and in Christ's preaching (Matth. iv. 17): *Repent, for the kingdom of heaven is at hand:* where *repentance* is expressed, *faith* is understood. But the parts of this *new contract* are most manifestly and formally set down there, where a certain ruler, bargaining as it were for the kingdom of God, asketh our Saviour (Luke xviii. 18): *Good Master, what shall I do to inherit eternal life?* But Christ first propounds one part of the price, namely, observation of the commandments, or obedience; which when he answered that he had kept, he adjoins the other, saying (verse 22): *Yet lackest thou one thing; Sell all that thou hast, and distribute to the poor, and thou shalt have treasure in heaven; and come, follow me.* This was matter of *faith.* He therefore not giving sufficient credit to Christ and his heavenly treasures, went away sorrowful. The same covenant is contained in these words (Mark xvi. 16): *He that believeth and is baptized, shall be saved; but he that believeth not, shall be damned:* where *faith* is expressed, *repentance* is supposed in those that are baptized. And in these words (John iii. 5): *Except a man be born again of water and the Holy Ghost, he cannot enter into the kingdom of heaven:* where, *to be born of water,* is the same with regeneration, that is to say, conversion to Christ. Now that *baptism* is required in the two places cited just before, and in divers others, we must understand, that what *circumcision* was to the *old covenant,* that *baptism* is to the *new.* Seeing therefore that was not of the essence, but served for a memorial of the *old covenant,* as a ceremony or sign (and was omitted in the wilderness); in like manner this also is used, not as pertaining to the essence, but in memory and for a sign of the *new covenant* which we make with God. And provided the will be not wanting, the act through necessity may be omitted; but *repentance* and *faith,* which are of the essence of the *covenant,* are always required.

8. In the *kingdom* of God after this life, there will be *no laws;* partly, because there is no room for laws, where there is none for sins; partly, because laws were given us from God, not to direct us in heaven, but unto heaven. Let us now therefore inquire what laws Christ established not himself; for he would not take upon him any legislative authority, as hath been declared above in art. 6; but propounded to us for his Father's. We have a place in Scripture, where he contracts all the laws of God published till that time, into two precepts. (Matth. xxii. 37, 38, 39, 40): *Thou shalt love the Lord thy God with all thine heart, with all thy soul, and with all thy mind; this is the greatest and first commandment. And the second is like unto it, Thou shalt love thy neighbour as thyself. On these two commandments hangs all the law and the prophets.* The first of these was given before by Moses in the same words (Deut. vi. 5); and the second even before Moses; for it is the natural law, having its beginning with rational nature itself: and both together is the sum

of all laws. For all the laws of divine natural worship are contained in these words, *Thou shalt love God;* and all the laws of divine worship due by the *old covenant,* in these words, *Thou shalt love thy God,* that is to say, *God,* as being the peculiar *King of Abraham* and his seed; and all the laws natural and civil, in these words, *Thou shalt love thy neighbour as thyself.* For he that loves God and his neighbour, hath a mind to obey all laws, both divine and human. But God requires no more than a mind to obey. We have another place where Christ interprets the laws, namely, the fifth, sixth, and seventh entire chapters of St. Matthew's Gospel. But all those laws are set down either in the *decalogue* or in the *moral law,* or are contained in *the faith of Abraham;* as that law of not putting away a wife is contained in *the faith of Abraham.* For that same, *two shall be one flesh,* was not delivered either by Christ first, or by Moses, but by Abraham, who first published the creation of the world. The laws therefore which Christ contracts in one place, and explains in another, are no other than those to which all mortal men are obliged, who acknowledge the God of Abraham. Beside these, we read not of any law given by Christ, beside the institution of the sacraments of *baptism* and the *eucharist.*

9. What may be said then of these kind of precepts, *Repent, Be baptized, Keep the Commandments, Believe the Gospel, Come unto me, Sell all that thou hast, Give to the poor, Follow me;* and the like? We must say that they are not *laws,* but a calling of us to the faith: such as is that of Isaiah (lv. 1): *Come; buy wine and milk without money and without price.* Neither if they come not, do they therefore sin against any law, but against prudence only; neither shall their infidelity be punished, but their former sins. Wherefore St. John saith of the unbeliever, *The wrath of God abideth on him;* he saith not, *The wrath of God shall come upon him.* And, *He that be-*

lieveth not, is already judged; he saith not, *shall be* judged, but *is already* judged. Nay, it cannot be well conceived, that remission of sins should be a benefit arising from *faith,* unless we understand also on the other side, that the punishment of sins is an hurt proceeding from *infidelity.*

10. From hence, that our Saviour hath prescribed no distributive laws to the subjects of princes, and citizens of cities; that is to say, hath given no rules whereby a subject may know and discern what is *his own,* what *another man's,* nor by what forms, words, or circumstances a thing must be *given, delivered, invaded, possessed,* that it may be known by right to belong to the *receiver, invader,* or *possessor:* we must necessarily understand that each single subject (not only with unbelievers, among whom Christ himself denied himself to be *a judge* and *distributor,* but even with Christians) must take those rules from his city, that is to say, from that man or council which hath the supreme power. It follows therefore, that by those laws; *Thou shalt not kill, Thou shalt not commit adultery, Thou shalt not steal, Honour thy father and mother;* nothing else was commanded, but that subjects, and citizens, should absolutely obey their princes in all questions concerning *meum* and *tuum, their own* and *others' right.* For by that precept, *Thou shalt not kill,* all slaughter is not prohibited; for he that said, *Thou shalt not kill,* said also (Exod. xxxv. 2): *Whosoever doth work upon the sabbath, shall be put to death.* No, nor yet all slaughter, the cause not being heard; for he said (Exod. xxxii. 27): *Slay every man his brother, and every man his companion, and every man his neighbour.* (Verse 28): *And there fell of the people about three thousand men.* Nor yet all slaughter of an innocent person; for Jephtha vowed (Judges xi. 31): *Whosoever cometh forth, &c. I will offer him up for a burnt offering unto the Lord;* and his vow was accepted of God. What then is forbidden?

Only this: that no man kill another, who hath not *a right to kill him*; that is to say, that no man kill, unless it belong to him to do so. The law of Christ therefore concerning killing, and consequently all manner of hurt done to any man, and what penalties are to be set, commands us to obey the city only. In like manner, by that precept, *Thou shalt not commit adultery*, all manner of copulation is not forbidden; but only that of lying with *another man's wife*. But the judgment, which is another man's wife, belongs to the city; and is to be determined by the rules which the city prescribes. This precept therefore commands both male and female to keep that faith entire, which they have mutually given according to the statutes of the city. So also by the precept, *thou shalt not steal*, all manner of invasion or secret surreption is not forbidden; but of *another man's only*. The subject therefore is commanded this only, that he invade not nor take away aught which the city prohibits to be invaded or taken away; and universally, not to call anything *murder, adultery,* or *theft,* but what is done contrary to the civil laws. Lastly, seeing Christ hath commanded us to *honour our parents,* and hath not prescribed with what rites, what appellations, and what manner of obedience they are to be honoured; it is to be supposed that they are to be honoured with the will indeed, and inwardly, as kings and lords over their children, but outwardly, not beyond the city's permission, which shall assign to every man, as all things else, so also *his honour.* But since the nature of justice consists in this, that every man have his own given him; it is manifest, that it also belongs to a Christian city to determine what is justice, what injustice, or a sin against justice. Now what belongs to a city, that must be judged to belong to him or them who have the sovereign power of the city.

11. Moreover, because our Saviour hath not showed subjects any other laws for the government of a city, be-

side those of nature, that is to say, beside the command
of obedience; no subject can privately determine who is
a public friend, who an enemy, when war, when peace,
when truce is to be made, nor yet what subjects, what authority and of what men, are commodious or prejudicial
to the safety of the commonweal. These and all like matters therefore are to be learned, if need be, from the city,
that is to say, from the sovereign powers.

12. Furthermore, all these things, to build castles,
houses, temples; to move, carry, take away mighty weights;
to send securely over seas; to contrive engines, serving
for all manner of uses; to be well acquainted with the face
of the whole world, the courses of the stars, the seasons
of the year, the accounts of the times, and the nature of
all things; to understand perfectly all natural and civil
rights; and all manner of sciences, which, comprehended
under the title of philosophy, are necessary partly to live,
partly to live well; I say, the understanding of these (because Christ hath not delivered it) is to be learnt from
reasoning; that is to say, by making necessary consequences, having first taken the beginning from experience. But men's reasonings are sometimes right, sometimes wrong; and consequently, that which is concluded
and held for a truth, is sometimes truth, sometimes error.
Now errors, even about these philosophical points, do
sometimes public hurt, and give occasions of great seditions and injuries. It is needful therefore, as oft as any
controversy ariseth in these matters contrary to public
good and common peace, that there be somebody to
judge of the reasoning, that is to say, whether that which
is inferred, be rightly inferred or not; that so the controversy may be ended. But there are no rules given by
Christ to this purpose, neither came he into the world to
teach *logic*. It remains therefore that the judges of such
controversies, be the same with those whom God by
nature had instituted before, namely, those who in each

city are constituted by the sovereign. Moreover, if a controversy be raised of the accurate and proper signification, that is, the definition of those names or appellations which are commonly used; insomuch as it is needful for the peace of the city, or the distribution of right, to be determined; the determination will belong to the city. For men, by reasoning, do search out such kind of definitions in their observation of diverse conceptions, for the signification whereof those appellations were used at diverse times and for diverse causes. But the decision of the question, whether a man do reason rightly, belongs to the city. For example, if a woman bring forth a child of an unwonted shape, and the law forbid to kill a man; the question is, whether the child be a man. It is demanded therefore, what a man is. No man doubts but the city shall judge it, and that without taking an account of Aristotle's definition, that man is a rational creature. And these things, namely, *right, politie,* and *natural sciences,* are subjects concerning which Christ denies that it belongs to his office to give any precepts, or teach any thing beside this only; that in all controversies about them, every single subject should obey the laws and determinations of his city. Yet must we remember this, that the same Christ, as God, could not only have taught, but also commanded what he would.

13. The sum of our Saviour's office was, to teach the way and all the means of salvation and eternal life. But justice and civil obedience, and observation of all the natural laws, is one of the means to salvation. Now these may be taught two ways; one, as *theorems,* by the way of natural reason, by drawing right and the natural laws from human principles and contracts; and this doctrine thus delivered, is subject to the censure of civil powers. The other, as laws, by divine authority, in showing the will of God to be such; and thus to teach, belongs only to him to whom the will of God is supernaturally known,

that is to say, to Christ. Secondly, it belonged to the office
of Christ to forgive sins to the penitent; for that was necessary for the salvation of men who had already sinned.
Neither could it be done by any other. For remission of
sins follows not repentance naturally, as a debt; but it
depends, as a free gift, on the will of God supernaturally
to be revealed. Thirdly, it belongs to the office of Christ
to teach all those commandments of God, whether concerning his worship, or those points of faith which cannot
be understood by natural reason, but only by revelation;
of which nature are those, *that he was the Christ; that
his kingdom was not terrestrial, but celestial; that there
are rewards and punishments after this life; that the soul
is immortal; that there should be such, and so many
sacraments;* and the like.

14. From what hath been said in the foregoing chapter,
it is not hard to distinguish between things *spiritual* and
temporal. For since by *spiritual,* those things are understood which have their foundation on the authority and
office of Christ, and, unless Christ had taught them, could
not have been known; and all other things are temporal;
it follows, that the definition and determination of what
is *just* and *unjust,* the cognizance of all controversies
about the *means of peace* and *public defence,* and the examination of doctrines and books in all manner of
rational science, depends upon *the temporal right;* but
those which are *mysteries of faith,* depending on Christ's
word and authority only, their judgments belong to *spiritual right.* But it is reason's inquisition, and pertains to
temporal right to define what is *spiritual,* and what
temporal; because our Saviour hath not made that distinction. For although St. Paul in many places distinguish
between *spiritual* things and *carnal* things; and calls
(Rom. viii. 5: 1 Cor. xii. 8–10) those things *spiritual,*
which are of the *spirit,* to wit, the *word of wisdom, the
word of knowledge, faith, the gift of healing, the working*

of miracles, prophecy, divers kind of tongues, interpretation of tongues; all supernaturally inspired by the Holy Ghost, and such as the *carnal* man understands not, but he only who hath known the mind of Christ (2 Cor. ii. 14–16); and those things *carnal*, which belong to worldly wealth (Rom. xv. 27); and the men *carnal men* (1 Cor. iii. 1–3): yet hath he not defined, nor given us any rules whereby we may know what proceeds from natural reason, what from supernatural inspiration.

15. Seeing therefore it is plain that our Saviour hath committed to, or rather not taken away from *princes*, and those who in each city have obtained the sovereignty, the supreme authority of judging and determining all manner of controversies about *temporal* matters; we must see henceforth to whom he hath left the same authority in matters *spiritual*. Which because it cannot be known, except it be out of *the word of God* and *the tradition of the Church*, we must enquire in the next place what *the word of God is,* what *to interpret it,* what a *Church* is, and what *the will and command of the Church.* To omit that the *word of God* is in Scripture taken sometimes for the *Son of God,* it is used three manner of ways. First, most properly for that which God hath spoken. Thus, whatsoever God spake unto Abraham, the patriarchs, Moses, and the prophets, our Saviour to his disciples, or any others; is *the word of God.* Secondly, whatsoever hath been uttered by men on the motion or by command of the Holy Ghost; in which sense we acknowledge the Scriptures to be the *word of God.* Thirdly, in the New Testament indeed, the *word of God* most frequently signifies the doctrine of the gospel, or the *word concerning God,* or *the word of the kingdom of God* by Christ. As where it is said (Matth. iv. 23) that Christ preached the *gospel of the kingdom:* where the apostles are said to preach *the word of God* (Acts xiii. 46): where

the *word of God* is called *the word of life* (Acts v. 20):
the word of the gospel (Acts xv. 7): *the word of faith*
(Rom. x. 8): *the word of truth,* that is to say (adding an
interpretation) *the gospel of salvation* (Eph. i. 13): and
where it is called *the word of the apostles;* for St. Paul
says (2 Thess. iii. 14): *If any man obey not our word,* &c.
Which places cannot be otherwise meant than of *the
doctrine evangelical.* In like manner, where the word of
God is said to be *sown, to increase,* and *to be multiplied*
(Acts xii. 24: and xiii. 49): it is very hard to conceive this
to be spoken of the *voice of God* or *of his apostles;* but
of their doctrine, easy. And in this third acception is all
that *doctrine of the Christian faith,* which at this day is
preached in pulpits and contained in the books of divines,
the word of God.

16. Now the sacred Scripture is entirely *the word of
God* in this second acception, as being that which we acknowledge to be inspired from God; and innumerable
places of it, in the first. And seeing the greatest part of it
is conversant either in the prediction of the *kingdom of
heaven,* or in prefigurations before the incarnation of
Christ, or in evangelization and explication after; the
sacred Scripture is also *the word of God,* and therefore
the canon and rule of all *evangelical doctrine,* in this
third signification; where *the word of God* is taken for
the word concerning God, that is to say, for *the gospel.*
But because in the same Scriptures we read many things
political, historical, moral, physical, and others which
nothing at all concern the mysteries of our faith; those
places, although they contain true doctrine, and are the
canon of such kind of doctrines, yet can they not be the
canon of the mysteries of Christian religion.

17. And truly, it is not the dead voice or letter of *the
word of God,* which is the canon of Christian doctrine;
but a true and genuine determination. For the mind is
not governed by Scriptures, unless they be understood.

There is need therefore of an interpreter to make the Scriptures canon, and hence follows one of these two things; that either the word of the interpreter is the word of God, or that the canon of Christian doctrine is not the word of God. The last of these must necessarily be false; for the rule of that doctrine which cannot be known by any human reason, but by divine revelation only, cannot be less than divine; for whom we acknowledge not to be able to discern whether some doctrine be true or not, it is impossible to account his opinion for a rule in the same doctrine. The first therefore is true, *that the word of an interpreter of Scriptures is the word of God.*

18. Now that interpreter whose determination hath the honour to be held for *the word of God*, is not every one that translates the Scriptures out of the Hebrew and Greek tongue, to his Latin auditors in Latin, to his French in French, and to other nations in their mother tongue; for this is not to interpret. For such is the nature of speech in general, that although it deserve the chief place among those signs whereby we declare our conceptions to others, yet cannot it perform that office alone without the help of many circumstances. For the living voice hath its interpreters present, to wit, time, place, countenance, gesture, the counsel of the speaker, and himself unfolding his own meaning in other words as oft as need is. To recall these aids of interpretation, so much desired in the writings of old time, is neither the part of an ordinary wit, nor yet of the quaintest, without great learning and very much skill in antiquity. It sufficeth not therefore for interpretation of Scriptures, that a man understand the language wherein they speak. Neither is every one an authentic interpreter of Scriptures, who writes comments upon them. For men may err; they may also either bend them to serve their own ambition; or even resisting, draw them into bondage by their forestallings; whence it will follow, that an erroneous sentence

must be held for *the word of God*. But although this
|might|not happen, yet as soon as these commentators are
departed, their commentaries will need explications; and
in process of time, those explications expositions; those
expositions new commentaries, without any end. So as
there cannot, in any written interpretation whatsoever,
be a canon or rule of Christian doctrine, whereby the controversies of religion may be determined. It remains, that
there must be some canonical interpreter, whose legitimate office it is to end controversies begun, by explaining the word of God in the judgments themselves; and
whose authority therefore must be no less obeyed, than
theirs who first recommended the Scripture itself to us
for a canon of faith; and that one and the same person be
an interpreter of Scripture, and a *supreme judge of all
manner of doctrines*.

19. What concerns the word *ecclesia*, or Church,
originally it signifies the same thing that *concio* or a
congregation does in Latin; even as *ecclesiastes* or church-
man, the same that *concionator* or preacher, that is to
say, he who speaks to the congregation. In which sense
we read in the Acts of the Apostles, of a *Church con-
fused*, and of a *lawful Church* (Acts xix. 32–39): that,
taken for a concourse of people meeting in way of tumult;
this, for a convocated assembly. But in holy writ by a
Church of Christians, is sometimes understood the assembly, and sometimes the Christians themselves, although not actually assembled, if they be permitted to
enter into the congregation and to communicate with
them. For example, *Tell it to the Church* (Matth. xviii.
17), is meant of a Church assembled; for otherwise it is
impossible to *tell* any thing to the Church. But *He laid
waste the Church* (Acts viii. 3), is understood of a
Church not assembled. Sometimes a Church is taken for
those who are baptized, or for the professors of the Christian faith, whether they be Christians inwardly or

feignedly; as when we read of somewhat said or written
to the Church, or said, or decreed, or done by the Church.
Sometimes for the elect only, as when it is called *holy and
without blemish* (Ephes. v. 27). But the elect, as they
are militant, are not properly called a Church; for they
know not how to assemble; but they are a *future Church*,
namely, in that day when severed from the reprobate they
shall be triumphant. Again, a Church may be sometimes
taken for all Christians collectively; as when Christ is
called *the head of his Church* (Ephes. v. 23); and
the head of his body the Church (Coloss. i. 18). Sometimes for its parts; as *the Church of Ephesus, the Church
which is in his house, the seven Churches*, &c. Lastly, a
Church, as it is taken for a company actually assembled,
according to the divers ends of their meeting, signifies
sometimes those who are met together to deliberate and
judge; in which sense it is also called a council and a
synod; sometimes those who meet together in the house
of prayer to worship God, in which signification it is
taken in the 1 Cor. xiv. 4, 5, 23, 28, &c.

20. Now a *Church*, which hath personal rights and
proper actions attributed to it, and of which that same
must necessarily be understood, *Tell it to the Church*,
and *he that obeys not the Church*, and all such like forms
of speech, is to be defined so as by that word may be understood a multitude of men, who have made a new
covenant with God in Christ, that is to say, a multitude
of them who have taken upon them the sacrament of
baptism; which multitude may both lawfully be called together by some one into one place, and, he so calling
them, are bound to be present either in person or by
others. For a multitude of men, if they cannot meet in
assembly when need requires, is not to be called *a person*.
For a Church can neither speak, nor discern, nor hear, but
as it is a congregation. Whatsoever is spoken by particular
men (to wit, as many opinions almost as heads), that is

the speech of one man, not of the Church. Furthermore, if an assembly be made, and it be unlawful, it shall be considered as null. Not any one of these therefore who are present in a tumult, shall be tied to the decree of the rest; but specially if he dissent. And therefore neither can such a Church make any decree; for then a multitude is said to decree somewhat, when every man is obliged by the decree of the major part. We must therefore grant to the definition of a Church, to which we attribute *things belonging to a person*, not only a possibility of assembling, but also of doing it lawfully. Besides, although there be some one who may lawfully call the rest together; yet if they who are called, may lawfully not appear; which may happen among men who are not subject one to another; that same *Church* is not *one person*. For by what right they, who being called to a certain time and place do meet together, are *one Church*; by the same, others flocking to another place appointed by them, are *another Church*. And every number of men of one opinion is a Church; and by consequence, there will be as many Churches as there are divers opinions; that is to say, the same multitude of men will at once prove to be *one*, and *many Churches*. Wherefore a Church is not one, except there be a certain and known, that is to say, a lawful power, by means whereof every man may be obliged to be present in the congregation, either himself in person, or by proxy; and that becomes *one*, and is capable of *personal* functions, by the union of a lawful power of convocating synods and assemblies of Christians; not by uniformity of doctrine; and otherwise it is a multitude, and *persons* in the plural, howsoever agreeing in opinions.

21. It follows what hath been already said by necessary connexion, that *a city of Christian men* and a *Church* is altogether the same thing, of the same men, termed by two names, for two causes. For the *matter of a city* and a

Church is one, to wit, the same Christian men. And the *form*, which consists in a lawful power of assembling them, is the same too; for it is manifest that every subject is obliged to come thither, whither he is summoned by his *city*. Now that which is called a *city*, as it is made up of *men*, the same, as it consists of *Christians*, is styled a *Church*.

22. This too is very coherent with the same points: *if there be many Christian cities, they are not altogether personally one Church.* They may indeed by mutual consent become one *Church*, but no otherwise than as they must also become one city. For they cannot assemble but at some certain time, and to some place appointed. But persons, places, and times, belong to civil right; neither can any subject or stranger lawfully set his foot on any place, but by the permission of the city, which is lord of the place. But the things which cannot lawfully be done but by the permission of the city, those, if they be lawfully done, are done by the city's authority. The *universal Church* is indeed one *mystical body*, whereof Christ is the head; but in the same manner that all men together, acknowledging God for the ruler of the world, are one kingdom and one city; which notwithstanding is neither one *person*, nor hath it one common action or determination. Furthermore, where it is said that *Christ is the head of his body the Church*, it manifestly appears that that was spoken by the Apostle of the elect; who, as long as they are in this world, are a *Church* only in *potentia*; but shall not actually be so before they be separated from the reprobate, and gathered together among themselves in the day of judgment. The Church of Rome of old was very great, but she went not beyond the bounds of her empire, and therefore neither was she *universal*; unless it were in that sense, wherein it was also said of the city of Rome, *Orbem jam totum victor Romanus habebat*; when as yet he had not the twentieth part of it. But after

that the civil empire was divided into parts, the single cities thence arising were so many Churches: and that power which the Church of Rome had over them, might perhaps wholly depend on the authority of those Churches, who having cast off the emperors, were yet content to admit the doctors of Rome.

23. They may be called *churchmen*, who exercise a public office in the Church. But of offices, there was one a *ministery*, another a *maistery*. The offices of the *ministers*, was to serve tables, to take care of the temporal goods of the Church, and to distribute, at that time when all propriety of riches being abolished they were fed in common, to each man his portion. The *maisters*, according to their order, were called some *apostles*, some *bishops*, some *presbyters*, that is to say, *elders*; yet not so, as that by the name of *presbyter*, the *age*, but the office might be distinguished. For Timothy was a *presbyter*, although a young man. But because for the most part the *elders* were received into the *maistership*, the word, denoting age, was used to signify the office. The same *maisters*, according to the diversity of their employments, were called some of them *apostles*, some *prophets*, some *evangelists*, some *pastors* or *teachers*. And the *apostolical* work indeed was universal; the *prophetical*, to declare their own revelations in the Church; the *evangelical*, to preach or to be publishers of the gospel among the infidels; that of the *pastors*, to teach, confirm, and rule the minds of those who already believed.

24. In the election of churchmen two things are to be considered; the election of the persons, and their *consecration* or institution, which also is called *ordination*. The first twelve apostles Christ himself both elected and ordained. After Christ's ascension, Matthias was elected in the room of Judas the traitor; the Church, which at that time consisted of a congregation of about one hundred and twenty men, choosing two men: *and they ap-*

pointed two, Joseph and Matthias: but God himself by lot approving of Matthias. And St. Paul calls these twelve *the first and great apostles;* also the apostles *of the circumcision.* Afterward were added two other apostles, Paul and Barnabas; ordained indeed by the doctors and prophets of the Church of Antioch (which was *a particular Church*) by the imposition of hands; but elected by the command of the Holy Ghost. That they were both apostles, is manifest in Acts xiii. 2, 3. That they received their apostleship from hence, namely, because they were separated, by command of the spirit, for the work of God from the rest of the prophets and doctors of the Church of Antioch, St. Paul himself shows; who calls himself, for distinction sake (Rom. i. 1), *an apostle separated unto the Gospel of God.* But if it be demanded further, *by what authority* it came to pass, that that was received for the command of the Holy Ghost, which those prophets and doctors did say proceeded from him; it must necessarily be answered, *by the authority of the Church of Antioch.* For the prophets and doctors must be examined by the Church, before they be admitted. For St. John (1 Epist. iv. 1) saith: *Believe not every spirit; but try the spirits, whether they are of God; because many false prophets are gone out into the world.* But by what Church, but that to which that epistle was written? In like manner St. Paul (Gal. ii. 14) reproves the Churches of Galatia, because they Judaized; although they seemed to do so by the authority of Peter. For when he had told them, that he had reprehended Peter himself with these words: *If thou being a Jew, livest after the manner of Gentiles, and not as do the Jews; why compellest thou the Gentiles to live as do the Jews:* not long after he questions them, saying (Gal. iii. 2): *This only would I learn of you: received ye the Spirit by the works of the law, or by the hearing of faith?* Where it is evident, that it was Judaism which he reprehended the Galatians for, not-

withstanding that the apostle Peter compelled them to
Judaize. Seeing therefore it belonged to the Church, and
not to Peter, and therefore also not to any man, to determine what doctors they should follow; it also pertained
to the authority of the Church of Antioch, to elect their
prophets and doctors. Now, because the Holy Ghost separated to himself the apostles Paul and Barnabas by the
imposition of hands from doctors thus elected, it is manifest, *that imposition of hands and consecration* of the
prime doctors in each Church, belongs to the doctors of
the same Church. But *bishops*, who were also called
presbyters, although all presbyters were not bishops, were
ordained sometimes by *apostles*; for Paul and Barnabas,
when they had taught in Derbe, Lystra, and Iconium, ordained *elders* in every Church (Acts xiv. 23): sometimes
by other bishops; for Titus was by Paul left in Crete, that
he should ordain *elders* in every city (Tit. i. 5). And
Timothy was advised (1 Tim. iv. 14) *Not to neglect the
gift that was in him, which was given him by prophecy
with the laying on of the hands of the presbytery.* And he
had rules given him concerning the election of *presbyters*. But that cannot be understood otherwise, than of
the ordination of those who were elected by the Church;
for no man could constitute a doctor in the Church, but
by the Church's permission. For the duty of the apostles
themselves was not to command, but to teach. And although they who were recommended by the apostles or
presbyters, were not rejected, for the esteem that was had
of the recommenders; yet seeing they could not be elected
without the *will* of the Church, they were also supposed
elected by the *authority* of the Church. In like manner
ministers, who are called *deacons*, were *ordained* by the
apostles; yet *elected* by the Church. For when the seven
deacons were to be elected and ordained, the apostles
elected them not: but, *look ye out*, say they (Acts vi. 3, 5,
6), *among you, brethren, seven men of honest report,*

&c.: *and they chose Stephen,* &c.: *and they set them before the apostles.* It is apparent therefore by the custom of the primitive Church under the apostles, that the *ordination* or *consecration* of all churchmen, which is done by *prayer* and *imposition of hands,* belonged to the *apostles* and *doctors;* but the *election* of those who were to be consecrated, *to the Church.*

25. Concerning the power of *binding* and *loosing,* that is to say, of *remitting* and *retaining of sins;* there is no doubt but it was given by Christ to the pastors then yet for to come, in the same manner as it was to the present apostles. Now the apostles had all the power *of remitting of sins* given them, which Christ himself had. *As the Father hath sent me,* says Christ (John xx. 21), *so send I you;* and he adds (verse 23): *Whose soever sins ye remit, they are remitted; and whose soever sins ye retain, they are retained.* But what *binding* and *loosing,* or *remitting* and *retaining of sins,* is, admits of some scruple. For first, to *retain* his sins, who being baptized into remission of sins, is truly penitent, seems to be against the very covenant itself of the New Testament; and therefore could not be done by Christ himself, much less by his pastors. And to *remit* the impenitent, seems to be against the will of God the Father, from whom Christ was sent to convert the world and to reduce men unto obedience. Furthermore, if each pastor had an authority granted him to *remit* and *retain* sins in this manner, all awe of princes and civil magistrates, together with all kind of civil government would be utterly destroyed. For Christ hath said it, nay even nature itself dictates, that *we should not fear them who slay the body, but cannot kill the soul; but rather fear him, who can cast both soul and body into hell* (Matth. x. 28). Neither is any man so mad, as not to choose to yield obedience rather to them who can remit and retain their sins, than to the powerfulest kings. Nor yet on the other side is it to be imagined, that *remission*

of sins is nothing else but an exemption from ecclesiastical punishments. For what evil hath excommunication in it, beside the eternal pains which are consequent to it? Or what benefit is it to be received into the Church, if there were salvation out of it? We must therefore hold, *that pastors have power truly and absolutely to forgive sins; but to the penitent: and to retain them; but of the impenitent.* But while men think that to repent, is nothing else, but that every one condemn his actions and change those counsels which to himself seem sinful and blameable; there is an opinion risen, that there may be repentance before any confession of sins to men, and that repentance is not an effect, but a cause of confession. And thence the difficulty of those, who say that the sins of the penitent are already forgiven in baptism, and their's who repent not, cannot be forgiven at all, is against Scripture, and contrary to the words of Christ, *whose soever sins ye remit,* &c. We must therefore, to resolve this difficulty, know in the first place, that a true acknowledgment of sin is repentance. For he that knows he hath sinned, knows he hath erred; but to will an error, is impossible; therefore he that knows he hath sinned, wishes he had not done it; which is to repent. Further, where it may be doubtful whether that which is done be a sin or not, we must consider, that repentance doth not precede confession of sins, but is subsequent to it: for there is no repentance but of sins acknowledged. The penitent therefore must both acknowledge the fact, and know it to be a sin, that is to say, against the law. If a man therefore think that what he hath done is not against the law, it is impossible he should repent of it. Before repentance therefore, it is necessary there be an application of the facts unto the law. But it is in vain to apply the facts unto the law without an interpreter: for not the words of the law, but the sentence of the law-giver is the rule of men's actions. But surely either one man, or some men are the interpreters of the law; for every man is not judge of his own fact, whether it be a sin or not. Wherefore the fact, of which we doubt whether it be a sin or not, must be unfolded before some man or men; and the doing of this is confession. Now when the interpreter of the law hath judged the fact to be a sin, if the sinner submit to his judgment and resolve with himself not to do so any more, it is repentance; and thus, either it is not true repentance, or else it is not antecedent, but subsequent to confession. These things being thus explained, it is not hard to understand what kind of power that of *binding* and *loosing* is. For seeing in remission of sins there are two things considerable; one, the *judgment* or *condemnation* whereby the fact is judged to be a sin; the other, when the party condemned does acquiesce and obey the sentence, that is to say, repents, *the remission of the sin;* or, if he repent not, *the retention:* the first of these, that is to say, the judging whether it be a sin or not, belongs *to the interpreter of the law,* that is, the *sovereign judge;* the second, namely, remission or retention of the sin, *to the pastor;* and it is that, concerning which the power *of binding* and *loosing* is conversant. And that this was the true meaning of our Saviour Christ in the institution of the same power, is apparent in Matth. xviii. 15–18, thus. He there speaking to his disciples, says: *If thy brother sin against thee, go and tell him his fault between him and thee alone.* Where we must observe by the way, that *if thy brother sin against thee,* is the same with, *if he do thee injury;* and therefore Christ spake of those matters which belonged to the civil tribunal. He adds, *if he hear thee not* (that is to say, if he deny that he hath done it, or if having confessed the fact, he denies it to be unjustly done), *take with thee yet one or two; and if he refuse to hear them, tell it to the Church.* But why to the Church, except that she might judge whether it were a sin or not? But if *he refuse to hear the Church;* that is, if he do not

submit to the Church's sentence, but shall maintain that
to be no sin, which she judges to be a sin; that is to say,
if he repent not (for certain it is, that no man repents
himself of that action which he conceives not to be a
sin); he saith not, *Tell it to the apostles;* that we might
know that the definitive sentence in the question,
whether it were a sin or not, was not left unto them; but
to the Church. *But let him be unto thee,* says he, *as an
heathen, or publican;* that is, as one out of the Church,
as one that is not baptized, that is to say, as one whose
sins are retained. For all Christians were baptized into
remission of sins. But because it might have been demanded, who it was that had so great a power, as that of
withholding the benefit of baptism from the impenitent;
Christ shows that the same persons, to whom he had
given authority to baptize the penitent into the remission of sins, and to make them of heathen men Christians, had also authority to retain their sins who by the
Church should be adjudged to be impenitent, and to
make them of Christian men heathens: and therefore
presently subjoins: *Verily I say unto you, whose soever
sins ye shall bind upon earth, they shall be bound also in
heaven; and whose soever sins ye shall loose upon earth,
they shall be loosed also in heaven.* Whence we may understand, that the power of binding and loosing, or of
remitting and retaining of sins, which is called in another
place the power of the keys, is not different from the
power given in another place in these words (Matth.
xxviii. 19): *Go, and teach all nations, baptizing them in
the name of the Father, and of the Son, and of the Holy
Ghost.* And even as the pastors cannot refuse to baptize
him whom the Church judges worthy, so neither can they
retain his sins whom the Church holds fitting to be absolved, nor yet remit his sins whom the Church pronounc-
eth disobedient. And it is the Church's part to judge of
the sin, the pastor's to cast out or to receive into the

Church those that are judged. Thus St. Paul to the Church of Corinth (1 Cor. v. 12): *Do not ye judge,* saith he, *of those that are within?* Yet he himself pronounced the sentence of excommunication against the incestuous person. *I indeed,* saith he (verse 3), *as absent in body, but present in Spirit,* &c.

26. The act of retaining sins is that which is called by the Church *excommunication,* and by St. Paul *delivering over to Satan.* The word *excommunication* sounding the same with ἀποσυνάγωγον ποιεῖν, *casting out of the synagogue,* seems to be borrowed from the Mosaical law; wherein they who were by the priest adjudged leprous, were commanded (Levit. xiii. 46) to be kept apart out of the camp, until by the judgment of the priest they were again pronounced clean, and by certain rites, among which the washing of the body was one, were purified. From hence in process of time it became a custom of the Jews, not to receive those who passed from Gentilism to Judaism, supposing them to be unclean, unless they were first *washed;* and those who dissented from the doctrine of the synagogue, they cast out of the synagogue. By resemblance of this custom, those that came to Christianity, whether they were Jews or Gentiles, were not received into the Church without baptism; and those that dissented from the Church, were deprived of the Church's communion. Now, they were therefore said *to be delivered over to Satan,* because all that was out of the Church, was comprehended within his kingdom. The end of this kind of discipline was, that being destitute for a time of the grace and spiritual privileges of the Church, they might be humbled to salvation; but the effect in regard of secular matters, that *being excommunicated,* they should not only be prohibited all congregations or churches, and the participation of the mysteries, but as being contagious they should be avoided by all other Christians, even more than heathen. For the apostle al-

lowed to accompany with heathen; but with these, *not so much as to eat* (1 Cor. v. 10–11). Seeing then the effect of *excommunication* is such, it is manifest, in the first place, that *a Christian city cannot be excommunicated.* For a Christian city is a Christian Church (as hath been declared above, in art. 21), and of the same extension; but a Church cannot be excommunicated. For either she must excommunicate herself, which is impossible; or she must be excommunicated by some other Church; and this, either *universal* or *particular.* But seeing *an universal Church* is no *person* (as hath been proved in art. 22), and therefore neither acts nor does any thing, it cannot *excommunicate* any man; and a particular Church by excommunicating another Church, doth nothing. For where there is not one common congregation, there cannot be any excommunication. Neither if some one Church (suppose that of Jerusalem), should have excommunicated another (suppose that of Rome), would it any more have excommunicated this, than herself: for he that deprives another of his communion, deprives himself also of the communion of that other. Secondly, *no man can excommunicate the subjects of any absolute government all at once, or forbid them the use of their temples or their public worship of God.* For they cannot be excommunicated by a Church, which themselves do constitute. For if they could, there would not only not remain a Church, but not so much as a *commonweal,* and they would be dissolved of themselves; and this were not *to be excommunicated* or *prohibited.* But if they be excommunicated by some other Church, that Church is to esteem them as heathen. But no *Christian Church,* by the doctrine of Christ, can forbid the heathen to gather together and communicate among themselves, as it shall seem good to their cities; especially if they meet to worship Christ, although it be done in a singular custom and manner: therefore also not the *excommuni-*

cated, who are to be dealt with as heathen. Thirdly, *a prince who hath the sovereign power, cannot be excommunicated.* For by the doctrine of Christ, neither one nor many subjects together can interdict their prince any public or private places, or deny him entrance into any assembly whatsoever, or prohibit him the doing of what he will within his own jurisdiction. For it is treason among all cities, for any one or many subjects jointly to arrogate to themselves any authority over the whole city. But they who arrogate to themselves an authority over him who hath the supreme power of the city, do arrogate the same authority over the city itself. Besides, a sovereign prince, if he be a Christian, hath this further advantage; that the city whose will is contained in his, is that very thing which we call a Church. The *Church* therefore excommunicates no man, but whom it excommunicates by the authority of the prince. But the prince excommunicates not himself; his subjects therefore cannot do it. It may be indeed, that an assembly of rebellious citizens or traitors may pronounce the sentence of excommunication against their prince; but not *by right.* Much less can one prince be excommunicated by another; for this would prove not an excommunication, but a provocation to war by the way of affront. For since that is not one Church, which is made up of citizens belonging to two absolute cities, for want of power of lawfully assembling them (as hath been declared before, in art. 22); they who are of one Church are not bound to obey another, and therefore cannot be excommunicated for their disobedience. Now, what some may say, that princes, seeing they are members of the universal Church, may also by the authority of the universal Church be excommunicated, signifies nothing: because *the universal Church* (as hath been showed in art. 22), is not *one person,* of whom it may be said that *she acted, decreed, determined, excommunicated, absolved,* and the like personal attributes;

neither hath she any governor upon earth, at whose command she may assemble and deliberate. For to be guide of the universal Church, and to have the power of assembling her, is the same thing as to be governor and lord over all the Christians in the world; which is granted to none, but God only.

27. It hath been showed above in art. 18, that the authority of *interpreting the Holy Scriptures* consisted not in this, that the interpreter might without punishment expound and explicate his sentence and opinion taken thence unto others, either by writing or by his own voice; but that others have not a right to do or teach aught contrary to his sentence; insomuch as *the interpretation* we speak of, is the same with *the power of defining* in all manner of controversies to be determined by sacred Scriptures. Now we must show that that power belongs to each Church; and depends on his or their authority who have the supreme command, provided that they be Christians. For if it depend not on the civil authority, it must either depend on the opinion of each private subject, or some foreign authority. But among other reasons, the inconveniences that must follow private opinions, cannot suffer its dependance on them. Of which this is the chief; that not only all civil obedience would be taken away (contrary to Christ's precept); but all human society and peace would be dissolved (contrary to the laws of nature). For seeing every man is his own interpreter of Scripture, that is to say, since every man makes himself judge of what is pleasing and displeasing unto God; they cannot obey their princes, before that they have judged whether their commands be conformable to the word of God, or not. And thus either they obey not, or they obey for their own opinion's sake; that is to say, they obey themselves, not their sovereign; civil obedience therefore is lost. Again, when every man follows his own opinion, it is necessary that the controversies which rise among them, will be-

come innumerable and indeterminable; whence there will
breed among men, who by their own natural inclinations
do account all dissension an affront, first hatred, then
brawls and wars; and thus all manner of peace and society would vanish. We have furthermore for an example, that which God under the old law required to be observed concerning the book of the law; namely, that it
should be transcribed and publicly used; and he would
have it to be the canon of divine doctrine, but the controversies about it not to be determined by private persons, but only by the priests. Lastly, it is our Saviour's
precept, that if there be any matter of offence between
private persons, they should *hear the Church.* Wherefore
it is the Church's duty to define controversies; it therefore belongs not to private men, but to the Church to
interpret Scriptures. But that we may know that the authority of *interpreting God's Word,* that is to say, of
determining all questions concerning God and religion,
belongs not to any foreign person whatsoever; we must
consider, first, what|esteem such a power carries in the
minds of the subjects, and their civil actions.|For no man
can be ignorant that the voluntary actions of men, by a
natural necessity, do follow those opinions which they
have concerning good and evil, reward and punishment.
Whence it happens, that necessarily they would choose
rather to obey those, by whose judgment they believe
that they shall be eternally happy or miserable. Now, by
whose judgment it is appointed what doctrines are necessary to salvation, by their judgment do men expect
their eternal bliss or perdition; they will therefore yield
them obedience in all things. Which being thus, most
manifest it is, that those subjects, who believe themselves
bound to acquiesce to a foreign authority in those doctrines which are necessary to salvation, do not *per se* constitute a city, but are the subjects of that foreign power.
Nor therefore, although some sovereign prince should by

writing grant such an authority to any other, yet so as he would be understood to have retained the civil power in his own hands, shall such a writing be valid, or transfer aught necessary for the retaining or good administration of his command. For by chap. II. art. 4, no man is said *to transfer his right, unless he give some proper sign, declaring his will to transfer it.* But he who hath openly declared his will to keep his sovereignty, cannot have given a sufficient sign of transferring the means necessary for the keeping it. This kind of writing therefore will not be a sign of will, but of ignorance in the contractors. We must consider next, how absurd it is for a city or sovereign to commit the ruling of his subjects' consciences to an enemy; for they are, as hath been showed above in chap. v. art. 6, in an hostile state, whosoever have not joined themselves into the unity of one person. Nor contradicts it this truth, that they do not always fight: for truces are made between enemies. It is sufficient for an hostile mind, that there is suspicion; that the frontiers of cities, kingdoms, empires, strengthened with garrisons, do with a fighting posture and countenance, though they strike not, yet as enemies mutually behold each other. Lastly, how unequal is it to demand that, which by the very reason of your demand you confess|belongs to another's right.|I am the interpreter of Scriptures to you, who are the subject of another|realm.| Why? By what covenants passed between you and me? By divine authority. Whence known? Out of holy Scripture: behold the book, read it. In vain, unless I may also interpret the same for myself. That interpretation therefore doth by right belong to me, and the rest of my private fellow-subjects; which we both deny. It remains therefore that in all *Christian Churches,* that is to say, in all *Christian cities,* the *interpretation* of sacred Scripture, that is to say, the right of determining all controversies,|depend on and derive from the authority of that man or council, which hath the sovereign power of the city.

28. Now because there are two kinds of controversies: the one about spiritual matters, that is to say, questions of faith, the truth whereof cannot be searched into by natural reason; such are the questions concerning *the nature and office of Christ, of rewards and punishments to come, of the sacraments, of outward worship,* and the like: the other, about questions of human science, whose truth is sought out by natural reason and syllogisms, drawn from the covenants of men, and definitions, that is to say, significations received by use and common consent of words; such as are all questions of right and philosophy; for example, when in matter of right it is questioned, whether there be *a promise* and *covenant,* or not, that is nothing else but to demand whether such words, spoken in such a manner, be by common use and consent of the subjects *a promise* or *covenant;* which if they be so called, then it is true that a contract is made; if not, then it is false: that truth therefore depends on the compacts and consents of men. In like manner, when it is demanded in philosophy, whether the same thing may entirely be in divers places at once; the determination of the question depends on the knowledge of the common consent of men, about the signification of the word *entire.* For if men, when they say a thing is entirely somewhere, do signify by common consent that they understand nothing of the same to be elsewhere; it is false that the same thing is in divers places at once. That truth therefore depends on the consents of men, and by the same reason, in all other questions concerning *right* and *philosophy.* And they who do judge that anything can be determined, contrary to this common consent of men concerning the appellations of things, out of obscure places of Scripture; do also judge that the use of speech, and at once all human society, is to be taken away. For

he who hath sold a whole field, will say he meant one whole ridge; and will retain the rest as unsold. Nay, they take away reason itself; which is nothing else but a searching out of the truth made by such consent. These kind of questions, therefore, need not be determined by the city by way of interpretation of Scriptures; for they belong not to God's *Word*, in that sense wherein *the Word of God* is taken for the *Word concerning God*; that is to say, for the *doctrine of the gospel.* Neither is he who hath the sovereign power in the Church, obliged to employ any *ecclesiastical doctors* for the judging of any such kind of matters as these. But for the deciding of questions of faith, that is to say, *concerning God,* which transcend human capacity, we stand in need of a divine blessing (that we may not be deceived at least in necessary points), to be derived from Christ himself by the imposition of hands. For, seeing to the end we may attain to eternal salvation we are obliged to a supernatural doctrine, and which therefore it is impossible for us to understand; to be left so destitute as that we can be deceived in necessary points, is repugnant to equity. This infallibility our Saviour Christ promised (in those things which are necessary to salvation) to his apostles until the day of judgment; that is to say, to the apostles, and pastors succeeding the apostles, who were to be consecrated *by the imposition of hands.* He therefore, who hath the sovereign power in the city, is obliged as a Christian, where there is any question concerning *the mysteries of faith,* to interpret the Holy Scriptures by *clergymen* lawfully ordained. And thus in Christian cities, the judgment both of *spiritual* and *temporal matters* belongs unto the civil authority. And that man or council who hath the supreme power, is head both of *the city* and *of the Church;* for a *Church* and *a Christian city* is but one thing.

XVIII

Concerning Those Things Which Are Necessary for Our Entrance into the Kingdom of Heaven

1. The difficulty propounded concerning the repugnancy of obeying God and men, is to be removed by the distinctions between the points necessary and not necessary to salvation. 2. All things necessary to salvation, are contained in faith and obedience. 3. What kind of obedience that is, which is required of us. 4. What faith is, and how distinguished from profession, from science, from opinion. 5. What it is to believe in Christ. 6. That that article alone, that Jesus is the Christ, is necessary to salvation; is proved from the scope of the evangelists. 7. From the preachings of the apostles. 8. From the easiness of Christian religion. 9. From this also, that it is the foundation of faith. 10. From the most evident words of Christ and his apostles. 11. In that article is contained the faith of the Old Testament. 12. How faith and obedience concur to salvation. 13. In a Christian city, there is no contradiction between the commands of God and of the city. 14. The doctrines which this day are controverted about religion, do for the most part relate to the right of dominion.

1. It was ever granted, that all authority *in secular matters* derived from him who had the sovereign power, whether he were one man or an assembly of men. That the same *in spiritual matters* depended on the authority of the *Church*, is manifest by the lastly foregoing proofs; and besides by this, that all Christian cities are Churches endued with this kind of authority. From whence a man, though but dull of apprehension, may collect, that in *a Christian city*, that is to say, in a city whose sovereignty belongs to a Christian prince or council, *all power, as well*

spiritual as secular, is united under Christ, and therefore it is to be obeyed in all things. But on the other side, *because we must rather obey God than men,* there is a difficulty risen, how obedience may safely be yielded to them, if at any time somewhat should be commanded by them to be done which Christ hath prohibited. The reason of this difficulty is, that seeing God no longer speaks to us by Christ and his prophets in open voice, but by the holy Scriptures, which by divers men are diversely understood; they know indeed what princes and a congregated Church do command; but whether that which they do command, be contrary to the word of God or not, this they know not; but with a wavering obedience between the punishments of temporal and spiritual death, as it were sailing between Scylla and Charybdis, they often run themselves upon both. But they who rightly distinguish between the things necessary to salvation, and those which are not necessary, can have none of this kind of doubt. For if the command of the prince or city be such, that he can obey it without hazard of his eternal salvation, it is unjust not to obey them; and the apostle's precepts take place (Col. iii. 20–22): *Children obey your parents in all things: servants in all things obey your masters according to the flesh.* And the command of Christ (Matth. xxiii. 2–3): *The Scribes and Pharisees sit in Moses' chair; all things therefore whatsoever they command you, that observe and do.* On the contrary, if they command us to do those things which are punished with eternal death, it were madness not rather to choose to die a natural death, than by obeying to die eternally: and then comes in that which Christ says (Matth. x. 28): *Fear not them who kill the body, but cannot kill the soul.* We must see, therefore, what all those things are, which are necessary to salvation.

2. Now all things necessary to salvation are comprehended in two virtues, *faith* and *obedience.* The latter of

these, if it could be perfect, would alone suffice to preserve us from damnation; but because we have all of us been long since guilty of disobedience against God in Adam, and besides we ourselves have since actually sinned, *obedience* is not sufficient without *remission of sins*. But this, together with our entrance into the kingdom of heaven, is the reward of *faith;* nothing else is requisite to salvation. For the kingdom of heaven is shut to none but sinners, that is to say, those who have not performed due *obedience* to the laws; and not to those neither, if they believe the necessary articles of the Christian faith. Now, if we shall know in what points obedience doth consist, and which are the necessary articles of the Christian faith; it will at once be manifest what we must do, and what abstain from, at the command of cities and of princes.

3. But by obedience in this place is signified not *the fact*, but the *will* and *desire* wherewith we purpose, and endeavour as much as we can, to obey for the future. In which sense the word *obedience* is equivalent to *repentance;* for the virtue of repentance consists not in the sorrow which accompanies the remembrance of sin; but in our conversion into the way, and full purpose to sin no more; without which that sorrow is said to be the sorrow not of a penitent, but a desperate person. But because they who love God cannot but desire to obey the divine law, and they who love their neighbours cannot but desire to obey the moral law; which consists (as hath been showed above in chap. III.) in the prohibition of *pride, ingratitude, contumely, inhumanity, cruelty, injury,* and the like offences, whereby our neighbours are prejudiced; therefore also *love*, or *charity*, is equivalent to *obedience*. Justice, also, which is a constant will of giving to every man his due, is equivalent with it. But that *faith and repentance* are sufficient for salvation, is manifest by the covenant itself of baptism. For they who were by Peter

converted on the day of *Pentecost*, demanding him, what they should do: he answered (Acts ii. 38): *Repent and be baptized every one of you, in the name of Jesus, for the remission of your sins.* There was nothing therefore to be done for the obtaining of baptism, that is to say, for to enter into the kingdom of God, but *to repent and believe in the name of Jesus;* for the kingdom of heaven is promised by the covenant which is made in baptism. Furthermore, by the words of Christ, answering the lawyer who asked him what he should do to inherit eternal life (Luke xviii. 20): *Thou knowest the commandments: Thou shalt not kill, thou shalt not commit adultery,* &c.: which refer to obedience; and (Mark x. 21): *Sell all that thou hast, and come and follow me:* which relates to faith. And by that which is said: *The just shall live by faith;* not every man, but the *just;* for *justice* is the same disposition of will which *repentance and obedience* are. And by the words of St. Mark (i. 15): *The time is fulfilled, and the kingdom of God is at hand; repent ye, and believe the gospel;* by which words is not obscurely signified, that there is no need of other virtues for our entrance into the kingdom of God, excepting those of *repentance and faith.* The obedience therefore which is *necessarily* required to salvation, is nothing else but *the will* or *endeavour* to obey; that is to say, of doing according to the laws of God; that is, the moral laws, which are the same to all men, and the civil laws; that is to say, the commands of sovereigns in *temporal* matters, and the ecclesiastical laws in *spiritual.* Which two kinds of laws are divers in divers cities and Churches, and are known by their promulgation and public sentences.

4. That we may understand what the *Christian faith* is, we must define *faith* in general; and distinguish it from those other acts of the mind, wherewith commonly it is confounded. The object of *faith* universally taken, namely, *for that which is believed,* is evermore a *proposi-*

tion, that is to say, a speech affirmative or negative, which we grant to be true. But because propositions are granted for divers causes, it falls out that these kind of concessions are diversely called. But we grant propositions sometimes, which notwithstanding we receive not into our minds; and this either for a time, to wit, so long, till by consideration of the consequences we have well examined the truth of them, which we call *supposing;* or also simply, as through fear of the laws, which is to *profess,* or *confess* by outward tokens; or for a voluntary compliance sake, which men use out of civility to those whom they respect, and for love of peace to others, which is *absolute yielding.* Now the propositions which we received for truth, we always grant for some reasons of our own; and these are derived either from the *proposition itself,* or from the *person propounding.* They are derived from the *proposition itself,* by calling to mind what things those words, which make up the proposition, do by common consent usually signify. If so, then the assent which we give, is called *knowledge* or *science.* But if we cannot remember what is certainly understood by those words, but sometimes one thing, sometimes another seem to be apprehended by us, then we are said to think. For example, if it be propounded that *two and three make five;* and by calling to mind, that the order of those numeral words is so appointed by the common consent of them who are of the same language with us (as it were, by a certain contract necessary for human society), that *five* shall be the name of so many unities as are contained in two and three taken together, a man assents that this is therefore true, because two and three together are the same with five: this assent shall be called knowledge. And to know this truth is nothing else, but to acknowledge that it is made by ourselves. For by whose will and rules of speaking the number | | is called two, | | | is called three, and | | | | | is called five; by their will also it comes to pass that this proposition is true, *two and three taken together make five*. In like manner if we remember what it is that is called *theft*, and what *injury*; we shall understand by the words themselves, whether it be true that *theft is an injury*, or not. *Truth* is the same with a *true proposition*; but *the proposition is true* in which the *word consequent*, which by logicians is called *the predicate*, embraceth *the word antecedent* in its amplitude, which they call *the subject*. And to *know truth* is the same thing as to *remember* that it was made by ourselves|by the very usurpation of the|words. Neither was it rashly nor unadvisedly said by Plato of old, *that knowledge was memory*. But it happens sometimes, that words although they have a certain and defined signification by constitution, yet by vulgar use either to adorn or deceive, they are so wrested from their own significations, that to remember the conceptions for which they were first imposed on things, is very hard, and not to be mastered but by a sharp judgment and very great diligence. It happens too that there are many words, which have no proper, determined, and everywhere the same signification; and are understood not by their own, but by virtue of other signs used together with them. Thirdly, there are some words of things unconceivable. Of those things, therefore, whereof they are the words, there is no conception; and therefore in vain do we seek for the truth of those propositions, which they make out of the words themselves. In these cases, while by considering the definitions of words we search out the truth of some proposition, according to the hope we have of finding it, we think it sometimes true, and sometimes false; either of which apart is called *thinking*, and also *believing*; both together, *doubting*. But when our reasons, for which we assent to some proposition, derive not from the *proposition itself*, but from the *person propounding*, whom we esteem so learned that he is not deceived, and we see no reason why he should deceive us; our assent, because it grows not from any confidence of our own, but from another man's knowledge, is called *faith*. And by the confidence of whom we do believe, we are said *to trust them*, or *to trust in them*. By what hath been said, the difference appears, first, between *faith* and *profession*; for that is always joined with inward assent; this not always. That is an inward persuasion of the mind, this an outward obedience. Next, between *faith* and *opinion*; for this depends on our own reason, that on the good esteem we have of another. Lastly, between *faith* and *knowledge*; for this deliberately takes a proposition broken and chewed; that swallows it down whole and entire. The explication of words, whereby the matter enquired after is propounded, is conducible to knowledge; nay, the only way *to know*, is by *definition*. But this is prejudicial to *faith*; for those things which exceed human capacity, and are propounded to be believed, are never more evident by explication, but, on the contrary, more obscure and harder to be credited. And the same thing befalls a man, who endeavours to demonstrate *the mysteries of faith* by natural reason, which happens to a sick man, who will needs chew before he will swallow his wholesome but bitter pills; whence it comes to pass, that he presently brings them up again; which perhaps would otherwise, if he had taken them well down, have proved his remedy.

5. We have seen therefore what it is *to believe*. But what is it *to believe in Christ*? Or what proposition is that, which is the object of our faith in Christ? For when we say, *I believe in Christ*, we signify indeed whom, but not what we believe. Now, *to believe in Christ* is nothing else but to believe that Jesus is the Christ, namely, he who according to the prophecies of Moses and the prophets of Israel, was to come into this world *to institute the kingdom of God*. And this sufficiently appears out of the words of Christ himself to Martha (John xi. 25–27): *I*

am, saith he, *the resurrection and the life; he that believeth in me, though he were dead, yet shall he live; and
whosoever liveth and believeth in me, shall never die. Believest thou this? She saith unto him, yea, Lord, I believe
that thou art the Christ the Son of God, which should
come into the world.* In which words, we see that the
question, *believest thou in me*, is expounded by the answer, *thou art the Christ.* To believe in Christ therefore
is nothing else but to believe Jesus himself, saying that he
is the Christ.

6. *Faith* and *obedience* both necessarily concurring to
salvation, what kind of obedience that same is, and to
whom due, hath been showed above in art. 3. But now
we must enquire what *articles of faith* are requisite. And
I say, that to a Christian* there is no other article of faith

---

* *I say, that to a Christian.* Although I conceive this assertion
to be sufficiently proved by the following reasons, yet I thought it
worth my labour to make a more ample explication of it; because I
perceive that being somewhat new, it may possibly be distasteful to
many divines. First therefore, when I say this article, *that Jesus is
the Christ*, is necessary to salvation; I say not that faith only is
necessary, but I require justice also, or that obedience which is due
to the laws of God; that is to say, a will to live righteously. Secondly,
I deny not but the profession of many articles, provided that that
profession be commanded by the Church, is also necessary to salvation. But seeing faith is internal, profession external, I say that the
former only is properly faith; the latter a part of obedience; insomuch
as that article alone sufficeth for inward belief, but is not sufficient
for the outward profession of a Christian. Lastly, even as if I had
said that true and inward repentance of sins was only necessary to
salvation, yet were it not to be held for a paradox; because we suppose justice, obedience, and a mind reformed in all manner of virtues
to be contained in it. So when I say that the faith of one article is
sufficient to salvation, it may well be less wondered at; seeing that
in it so many other articles are contained. For these words, *Jesus is
the Christ*, do signify that Jesus was that person, whom God had
promised by his prophets should come into the world to establish
his kingdom; that is to say, that Jesus is the Son of God, the creator
of heaven and earth, born of a virgin, dying for the sins of them who
should believe in him; that he was Christ, that is to say, a king;
that he revived (for else he were not like to reign) to judge the
world, and to reward every one according to his works (for otherwise

requisite as *necessary* to salvation, but only this, *that Jesus is the Christ.* But we must distinguish, as we have already done before in art. 4, between *faith* and *profession.* A *profession,* therefore, of more articles, if they be commanded, may be necessary; for it is a part of our *obedience* due to the laws. But we enquire not now what *obedience,* but what *faith* is necessary to salvation. And this is proved, first, out of the scope of the Evangelists, which was, by the description of our Saviour's life, to establish this one article: and we shall know that such was the scope and counsel of the Evangelists, if we observe but the history itself. St. Matthew (chap. i.), beginning at his genealogy, shows that Jesus was of the lineage of David, born of a virgin: chap. ii., that he was adored by the *wise men* as king of the Jews; that Herod for the same cause sought to slay him: chap. iii., iv., that his kingdom was preached both by John the Baptist and himself: chapters v., vi., vii., that he taught the laws, not as the Scribes, but as one having authority: chapters viii., ix., that he cured diseases miraculously: chap. x., that he sent his apostles, the preachers of his kingdom, throughout all the parts of Judea to proclaim his kingdom: chap. xi., that he commanded the messengers, sent from John to enquire whether he were the Christ or not, to tell him what they had seen, namely, the miracles which were only

---

he cannot be a king); also that men shall rise again, for otherwise they are not like to come to judgment. The whole symbol of the apostles is therefore contained in this one article. Which, notwithstanding, I thought reasonable to contract thus; because I found that many men for this alone, without the rest, were admitted into the kingdom of God, both by Christ and his apostles; as the thief on the cross, the eunuch baptized by Philip, the two thousand men converted to the Church at once by St. Peter. But if any man be displeased that I do not judge all those eternally damned, who do not inwardly assent to every article defined by the Church, and yet do not contradict, but, if they be commanded, do submit: I know not what I shall say to them. For the most evident testimonies of Holy Writ, which do follow, do withhold me from altering my opinion.

compatible with Christ: chap. xii., that he proved and declared his kingdom to the Pharisees and others by arguments, parables, and signs; and the following chapters to xxi., that he maintained himself to be the Christ against the Pharisees: chap. xxi., that he was saluted with the title of king, when he entered into Jerusalem: chaps. xxii., xxiii., xxiv., xxv., that he forewarned others of *false Christs;* and that he showed in parables what manner of kingdom his should be: chaps. xxvi., xxvii., that he was taken and accused for this reason, because he said he was a king; and that a title was written on his cross, *this is Jesus the king of the Jews:* lastly, chap. xxviii., that after his resurrection, he told his apostles that all power was given unto him both in heaven and in earth. All which tends to this end; that we should believe Jesus to be the Christ. Such therefore was the scope of St. Matthew in describing his gospel. But such as his was, such also was the rest of the Evangelists; which St. John sets down expressly in the end of his gospel (John xx. 31): *These things,* saith he, *are written, that ye may know that Jesus is the Christ, the Son of the living God.*

7. Secondly, this is proved by the preaching of the apostles. For they were the proclaimers of his kingdom; neither did Christ send them to preach aught but the kingdom of God (Luke ix. 2: Acts x. 42). And what they did after Christ's ascension, may be understood by the accusation which was brought against them (Acts xvii. 6–7): *They drew Jason,* saith St. Luke, *and certain brethren unto the rulers of the city, crying, these are the men that have turned the world upside down, and are come hither also, whom Jason hath received; and these all do contrary to the decrees of Cæsar, saying that there is another king, one Jesus.* It appears also, what the subject of the apostle's sermon was, out of these words (Acts xvii. 2–3): *Opening and alleging out of the Scriptures* (to wit, of the Old Testament) *that Christ must needs*

*have suffered and risen again from the dead; and that this
Jesus is the Christ.*

8. Thirdly, by the places, in which the easiness of those
things, which are required by Christ to the attaining of
salvation, is declared. For if an internal assent of the mind
were necessarily required to the truth of all and each
proposition, which this day is controverted about the
Christian faith, or by divers churches is diversely defined;
there would be nothing more difficult than the Christian
religion. And how then would that be true (Matth. xi.
30): *My yoke is easy and my burden light;* and that
(Matth. xviii. 6): *little ones do believe in him;* and that
(1 Cor. i. 21): *it pleased God by the foolishness of
preaching, to save those that believe?* Or how was the
thief hanging on the cross sufficiently instructed to salvation, the confession of whose faith was contained in these
words: *Lord, remember me when thou comest into thy
kingdom?* Or how could St. Paul himself, from an enemy,
so soon become a doctor of Christians?

9. Fourthly, by this, that that article is the foundation
of faith; neither rests it on any other foundation. Matth.
xxiv. 23, 24: *If any man shall say unto you, Lo here
is Christ, or he is there; believe it not. For there shall arise
false Christs and false prophets, and shall show great signs
and wonders,* &c. Whence it follows, that for the faith's
sake which we have in this article, we must not believe
any signs and wonders. Gal. i. 8: *Although we or an angel
from heaven,* saith the apostle, *should preach to you any
other gospel, than what we have preached; let him be ac-
cursed.* By reason of this article, therefore, we might not
trust the very apostles and angels themselves, and therefore, I conceive, not the Church neither, if they should
teach the contrary. 1 John iv. 1–2: *Beloved, believe not
every spirit, but try the spirits whether they are of God;
because many false prophets are gone out into the
world. Hereby know ye the spirit of God; every spirit that*

confesseth Jesus Christ is come in the flesh, is of God, &c.
That article therefore is the measure of the spirits,
whereby the authority of the doctors is either received,
or rejected. It cannot be denied, indeed, but that all who
at this day are Christians, did learn from the doctors that
it was Jesus, who did all those things whereby he might
be acknowledged to be the Christ. Yet it follows not, that
the same persons believed that article for the doctor's or
the Church's, but for Jesus' own sake. For that article
was before *the Christian Church* (Matth. xvi. 18), although all the rest were after it; and the Church was
founded upon it, not it upon the Church. Besides, this
article, that *Jesus is the Christ,* is so fundamental, that
all the rest are by St. Paul (1 Cor. iii. 11–15) said to be
built upon it: *For other foundation can no man lay, than
that which is laid; which is Jesus Christ;* that is to say,
that *Jesus is the Christ. Now if any man build upon this
foundation, gold, silver, precious stones, wood, hay,
stubble; every man's work shall be made manifest; if any
man's work abide, which he hath built thereupon, he
shall receive a reward; if any man's work shall be burnt,
he shall suffer loss, but he himself shall be saved.* From
whence it plainly appears, that by *foundation* is understood this article, *that Jesus is the Christ:* for gold, and
silver, precious stones, wood, hay, stubble, whereby the
doctrines are signified, are not built upon the person of
Christ: and also, that false doctrines may be raised
upon this foundation; yet not so as they must necessarily
be damned who teach them.

10. Lastly, that this article alone is needful to be inwardly believed, may be most evidently proved out of
many places of holy Scripture, let who will be the interpreter. John v. 39: *Search the Scriptures; for in them
ye think ye have eternal life; and they are they which testify of me.* But Christ meant the Scriptures of the Old
Testament only; for the New was then not yet written.

Now, there is no other testimony concerning Christ in the Old Testament, but that an eternal king was to come in such a place, that he was to be born of such parents, that he was to teach and do such things whereby, as by certain signs, he was to be known. All which testify this one thing; that Jesus who was so born, and did teach and do such things, was the Christ. Other faith then was not required to attain eternal life, besides this article, John xi. 26: *Whosoever liveth and believeth in me, shall never die.* But to believe in Jesus, as is there expressed, is the same with believing that Jesus was the Christ. He therefore that believes that, shall never die; and by consequence, that article alone is necessary to salvation. John xx. 31: *These are written, that ye might believe that Jesus is the Christ, the Son of God; and that believing, ye might have life through his name.* Wherefore he that believes thus, shall have eternal life; and therefore needs no other faith. 1 John iv. 2: *Every spirit, that confesseth that Jesus Christ is come in the flesh, is of God.* And 1 John v. 1: *Whosoever believeth that Jesus is the Christ, is born of God.* And verse 5: *Who is he that overcometh the world, but he that believeth that Jesus is the Son of God?* If therefore there be no need to believe anything else, to the end a man may be *of God, born of God, and overcome the world,* than that Jesus is the Christ; that one article then is sufficient to salvation. Acts viii. 36–37: *See, here is water; what doth hinder me to be baptized? And Philip said, If thou believest with all thine heart, thou mayest. And he answered and said, I believe that Jesus Christ is the Son of God.* If then this article being believed with the whole heart, that is to say, with inward faith, was sufficient for baptism; it is also sufficient for salvation. Besides these places, there are innumerable others, which do clearly and expressly affirm the same thing. Nay, wheresoever we read that our Saviour commended the faith of any one, or that he said, *thy faith hath saved thee,* or that he healed any one for his faith's sake; there the proposition believed was no other but this, *Jesus is the Christ,* either directly or consequently.

11. But because no man can believe *Jesus to be the Christ,* who, when he knows that by Christ is understood that same king, who was promised from God by Moses and the prophets for to be the king and Saviour of the world, doth not also believe Moses and the prophets; neither can he believe these, who believes not that God is, and that *he governs the world;* it is necessary, that the faith of God and of the Old Testament be contained in this faith of the New. Seeing therefore that atheism, and the denial of the Divine Providence, were the only treason against the Divine Majesty in the kingdom of God by nature; but idolatry also in the kingdom of God by the old covenant; now in this kingdom, wherein God rules by way of a new covenant, apostacy is also added, or the renunciation of this article once received, that Jesus is the Christ. Truly other doctrines, provided they have their determination from a lawful Church, are not to be contradicted; for that is the sin of disobedience. But it hath been fully declared before, that they are not needful to be believed with an *inward faith.*

12. *Faith* and *obedience* have divers parts in accomplishing the salvation of a Christian; for this contributes the *power* or *capacity,* that the *act;* and either is said to justify in its kind. For Christ forgives not the sins of all men, but of the *penitent* or the *obedient,* that is to say, the *just.* I say not the *guiltless,* but the *just;* for *justice* is a will of obeying the laws, and may be consistent with a sinner; and with Christ, the will to obey is obedience. For not every man, but *the just shall live by faith. Obedience* therefore *justifies,* because it *maketh just;* in the same manner as temperance maketh temperate, prudence prudent, chastity chaste; namely, essentially; and puts a man in such a state, as makes him capable of pardon.

Again, Christ hath not promised forgiveness of sins to all just men; but only *those of them who believe him to be the Christ*. *Faith* therefore *justifies* in such a sense as a judge may be said to *justify*, who *absolves*, namely, by the *sentence* which *actually* saves a man; and in this acception of justification (for it is an equivocal term) *faith alone* justifies; but in the other, *obedience only*. But neither obedience alone, nor faith alone, do *save* us; but both together.

13. By what hath been said hitherto, it will be easy to discern what the duty of Christian subjects is towards their sovereigns; who, as long as they profess themselves Christians, cannot command their subjects to deny Christ, or to offer him any contumely: for if they should command this, they would profess themselves to be no Christians. For seeing we have showed, both by natural reason and out of holy Scriptures, that subjects ought in all things to obey their princes and governors, excepting those which are contrary to the command of God; and that the commands of God, in a Christian city, concerning *temporal affairs*, that is to say, those which are to be discussed by human reason, are the laws and sentence of the city, delivered from those who have received authority from the city to make laws and judge of controversies; but concerning spiritual matters, that is to say, those which are to be defined by the holy Scripture, are the laws and sentences of the city, that is to say, the Church (for a Christian city and a Church, as hath been showed in the foregoing chapter, art. 10, are the same thing), delivered by pastors lawfully ordained, and who have to that end authority given them by the city; it manifestly follows, that in a Christian commonweal obedience is due to the sovereign in all things, as well *spiritual* as *temporal*. And that the same obedience, even from a Christian subject, is due in all *temporal matters* to those princes who are no Christians, is without any controversy;

but in *matters spiritual,* that is to say, those things which concern God's worship, some Christian Church is to be followed. For it is an hypothesis of the Christian faith, that God speaks not in things supernatural but by the way of Christian interpreters of holy Scriptures. But what? Must we resist princes, when we cannot obey them? Truly, no; for this is contrary to our civil covenant. What must we do then? Go to Christ by martyrdom; which if it seem to any man to be a hard saying, most certain it is that he believes not with his whole heart, *that Jesus is the Christ, the Son of the living God;* for he would then desire to be dissolved, and to be with Christ; but he would by a feigned Christian faith elude that obedience, which he hath contracted to yield unto the city.

14. But some men perhaps will wonder, if (excepting this one article, that Jesus is the Christ, which only is necessary to salvation in relation to internal faith) all the rest belong to obedience; which may be performed, although a man do not inwardly believe, so he do but desire to believe, and make an outward profession, as oft as need requires, of whatsoever is propounded by the Church; how it comes about that there are so many tenets, which are all held so to concern our faith, that except a man do inwardly believe them, he cannot enter into the kingdom of heaven. But if he consider that, in most controversies, the contention is about human sovereignty; in some, matter of gain and profit; in others, the glory of wits: he will surely wonder the less. The question about *the propriety of the Church,* is a question about the *right of sovereignty.* For it being known what a *Church* is, it is known at once to whom the rule over Christians doth belong. For if every Christian city be that Church, which Christ himself hath commanded every Christian, subject to that city, to hear; then every subject is bound to obey his city, that is to say, him or them who have the supreme power, not only *in temporal,* but also *in spiritual mat-*

ters. But if every Christian city be not that Church, then is there some other Church more universal, which must be obeyed. All Christians therefore must obey that Church, just as they would obey Christ, if he came upon earth. She will therefore rule either by the way of monarchy, or by some assembly. This question then concerns the *right of ruling.* To the same end belongs the question concerning *infallibility.* For whosoever were truly and internally believed by all mankind, that he could not err, would be sure of all dominion, as well *temporal* as *spiritual,* over all mankind, unless himself would refuse it. For if he say that he must be obeyed in *temporals,* because it is supposed he cannot err, that right of dominion is immediately granted him. Hither also tends the privilege of interpreting Scriptures. For he to whom it belongs to interpret the controversies arising from the divers interpretations of Scriptures, hath authority also simply and absolutely to determine all manner of controversies whatsoever. But he who hath this, hath also the command over all men who acknowledge the Scriptures to be the word of God. To this end drive all the disputes about *the power of remitting and retaining sins;* or *the authority of excommunication.* For every man, if he be in his wits, will in all things yield that man an absolute obedience, by virtue of whose sentence he believes himself to be either saved or damned. Hither also tends the power of *instituting societies.* For they depend on him by whom they subsist, who hath as many subjects as monks, although living in an enemy's city. To this end also refers the question concerning the *judge of lawful matrimony.* For he to whom that judicature belongs, to him also pertains the knowledge of all those cases which concern the inheritance and succession of all the goods and rights, not of private men only, but also of sovereign princes. And hither also in some respect tends the *virgin life of ecclesiastical persons;* for unmarried men have less coherence than others

with civil society. And besides, it is an inconvenience
not to be slighted, that princes must either necessarily
forego the priesthood, which is a great bond of civil obedience; or have no hereditary kingdom. To this end also
tends the *canonization of saints*, which the heathen called
apotheosis. For he that can allure foreign subjects with
so great a reward, may bring those who are greedy of
such glory, to dare and do anything. For what was it but
an honourable name with posterity, which the Decii and
other Romans sought after; and a thousand others, who
cast themselves upon incredible perils? The controversies about *purgatory*, and *indulgences*, are matter of gain.
The questions of *free-will*, *justification*, and *the manner
of receiving Christ in the sacrament*, are philosophical.
There are also questions concerning some rites not introduced, but left in the Church not sufficiently purged from
Gentilism. But we need reckon no more. All the world
knows that such is the nature of men, that dissenting in
questions which concern their *power*, or *profit*, or *pre-
eminence of wit*, they slander and curse each other. It is
not therefore to be wondered at, if almost all tenets, after
men grew hot with disputings, are held forth by some or
other to be *necessary* to salvation and for our entrance
into the kingdom of heaven. Insomuch as they who hold
them not, are not only condemned as guilty of disobedience; which in truth they are, after the Church hath once
defined them; but of infidelity: which I have declared
above to be wrong, out of many evident places of Scripture. To which I add this one of Saint Paul's (Rom. xiv.
3, 5): *Let not him that eateth, despise him that eateth
not, and let not him that eateth not, judge him that eateth; for God hath received him. One man esteemeth one
day above another, another esteemeth every day alike.
Let every man be fully persuaded in his own mind.*

APPENDIX

The following lists variants from the Molesworth and 1651 editions. Obvious typographical errors, minor changes that do not affect the sense of the passage in question, and matters of punctuation are not listed. The page numbers are those of the current edition, referring to words or passages in the text, marked with vertical lines.

p. 110: The 1651 edition has "so".

p. 111: The 1651 edition has "before".

p. 115: Molesworth has "is so far from being a matter scornfully to be looked upon, that one has neither the power nor the wish".

p. 116: Molesworth has "For if it be contrary to right reason that I should judge of mine own peril, say, that another man is judge."

p. 116: The 1651 edition has "*mere*".

p. 117: The 1651 edition has "owns".

p. 118: The 1651 edition has "destroyed".

p. 122: Molesworth has "own consent,".

p. 122: Molesworth has "with the greatest unaninimity and earnestness".

p. 122: Molesworth has "which is done *wrong*,".

p. 128: The 1651 edition has "incertainty".

p. 129: The bracketed word, translated by Molesworth, did not appear in the 1651 edition.

p. 135: The 1651 edition has "answerable".

p. 136: The 1651 edition has "contracts".

p. 143: Molesworth has "master".

p. 143: Molesworth has "always or often".

p. 166: Molesworth has "trite".

p. 173: Molesworth has "is no body should have".

p. 174: Molesworth has "each".

p. 175: The 1651 edition has "it's one;".

p. 182: The 1651 edition has "mediately".

p. 205: The 1651 edition has "or slaves, and".

p. 206: The 1651 edition has "deprived him of;".

p. 223: The 1651 edition has "is common to".

p. 223: Molesworth has "equally".

p. 228: The 1651 edition has "politie.".

p. 244: The bracketed passages, translated by Molesworth, did not appear in the 1651 edition.

p. 246: The 1651 edition has "adversary opinion".

p. 257: The 1651 edition has "not the propriety of".

p. 261: The 1651 edition has "holds".

p. 264: The 1651 edition has "its reason good".

p. 266: The 1651 edition has "are only".

p. 280: The 1651 edition has "shall not obey".

p. 280: The 1651 edition has "accused".

p. 299: Molesworth has "many".

p. 299: Molesworth has "many".

p. 309: The Latin (Warrender) has "visible".

p. 325: The Latin reads "The priest could do by right only what God commanded. But the king could do by right whatever each person could do by right in respect to himself. For" [Translation by Edwin Curley].

p. 325: Molesworth has "*laws* to the *facts.*".

p. 329: The Latin (Warrender) reads "morality,".

p. 335: The 1651 edition has "hear not my words, and keep them,".

p. 350: The 1651 edition has "could".

p. 365: Molesworth has "weight such a power has in the minds of the citizens, and their actions.".

p. 366: Molesworth has "to be the right of another.".

p. 366: Molesworth has "state.".

p. 366: ", that is to say, the right of determining all controversies,", translated by Molesworth, did not appear in the 1651 edition.

p. 374: The 1651 edition has "in the common use of".

Hackett Publishing Company wishes to express its appreciation to Mark Rooks of InteLex Corporation for making available a complete list of variants, from which this appendix was derived.